COMIC BOOK FILM STYLE

COMIC BOOK FILM STYLE

CINEMA AT 24 PANELS PER SECOND

DRU JEFFRIES

UNIVERSITY OF TEXAS PRESS 〰 AUSTIN

Requests for permission to reproduce material from
this work should be sent to:
    Permissions
    University of Texas Press
    P.O. Box 7819
    Austin, TX 78713-7819
    http://utpress.utexas.edu/index.php/rp-form

The paper used in this book meets the minimum requirements
of ANSI/NISO Z39.48-1992 (R1997) (Permanence of Paper). ∞

LIBRARY OF CONGRESS CATALOGING-IN-PUBLICATION DATA

Names: Jeffries, Dru, author.
Title: Comic book film style : cinema at 24 panels per second /
    Dru Jeffries.
Description: First edition. | Austin : University of Texas Press,
    2017. | Includes bibliographical references and index.
Identifiers: LCCN 2017000691
    ISBN 978-1-4773-1325-1 (cloth : alk. paper)
    ISBN 978-1-4773-1450-0 (pbk. : alk. paper)
    ISBN 978-1-4773-1326-8 (library e-book)
    ISBN 978-1-4773-1327-5 (non-library e-book)
Subjects: LCSH: Comic books, strips, etc.—History and
    criticism. | Motion pictures and comic books. | Motion
    pictures—Production and direction. | Film adaptations—
    History and criticism. | Motion picture industry—History
    and criticism.
Classification: LCC PN6725 .J43 2017 | DDC 741.5/9—dc23
LC record available at https://lccn.loc.gov/201700 0691

doi:10.7560/313251

CONTENTS

ACKNOWLEDGMENTS

One's first book doesn't materialize easily or painlessly; thankfully, the process of researching, writing, and revising *Comic Book Film Style* was made as smooth as possible thanks to the remarkable support, wisdom, and friendship I received throughout from my family, friends, and colleagues. First I must express my profound gratitude to Martin Lefebvre, whose mentorship and friendship have been truly invaluable from the very outset of this project, throughout my doctoral studies, and beyond. I also want to thank Charlie Keil for his encouragement, counsel, and seemingly endless reservoir of warmth over the years; you make academia feel like the supportive and truly collegial environment that it could and should be. I'd also like to recognize Marc Steinberg, Luca Caminati, Darren Wershler, and Will Brooker, whose instructive comments on previous versions of this project helped give shape to the book that it ultimately became. Rob King and Philippa Gates supervised earlier research projects that led to *Comic Book Film Style* and deserve credit for planting seeds and leading me in productive directions. I'd also like to acknowledge the rest of my colleagues at Concordia University, the University of Toronto, and Wilfrid Laurier University, as well as the Social Sciences and Humanities Research Council, who saw fit to fund my research multiple times over the years. Special thanks, finally, to Jim Burr, Lindsay Starr, Lynne Chapman, Sarah McGavick, Nancy Warrington, everyone at the University of Texas Press, and my two anonymous readers, whose suggestions improved my manuscript immensely. The blame for any errors that may remain in this book should be directed entirely at the author.

There are obviously many more people whose impact on this book cannot be as directly quantified as those cited above but who are equally worthy of my thanks. Jeff Gross talked things through with me every morning on his walk to work—and still does (sometimes we even talk about my research). Tony Fong read drafts and offered moral support even when his own work commitments were overwhelming already. Since 2011, I've also cohosted a podcast on the subject of comic book films, which has allowed me to ramble long enough to land on some of the ideas that appear in this book. My cohosts all deserve credit for putting up with me (and I hope I didn't inadvertently steal any of their ideas): Dave Babbitt, James Hrivnak, Andrew Kannegiesser, and Chris Martin. Speaking of putting up with me, nobody has done so to such a tremendous extent as Giselle Kraus, whose love and profound empathy make me better with every day. To paraphrase the great Sam Cooke: You're the apple of my eye / You're cherry pie / You're coconut cake and vegan ice cream.

Portions of chapter 4 have been published previously as "Comics at 300 Frames per Second: Zack Snyder's *300* and the Figural Translation of Comics to Film" in *Quarterly Review of Film and Video* 31, no. 3 (2014). My thanks to the journal's editors for permission to include some of that material here.

This book is dedicated with all my love to my parents, Pat and Rick, and to my sisters, Amanda and Emily. I love the shit out of you.

COMIC BOOK FILM STYLE

INTRODUCTION

For *The Warriors'* 2005 home video release, director Walter Hill produced a new version of the 1979 cult film, dubbed the "Ultimate Director's Cut." Hill claimed that this new version better reflected his original intentions for the film, which was conceived as "a comic book rock 'n' roll version of the Xenophon story [*Anabasis*]."[1] Of the three central elements in this description—the medium of comics, rock 'n' roll music, and an ancient Greek text—rock music is the only one that was explicitly present in the original version of the film, motivated on the soundtrack by the radio deejay who functions as a diegetic narrator. Hill's main intervention in the revised version is to integrate the two missing elements into the film in similarly literal ways: the 2005 cut opens with a new prologue, narrated by Hill himself, that plainly states the narrative's relation to Xenophon, accompanied by a series of comic book–style images. In addition to this opening gambit, the body of the film itself is peppered with comic book flourishes, particularly in transitional moments between scenes. In such moments, the cinematographic images freeze, dissolve into drawn versions of the same images, and sometimes include textual captions that narrate changes of location or time (e.g., "Meanwhile") or characters' unspoken internal monologues (e.g., "Holy shit!"). Often, the (virtual) camera tracks out of these images, revealing their placement within a grid of juxtaposed images, purposefully recalling the structure of a comic book page. The cumulative suggestion of these stylistic additions is clear: whereas *The Warriors* '79 simply presents a cinematic representation of a live-action fictional storyworld, *The Warriors* '05 presents a comic book storyworld brought to life through live-action cinema. The relevant difference between these two versions lies not in their narrative content but rather in how that content is mediated—or remediated, as the case may be—for the viewer.

This is merely one example of the much broader phenomenon that will be explored at length in this book, which I dub *comic book film style*. This designation refers to the results of an intermedial relationship between comics and film, whereby the latter medium appropriates and transforms certain of the formal attributes unique to the former as a means of stylization. While this phenomenon has inarguably been most visible in Hollywood cinema since the 1990s, a distinctly comic book–influenced film style can be found in various examples dating back to the mid-1960s at least, and adaptations of popular newspaper comic strips are among the earliest fiction films of the silent era. This is not to imply that all comic book adaptations necessarily have an interest in comics' medium-specific formal characteristics. Indeed, one common way that critics measure the "success" of a comic book film adaptation is the degree to which it renounces any residual trace of the comic book medium. One need look no further than reviews of one of the most successful comic book adaptations of all time, Christopher Nolan's *The Dark Knight* (2008), which was lauded by critics for the specifically "cinematic" qualities that allowed it to "transcend" its comic book origins.[2] Similarly, Roger Ebert's summation of *Superman III* (1983) illustrates the common view that a comic book–influenced cinema is an artistically impoverished one: "It's a cinematic comic book, shallow, silly, filled with stunts and action, without much human interest."[3]

If it's so undesirable, why devote a book to understanding comic book film style? To answer the question, one must understand why it is derided in the first place. Certainly one factor that contributes to the generally low opinion of comic book film style is the prevailing wisdom that films adapted from other media ought to replace the stylistic choices made in the text's original medium with cinematic equivalents: by this logic, a comics' dialogue, presented via text contained in speech balloons, should be replaced in a film adaptation by recorded dialogue, presented via synchronized sound. At a press junket for *Marvel's The Avengers* (2012), the film's writer/director, Joss Whedon, echoed this logic, stating that the key to making a good comic book adaptation was "capturing the essence of the comic and being true to what's wonderful about it, while remembering that it's a movie and not a comic. . . . You have to give the spirit of the thing and then step away from that, and create something cinematic and new."[4] In other words, a "good" adaptation will disavow those elements of the original that would seem alien in a cinematic context, favoring the conventions of cinema rather than comics wherever they come into conflict. Comic book film style thereby goes against the grain of "good" adaptation practice by retaining, if not privileging, the aesthetics of the original medium at the expense of cinematic convention.

This provides us with a good starting point from which to sketch a definition of comic book film style. As a primary principle, *comic book film style can be described as a set of self-reflexive gestures in which the different representational abilities of comics and film are put on simultaneous display in a cinematic work.* This occurs through what Jay David Bolter and Richard Grusin define as remediation, referring to the dialectical process through which one medium takes the form of another medium as its content or style, effectively resulting in the representation of one medium within another.[5] Remediating comic book form into cinematic style inserts an additional layer of mediation between the diegetic world and its cinematic representation. In other words, the storyworld is filtered through both comics and cinema before it reaches the viewer's perception, resulting in self-consciously stylized or "hypermediated" representations, as opposed to a logic of transparency or "immediacy."[6] While the mise-en-scène (i.e., lighting, costumes, sets, makeup, actors, etc.) may also be stylized, it's important to note that comic book film style overwhelmingly exists in that layer of mediation between the storyworld and the viewer: it is something that is *imposed upon* the diegesis, not something that emerges from it. Set design, for instance, certainly contributes to a film's overall look and aesthetic sensibility, but the stylization of sets falls under the realization of comic book content rather than the remediation of comics' form. Illustrative examples include the nearly abstract use of color in the film adaptation of *Sin City* (2005), which constantly calls attention to its own artificiality, or the use of slow motion in *300* (2006), which abstracts diegetic duration from viewed duration. We should then add that *comic book film style is nondiegetic, but it influences and conditions our access to the diegetic world on display in the film in various ways.*

As we'll discover over the following chapters, film and comics have distinctive and in some respects radically oppositional formal systems. The integration of comics' formal or conventional characteristics into a film thus results in some unusual and innovative effects, especially compared to what we expect from mainstream Hollywood filmmaking. Such ostentatious stylistic gestures can't help but call attention to themselves as artificial impositions on the representation, possibly even to such an extent that they disrupt the illusion created by the film. It follows from all of this that comic book film style represents a challenge to classical film style as influentially articulated by David Bordwell, Janet Staiger, and Kristin Thompson in *The Classical Hollywood Cinema*, or even "intensified continuity" as defined later by Bordwell. These approaches to film narration are defined by their strategic deployment of conventions in ways that are meant to produce particular effects—narrative immersion chief among them—without triggering the viewer's awareness that he or she is being manipulated into this state through deliberate stylistic choices. In Jared Gardner's words, classical style "trained audiences to privilege continuity, resolution, and closure—and to reject as 'bad film' the fragments, the gaps, the illogical connections" that might otherwise flourish.[7] Here we find another potential mark against comic book film style. In contrast to the classical mode, comic book film style deliberately and self-consciously puts style at the forefront of the viewer's experience of the film, often at the expense of narrative immersion. In this way, comic book film style harkens back to what Tom Gunning has called a "cinema of attractions" style of engagement in which the representational apparatus becomes a central source of aesthetic pleasure, on equal footing with the representations themselves. Therefore, *comic book film style's interest in remediating comics and its concomitant emphasis on intermedial aesthetics represent a nonclassical approach to film style.* This is not to say that such films are narratively incoherent or even stylistically excessive, since excess is typically defined by "arbitrary rather than logical" narration.[8] Comic book film style is decidedly not arbitrary; it is directed toward a particular purpose and is meant to achieve particular effects, but they are simply not motivated by or otherwise related to the narrative. Finally, then, we can add that *comic book film style is not motivated by narrative but instead by an intermedial relationship to and aesthetic interest in comics.*

Even if comic book film style can be and often is derided as an "improper" approach to film adaptation or for its "failure" to adhere to a logic of classical narrative immersion, it's nevertheless important to understand the forces that are shaping the ongoing evolution of film style. As Bordwell writes, "The way movies look has a history; this history calls out for analysis and explanation; and the study of this domain—the history of film style—presents inescapable challenges to anyone who wants to understand cinema."[9] The comic book film has been described without hyperbole as "Hollywood's leading genre"[10] today, and it follows that the comic book medium would exert a particularly strong influence on how film style evolves going forward. The self-consciously stylized techniques of today, originating in comics and transformed by processes of remediation, may well become the entrenched cinematic conventions of tomorrow.

It's my contention that this stylistic influence is both the most interesting attribute of comic book cinema and the one that is most often overlooked. Several significant studies of contemporary film style cite comics as an important source of material for Hollywood blockbusters in particular, but rarely is style singled out as a unique or notable feature of these films. For instance, Bordwell devotes a long paragraph to "comic-book movies" in *The Way Hollywood Tells It* but doesn't consider them to represent a special case in terms of style;[11] similarly, in *New Hollywood Cinema*, Geoff King discusses comic book adaptations like *Batman* (1989) as exemplars of blockbuster franchising in the age of media conglomeration,[12] but he seems to consider the "mainstream comic-book caper" as a sort of stylistic blank slate against which "some of the darker and quirkier dimensions of the developing [Tim] Burton style" stand out.[13] Indeed, King seems to deny the existence or possibility of a distinctive comic book film style, as evidenced by the way he opens the same book: "A complex American 'art' cinema of innovation and experimentation, or the simplistic world of the comic-book blockbuster? . . . Unsettling departures from 'classical' Hollywood style, or superficial glitz and over-insistent rhetoric drawn from advertising and MTV?"[14] While King is attempting to demonstrate the breadth and contradictory nature of "New Hollywood" cinema, the present volume should make it clear that comic book film style also simultaneously and consistently embodies both sides of these binaries. Such a singular feat should make it worthy of extended interrogation on its own.

Defining the Comic Book Film: Genre, Adaptation, or Style?

The broader category from which comic book film style emerges—the "comic book film"—is itself somewhat confused: untangling this knot is a necessary first step toward better defining and justifying the scope of the present project. In order to do so, it's productive to return briefly to *The*

Warriors. Based on comments made in conjunction with the release of the "Ultimate Director's Cut," Walter Hill clearly conceptualized the film from the ground up as a "comic book film," despite the fact that its source text was not a comic book but rather a novel (which was itself inspired by Xenophon). Hill's interest in comics was therefore not intertextual in nature, since he wasn't looking to specific comic books for narrative inspiration; rather, he was interested in the unique aesthetic appeal of the medium more generally. In an oral history of his film, the director stated:

> I don't think you can understand the movie without understanding my infatuation with the American comic book. It was the height of my creative interest in that art form. I wanted to divide the movie into chapters and then have each chapter come to life starting with a splash panel. It was a low budget movie and there was very little time for post-production because we had a fixed release date that we agreed upon.[15]

Due to these pressures, Hill was unable to integrate the medium of comics into *The Warriors'* stylistic system to the extent that he had hoped, thereby losing what he had considered an essential aspect of the film's meaning. His interest in imbuing the film with a comic book aesthetic was limited in the original version to a few animated "page curl" wipes that may evoke the readerly experience of comics for some viewers, but that might just as equally point to the film's origins as a novel.

Despite the director's own misgivings, however, *The Warriors'* comic book influence was noted by some critics prior to the release of the "Ultimate Director's Cut." These comments are, in my view, particularly illuminating. Jake Horsley described *The Warriors* as "about as close to comic book kineticism as the movies had ever got"[16] and "one of the first American movies to come up with a genuine comic book nihilism";[17] Andy Johnson wrote that "one of the things which makes the film so unique is the vivid, comic book–style depiction of . . . New York";[18] Andrew Tutor focused on *The Warriors'* color palette, writing that the film "is rendered with the use of the strong reds, yellows, and blues of comic book design. In its subway scenes especially, colors leap from the screen much as, say, a Roy Lichtenstein picture leaps from the canvas, its direct assault on our vision as basic as that of a comic strip";[19] and Elayne Chaplin asserted that "the cliche-ridden plot . . . along with the formal elements of the film (such as the jagged, page-turn wipes that growl across the screen to mark the transitions between sequences) combine to emphasise its comic book sensibility."[20] Comments such as these suggest that the film's narrative and whatever stylization was present in its original iteration already evoked comics for a certain segment of the viewing audience. But what exactly are these writers saying about *The Warriors* and, more importantly, about comic books as a medium? Reading these quotations closely offers a clue: on a grammatical level, these assessments of the film overwhelmingly use "comics" or "comic book" not as a noun, which would refer to the medium of comics or to specific comic book texts, but rather as an adjective that modifies some other quality that is present in the film. This is similar to how the New Critics used the words "comic book" as "shorthand for all that was degraded and degenerate about contemporary mass culture"; like some of the above descriptions of *The Warriors*, they would wield an entire medium as a pejorative, denigrating everything disposable about mass culture as "comic book culture."[21] In such statements, the comic book medium is invoked obliquely at best. As *The Warriors'* critics describe it, the film's *comic book* kineticism and *comic book* nihilism work in tandem with its *comic book–style* depiction of New York to create an overall *comic book* sensibility. In short, "comic book" is being deployed by these writers not to reference the formal or textual specificities of the medium that Scott McCloud has influentially defined as "juxtaposed . . . images in deliberate sequence,"[22] but rather to flag—and sometimes deride—certain narrative or stylistic attributes ("kineticism," "nihilism," "vivid," "cliché-ridden") that they personally associate with comics.

So what's wrong with this? To start, comics aren't inherently kinetic—indeed, their basis in static art renders this a somewhat strange and perhaps even paradoxical association. Similarly, there isn't anything inherently nihilistic about stories told through text and images juxtaposed in space. Likewise, comics imagery may be vivid, but it may equally be bland; color is strongly associated with comics, but there is an equally rich history of monochromatic comics. And finally, comics narratives may be cliché-ridden—a trait they share with no less than *every other storytelling medium*—but they may equally be innovative, unique, or even nonnarrative in orientation. In short, these descriptions traffic exclusively in sweeping generalizations about the medium of comics that would likely not have passed muster had they been made with reference to literature or music, for instance. Indeed, the qualities invoked have little to do with the inherent or essential qualities of the medium as a whole and likely have much more to do with specific experiences that these authors have had with particular texts or, at most, genres. After all, a comic can be anything from two crudely sketched panels to thousands of ornately composed pages; comics' visual style can vary from abstract and caricatured to painterly or even photographic, from monochromatic to full-color and every variation between; a comic's narration may be entirely visual ("silent") or heavily reliant on text. No one of these myriad options defines or exhausts the potential of comics, which is not a *genre* centered around a specific type of narrative content and style, but rather a *medium* capable of infinite variation.[23]

Given how loosely the medium is often invoked, it's not surprising that there would be some confusion over what precisely constitutes a comic book film. Generally speaking, any superhero-centered film is likely to be dubbed a comic book film, even if it is not a comic book adaptation and doesn't betray any stylistic interest in comics.[24] As Liam Burke notes, "the term 'comic book adaptation' [has become] synonymous with 'superhero movie.'"[25] The adaptation scholar Thomas Leitch makes this mistake, describing Pixar's animated superhero film *The Incredibles* (2004) as a comic book movie, and Geoff King goes even further afield when he classifies the science-fiction adventure *Star Wars* (1977) as a "comic book blockbuster."[26] Pervasive though it may be, defining the comic book movie category in this way is plainly wrong, since superhero or other "hero's journey" narratives don't necessarily have anything to do with comics as a medium.

Conversely, "comic book film" is also used as a generic shorthand for any film adapted from comic book source material, be it a direct adaptation of a particular text (e.g., *300*) or a loose adaptation of characters and story-worlds that originated in comics (e.g., *Batman*). This is how David Hughes,[27] Leitch,[28] and Bordwell[29] define the comic book film, to name just a few. On the face of it, this is a much more plausible definition, since it is based on an empirical relationship between a given film and a comic book. Films adapted from comic books are, in a real sense, comic book films insofar as they possess certain demonstrable similarities with particular comic book texts. The question becomes, then, whether adaptation theory offers the most useful set of tools with which to approach comic book films. On this front, I believe the answer is no. The traditional concerns of adaptation theory have dominated the discourse surrounding comic book films to date. As Leitch, who is perhaps the most self-aware adaptation scholar today, notes, "since its inception half a century ago, adaptation studies has been haunted by concepts and premises it has repudiated in principle but continued to rely on in practice."[30] The so-called "fidelity discourse" is often the first of these to be disavowed, only to rear its ugly head in subtler forms: "the field is still haunted by the notion that adaptations *ought to* be faithful to their ostensible sourcetexts."[31] Evaluating a film not for what it *is* but for what *you think it should be* is fine for fans, but it is a faux-pas for film critics and scholars. For those who remain drawn to the phenomenon of film adaptation as an object of serious study, it's clear why they would want to distance themselves from such practices, but it seems as though there's a magnetic field inherent in adaptation theory that pulls scholars into these kinds of orbits—or, more accurately, black holes.

Despite having been declared a "chimera" by Robert Stam[32] and disowned by most other scholars working within the field of adaptation studies, the concept of fidelity continues to pervade scholarship relating to comic book film adaptations, from Greg M. Smith's claim that the animated television adaptation of Image Comics' *The Maxx* "is as literal an adaptation of the comic book as is imaginable"[33] to Bob Rehak's pronouncement that Zack Snyder's live-action adaptation of "*Watchmen* simply takes faithfulness and fidelity to a cosmic degree."[34] Fidelity discourse is an unfortunate remnant of adaptation theory's origins as an evaluative schema, based on the premise that the original work represents a standard of quality to which the film adaptation must strive. As Stam amusingly points out, deviations from the original version tend to be met with hostility: "The language of criticism dealing with the film adaptation of novels has often been profoundly moralistic, awash in terms such as *infidelity, betrayal, deformation, violation, vulgarization,* and *desecration,* each accusation carrying its specific charge of outraged negativity."[35]

What's particularly problematic about fidelity discourse is that it can't be applied with any standard of rigor or empiricism. A film adaptation can be praised as faithful by one person and denounced as sacrilege by another, simply because these viewers value different aspects of the original work. As the claims above by Smith and Rehak demonstrate, visual fidelity tends to be privileged above other considerations in assessments of comic book film adaptations. But as Dan Hassler-Forest argues, superficial visual correspondences between original and adaptation do not necessarily amount to perfect fidelity. To judge a film like *300* as "faithful" to its source text, he argues, is to privilege the film's visuals at the expense of its ideological content, the latter of which is quite distinct from its comic book counterpart.[36] Pascal Lefèvre's article "Incompatible Visual Ontologies?" advances the view that the various formal dissimilarities between comics and film render fidelity impossible—following Stam, fidelity is a chimera, a pipe dream that will not and cannot be achieved—and that fans should therefore be tolerant of the inevitable differences between original and adaptation.[37] Most recently, Burke has attempted to rescue fidelity discourse, arguing that it remains "a marker of quality for many audiences"[38] and is therefore key to understanding how these films succeed or fail with viewers. Citing J. D. Connor, he claims that adaptation scholars must continue to grapple with fidelity based on "the role [it] plays in the layman's discussion."[39] Indeed, it seems to me that discussions of fidelity are *only* useful in such contexts, but then we're shifting our focus from the films themselves to fan discourse surrounding their reception. Ultimately, I don't believe that the concept of fidelity can play any useful role in academic criticism that attempts to analyze the films as texts in and of themselves.

While discussing Burke's approach, it's worth noting that he does not simply define the comic book film as adaptation. In his book—titled, ironically, *The Comic Book Film Adaptation*—he offers a definition that is far more prescriptive in terms of content than either of the possible definitions mentioned above. According to him, the comic book film is a unique genre unto itself that "follows a vigilante or outsider character engaged in a form of revenge narrative, and is pitched at a heightened reality with a visual style marked by distinctly comic book imagery."[40] The number of comic book film adaptations that fall outside of even these broadly sketched lines, however, is considerable, to say nothing about films that have an aesthetic interest in remediating comics but that aren't adaptations of a particular comic book. Moreover, many comic book adaptations satisfy Burke's content description but not the stylistic one, or vice versa, and the criteria relating to film style ("heightened reality," "comic book imagery") are nebulous at best. This definition treats the "comic book" in "comic book film" in the same loose, adjectival way that plagued descriptions of *The Warriors*, where what is being invoked is not anything specific or central to the medium itself but rather a series of more general qualities that can appear in any storytelling medium. Surely there is nothing about the history or form of sequential art that predisposes or limits it to narratives about revenge; or stories centered on vigilante or outsider characters; or, given the existence of avant-garde and abstract comics, even to narrative at all! In artificially yoking these qualities to the comic book medium, Burke's definition creates an arbitrary and fallacious association between a particular kind of narrative and style and the medium of comics.

Despite the vague allusion to "comic book imagery," Burke's definition also seems divorced from the medium of comics itself; while he correctly states that "a comic book movie does not need to actually be based on a comic book to be included in this genre," he then elaborates that "it simply needs to adopt elements synonymous with the comic book movie."[41] By this circular logic, a given movie can be described as a comic book film if it is sufficiently similar to other comic book movies, even if it has no intertextual or intermedial relationship to actual comics. As an example, he cites *The League of Extraordinary Gentlemen* (2003) as a film that is "significantly modified [from its source material] to meet the conventions of the [comic book film] genre."[42] The implication is presumably that a more "faithful" adaptation of the original comics would *not* have met Burke's definition of a comic book film, and that the film needed to distance itself from the narrative and visual approach of its actual comic book source material in order to satisfy the requirements of the genre! Burke's definition is clearly broken: indeed, it's so divorced from the actual medium of comics and the unlimited variety of narratives that they can contain that adaptations of unconventional (read: not superhero) comics must downplay their relationship to their source material to be considered proper comic book films.

Burke's definition embodies a fundamental difficulty of genre identification and recognition discussed by Andrew Tudor. Using the western genre as his example, Tudor claims that "most writers tend to assume that there is some body of films we can safely call the western and then move on to the real work—the analysis of the crucial characteristics of the already recognized *genre*."[43] But genre theorists then find themselves trapped in a logic loop: to discuss films as belonging to a particular genre, they have to first assume that they belong in that category, which is a conclusion that cannot be safely made *before* analysis takes place. As Tudor might observe, Burke leans "on a common cultural consensus as to what constitutes" a comic book film—namely superhero films and most comic book adaptations—and then reverse engineers a restrictive definition based on what few consistencies those films offer. I think this is where he first errs: that is, with the initial premise that there is a distinct and unique genre to be found within the glut of so-called "comic book films" in contemporary Hollywood. The fact that the conventions he cites as definitive of the comic book film have so little to do with the actual medium of comics should rightly cause us to question the legitimacy of the genre. To me, his definition begs a series of questions: If comic books themselves aren't limited to a tightly circumscribed narrative genre, why should comic book films be? How can the sole criterion for consideration as a comic book film be anything other than a significant interest in or aesthetic debt to the form and content of *comic books*? Why should anything other than the cinematic representation of comics' medium-specific qualities and conventions—or even of comics themselves—be considered central to our definition of the comic book film?

When defining the comic book film, then, we should not start with films that we assume to be examples of the genre a priori, but instead with definitions of the comic book medium. Such a definition might rightly mention the simultaneous presence of sequential static images, the hybridity of words and pictures (e.g., in word balloons), or the multiframe as an organizing visual principle, to cite just a few of the medium's notable characteristics. However, it could not justifiably mention superheroes, even though the genre has been closely associated with comics for much of its history, because superheroes—or any specific narrative content, for that matter—are not a defining trait of the medium. If it's to be meaningful and valuable as a designation, the "comic book" in "comic book film" can't mean something different to each viewer based on their own individual perceptions of what kinds of stories comics tell—denoting nihilism to one person, clichéd narratives to the next, and vigilante protagonists to another. Its meaning must be concrete rather than abstract, based on the medium-specific qualities that define comics as a unique art; in short, it must mean *comic book*. Properly speaking, then, the comic book film ought to exclusively designate films that *remediate* comic books as an art form, rather than those that merely *adapt* comics narratives (or, more loosely, the kinds of narratives that we reductively associate with comics). Some of the most ambitious cases of comic book film style are not superhero films, adaptations, or revenge narratives with vigilante protagonists—films like George A. Romero's *Creepshow* (1982), Alain Resnais's *I Want to Go Home* (1989), Kurt Wimmer's *Ultraviolet* (2006), Randall Miller's *CBGB* (2013), and the director's cut of *The Warriors*. Nevertheless, all of these films integrate recognizable elements of the comic book medium into their representational styles. Indeed, these films are arguably more invested in the comic book *as a medium* than the vast majority of direct adaptations.

To focus on the "comic book" in "comic book film," we must distance ourselves from the ways of thinking that so confused this category in the first place. This means moving away from conceptualizing the comic book film as a genre with prescribed content—be it superheroes or something slightly broader—or as a mode of adaptation, and toward considering it as an intermedial approach to film style. Instead of asking what generic qualities films adapted from or otherwise related to comic book narratives share, we should instead ask: What concrete influence has the comic book medium exerted on films, and how does such an influence manifest? How have different films approached the challenges involved in remediating comic books? And what do these various approaches reveal about the two media involved? An analytical approach based on close textual readings and informed by remediation theory gets to the heart of this matter and reveals the stylistic complexity of the comic book film.

Revising Remediation

The theory of remediation as defined by Bolter and Grusin is imperfect and requires some nuancing to be a maximally effective tool for articulating the nuances of comic book film style. As their book's subtitle makes clear, remediation is meant as a tool for "understanding new media," and its biases definitely veer toward the digital for reasons that I will discuss shortly. First, however, it's necessary to provide a brief overview of their argument and terminology to discover which elements of their theory require revision. For Bolter and Grusin, the phenomenon of remediation is not only dialectical but also dialogic: every medium is born and lives alongside every other medium in a kind of dynamic pool, similar to what the Russian literary theorist Mikhail Bakhtin imagines for linguistic utterances,[44] wherein each individual articulation—of language or, in this case, of media—can only be understood through its countless associations and resonances with and against other like articulations. No medium exists in a vacuum, and all media come into being and evolve through acts of intermedial appropriation. Unlike Bakhtin, however, Bolter and Grusin imagine a single Platonic ideal toward which all media necessarily strive: implicit or explicit in every act of media appropriation is a claim that the colonizing medium improves upon the colonized by giving its user more or better access to "the real."[45] Perhaps they limit their focus to new digital media because this trajectory doesn't hold up when applied to old media. Though new media have overwhelmingly followed this particular path, there is simply no reason why any medium—old or new—ought to *necessarily* evolve in a single, unified direction. The history of modern painting offers a compelling counterexample of a medium that has evolved without a singular or unified trajectory, with movements embracing new forms of realism being succeeded by radical breaks with representationalism altogether (e.g., the post–World War II abstract expressionist movement, which followed a period of social realism). Because painting is widely accepted as a medium without an inherent predisposition toward any single style of aesthetic expression, it has been mobilized in a variety of ways, by a variety of artists, toward a variety of ends. It has moved hither and thither, refusing to follow a straight line, and thus refusing to satisfy a teleology. In short, there is no Platonic ideal that the history of painting collectively strives toward. Moreover, Bolter and Grusin also tend to conflate the concepts of "realism"—such as that advanced by André Bazin or Stanley Cavell with regard to the cinema—"immediacy," and "the real." They refute Bazin's claim that the cinema satisfies "our obsession with realism" on the basis that digital technologies have since increased our access to "the real,"[46] rendering the cinema of yesteryear antiquated and out of step with reality as perceived by contemporary eyes. However, Bazin and Cavell are discussing a different phenomenon than Bolter and Grusin: realism, unlike immediacy, is a *style*, a conscious deployment of form used in the production of artworks; "the real" is precisely that which art—even realist art—is not.

Comic books represent another blind spot of their teleological argument. In the early days of the medium, comics may have been viewed as a remediation of drawing, taking individual drawn images and "improving" them by placing discrete images in sequence to form relationships, be they narrative or otherwise; likewise, it could be viewed as a remediation of the novel, taking its approach to narrative and its linear, printed format and "improving" it with the addition of visual images. In neither case, however, is it clear that comics are "[refashioning the older medium] in the name of the real."[47] The mental images evoked by a skilled novelist's prose may be more detailed, nuanced, "realistic," or more immediate than the static, often crude drawings of early comics, but it's ultimately an apples-to-oranges-style comparison; likewise, the sequential drawings of comics are undoubtedly adding *something* to the individual drawing, but there's no reason why the sequential nature of comics should necessarily be mobilized in pursuit of "the real." Cinema provides a similar case. Though cinema has largely been understood as progressing (by virtue of technological "improvements" such as sound, color, and 3-D) toward greater and greater realism, there is no reason why it must be thus. As we'll see throughout the chapters to follow, the remediation of comic books by the cinema overwhelmingly produces a marked increase in self-conscious mediation, an increased visibility and awareness of the cinematic apparatus, and a more qualified relationship to "the real." Ultimately, Bolter and Grusin's insistence that media evolve toward "the real" is misplaced and limiting, and therefore doesn't factor into my use of remediation.

The dialectic between immediacy (in which the means of representation are completely effaced or transparent, seemingly placing the user in the immediate presence of what is being represented) and hypermediacy (in which the means of representation are of equal representational significance to that which is being represented through them) is also central to Bolter and Grusin's theory. They write that

> although each medium promises to reform its predecessors by offering a more immediate or authentic experience, the promise of reform inevitably leads us to become aware of the new medium as a medium. Thus, immediacy leads to hypermediacy. The process of remediation makes us aware that all media are at one level a "play of signs," which is a lesson that we take from poststructuralist literary theory.[48]

Indeed, it is a lesson that we can learn much earlier, for instance from the formalist theory of art advanced by Viktor Shklovsky in his 1917 essay "Art as Device":

> In order to return sensation to our limbs, in order to make us feel objects, to make a stone feel stony, man has been given the tool of art. The purpose of art, then, is to lead us to a knowledge of a thing through the organ of sight instead of recognition. By "enstranging" objects and complicating form, the device of art makes perception long and "laborious." The perceptual process in art has a purpose all its own and ought to be extended to the fullest. *Art is a means of experiencing the process of creativity. The artifact itself is quite unimportant.*[49]

Both articulations of this idea express a circular process whereby the conventions of a given system of representation are first "enstranging" or hypermediated; then, as we become accustomed to their particular brand of mediation, they become more immediate or invisible, thereby necessitating a new set of conventions to renew our perceptual and aesthetic experience. For Shklovsky, this was the process through which individual art forms maintained their vibrancy and urgency; for Bolter and Grusin, it is the process through which new media come into being and solidify their unique identities.

The deep similarities between these two theories speak to remediation's concern with the formal and stylistic qualities of media and suggest that remediation might be a useful tool for identifying and conceptualizing stylistic innovations that have an intermedial basis. In using it to these ends, however, one inevitably subverts Bolter and Grusin's intentions: where remediation as they theorized it insists on media's relationship to "the real" and strives for immediacy, a formalist approach to remediation privileges hypermediacy and is concerned with aestheticization rather than a representation's relationship to a real-world referent. My rearticulation of remediation removes this insistence on immediacy and "the real": in my usage, remediation should be understood to refer only to a medium's appropriation of "the techniques, forms, and social significance of other media" and the concomitant "[attempt] to rival or refashion them" using its own native representational system, resulting in a hybridized, intermedial, and properly dialogic expression. Rather than insist on a more immediate relationship to the real in this combination, remediation may (and most often does) result in a more thoroughly and self-consciously mediated aesthetic experience.

How might remediation relate to adaptation? In Bolter and Grusin's own words, an adaptation is a text in which "the content has been borrowed, but the medium has not been appropriated or quoted."[50] A remediation is essentially the inverse, wherein the medium is the focus of the appropriation and the content is irrelevant. Of course, it's also possible for a text to adapt and remediate simultaneously. For this reason, remediation scholars need to be careful to avoid falling back into the unproductive tendencies of adaptation theory. Indeed, Bolter himself has invoked the evaluative language associated with adaptation when discussing Robert Rodriguez's *Sin City* as a remediation: "The style of the film *Sin City* perfectly matches the dark vision of the original comic book: the film is probably the *most faithful remediation* of a comic book in the history of the genre."[51] While remediation is undoubtedly a superior logic with which to confront the specific problems presented by comic book film style, it also represents a much-needed escape from the baggage associated with adaptation studies: to continue to fall back on fidelity discourse in this new context is surely less than ideal. Remediation provides a means of addressing the specific formal problems raised by intermedial films such as *Sin City*; to abandon the analysis at the mere recognition of superficial resemblances between the two versions squanders the theoretical promise of remediation for formal and stylistic analysis.

To deploy remediation as a nuanced analytical tool, we must also further tailor it to the specificities of the comic book film. This is precisely the task of chapter 1, "The Six Modes of Interaction between Comics and Film," in which I establish a schema of six unique modes of intertextual and intermedial relations that exhaustively reflect the ways in which comic book films incorporate aspects of the comic book medium into their stylistic systems. Drawing on Sylvain White's *The Losers* (2010) for illustrative examples throughout, I define and demonstrate each of the comic book film's six modes of interaction: (1) diegetic intertextuality, (2) compositional intertextuality, (3) explicit intermediality, (4) expressive intermediality, (5) formal intermediality, and (6) figural intermediality. These six categories provide the conceptual framework that will be used throughout the chapters to follow and that I hope will be adopted as a means of analyzing intermedial film style more generally. The chapter also functions as a thorough close reading of *The Losers* from a stylistic perspective.

The next three chapters each focus on a specific site of what Pascal Lefèvre would describe as "irreconcilable ontological difference" between comics and film. Such dissimilarities between the two media make adaptation difficult per Lefèvre,[52] insofar as perfectly faithful, perfectly equivalent adaptations are impossible by definition. From a more positive viewpoint, however, these dissimilarities are precisely the lifeblood of comic book film style, presenting opportunities for creative filmmakers to appropriate various formal and conventional attributes associated with an ontologically alien medium into their films, thereby producing unusual and occasionally influential articulations of cinematic style.

Chapter 2, "Vandalizing the Fourth Wall: Word-Image Hybridity and a Comic Book Cinema of Attractions," explores the difference between the sound of film and the "silence" of comics. Such a starkly articulated difference between the two media, however, ignores the considerable chunk of film history that precedes the technological integration of synchronized film sound. Appropriately, it is in this preclassical period of silent filmmaking that we find the closest cinematic equivalent to comic books' insistence on representing sound through graphically rendered text. Through analyses of *Batman: The Movie* (1966), *American Splendor* (2003), and *Super* (2010), I argue that remediating comics' hybridization of image and text—including speech and thought balloons, captions, and onomatopoeia—results in a contemporary articulation of the preclassical cinema of attractions that deliberately eschews the "invisibility" of film style; instead, the visual plane becomes a more playful territory upon which diegetic and nondiegetic elements interact, putting style on flamboyant display and laying bare the artifice of both media. Like comics, comic book film style puts the processes through which worlds are represented, stories are told, and meaning is created on spectacular and self-conscious display.

This line of inquiry continues in chapter 3, "These Panels Have Been Formatted to Fit Your Screen: Remediating the Comics Page through the Cinematic Frame," which explores various attempts at appropriating the comics panel's plasticity and the comics page's multiplicity within the film frame. The differences between the panel and the frame are often misunderstood and oversimplified by comics and film scholars alike: this chapter begins by setting the record straight and laying out how each works in its respective medium. What happens, then, when the film frame is treated as a panel, or contains multiple panels? Films like *Superman* (1978), *Creepshow*, and *The Dark Knight* present "holistic" approaches to remediating the structure and flexibility of the comic book page, while movies like *Hulk* (2003) and *The Green Hornet* (2011) employ split screen in ways that challenge the technique's usual cinematic use. These and other case studies represent the space between simultaneity and sequentiality, continuity and discontinuity, subjectivity and omniscience—in short, between comics' hypervisible mode of narration and the invisible narration usually associated with classical film style.

The fourth chapter, "The Privileged Instant: Remediating Stasis as Movement," examines the role played by duration and temporality in comic book film style. Since comics consist entirely of static images and cinema features images that move, their respective relationships to time could hardly be more different. But just as comics can represent sound while remaining a "silent" medium, so too can they represent movement without necessarily containing moving images. As is the case with the remediation of comics' "sound," the aesthetic conventions that communicate movement may also be remediated cinematically. Each panel in a comic represents a "privileged instant," often a composite that spans a duration of time; film has various methods for privileging specific instants in a similar way. Using examples from films like *Spider-Man 2* (2004) and *Daredevil* (2003), I explore the practice of compositional mimesis, whereby specific panels from comics are restaged for a film, resulting in an indexical relationship between the film version and its comic book referent, comparable to a *tableau vivant*. Motion lines, a convention used to suggest the speed and trajectory of movement in comics, can also be remediated for film using various effects, as seen in films like *Superman* and *V for Vendetta* (2005). Finally, selective slow motion (also known as speed ramping) is used in films like *300*, *Wanted* (2008), and *Avengers: Age of Ultron* (2015) to re-create the elastic temporality of comics and, more specifically, to remediate the reader's internal negotiation of the productive space between the static images that co-occupy each comic book page (known in comics scholarship as "gutters"). In different ways, all of these techniques complicate cinema's relationship to time by appealing to the looser experience of "panel time," wherein past, present, and future can coexist, and iconic moments are presented in ways that linger before the reader's perception.

Chapter 5 demonstrates that the six modes of intermedial interaction defined in chapter 1 can be applied to a broader array of media. The chapter title, "The Polymedial Comic Book Film," refers to films that remediate comics that themselves remediate a host of other media, effectively synthesizing an entire media ecology into a single aesthetic. I focus on two in-depth case studies: *Scott Pilgrim vs. the World* (2010) and *Watchmen: The Ultimate Cut* (2009). Both of these films are suffused with the kinds of intertextuality and intermediality described in previous chapters, but they also represent the "post-cinematic" approach to filmmaking endemic to contemporary image-saturated digital culture, making them particularly dense case studies of cinematic remediation. These films advance the discussions begun in previous chapters into new territories that are opened up largely as a result of the aesthetic flexibility afforded by digital technology, which is alternately used to reflect a media-saturated world (in *Scott Pilgrim*) and to traverse multiple platforms for transmedia distribution (in *Watchmen*). Even in this "new media" context, the comic book medium remains the prism through which other media are filtered in these films, demonstrating the continued relevance of comics—certainly not "new media" by any standard definition—in an increasingly digital and post-cinematic era. The overt stylization of these films and their total embrace of ostentatiously hypermediated representations make them among the purest and richest examples of comic book film style, wherein the content, form, and conventions of comics are superimposed on the diegetic worlds represented cinematically, thoroughly and self-consciously conditioning the viewer's experience of them. Finally, the book's conclusion examines the notion of world-building in relation to comic book film franchises, and looks forward to the future of comic book film style using three brief analyses of recent films.

Salient issues related to the comic book film remain beyond the scope of the present study. Most significantly, I have chosen to limit my analysis to the ways in which films have remediated comics and not also vice versa. This unidirectional focus should not imply that cinema has not also exerted a powerful influence on the style and formal development of comics, but rather that this influence is sufficiently rich, nuanced, and complex that the subject would be better explored in a monograph all its own. Analyses of comics' formal system—such as Thierry Groensteen's *System of Comics*, for example—are sufficiently indebted to concepts and terminology ported over from film studies that such a project would be a natural extension of the work already being done in the field. I also want to stress that focusing specifically on the cinematic side of this intermedial dialogue does not undermine the inherently dialectical nature of comic book film style, which is always the product of thesis (the prevailing stylistic tendencies of mainstream cinema) and antithesis (the particular formal features and conventions of comics) creating a new synthesis (comic book film style); it is always a complex dialogic interaction, never a simple process of intermedial transference. Finally, I don't mean to imply that comics and film are somehow privileged or special cases within the broader contemporary media ecology: the boundaries between media have always been fluid, and there is no pure or unique "essence" to either cinema or comics that exists in a vacuum, safe from the influence of other media. As Bolter and Grusin put it:

> No medium today, and certainly no single event, seems to do its cultural work in isolation from other media, any more than it works in isolation from other social and economic forces. What is new about new media comes from the particular *ways* in which they refashion older media and the ways in which older media refashion themselves to answer the challenges of new media.[53]

The dialogic interaction between comics and film is itself not new, but it has certainly reached the point where its effects can no longer be ignored if we want to have a coherent and comprehensive account of contemporary film style.

I have also limited my case studies to English-language, predominantly American live-action films. While other national cinemas certainly adapt and remediate comics, the category of "comic book film" is undoubtedly dominated by Hollywood productions, with superhero blockbusters being the most visible in the present moment. Italian, Japanese, and Franco-Belgian comic book films—to name only three alternative production contexts—are equally deserving of study, and could be productively considered within the framework that I establish here. I would certainly be curious as to how the results of such studies might enrich or complicate my own conclusions. Animated films are also excluded from my corpus on the basis that the remediation of drawn images into live action represents, for me, one of the most compelling differences between the media of comics and film. Due to their mutual reliance on illustration, there is less of an inherent difference between representations made for comic books and those made for animated films, at least when compared to photographic (or seemingly photographic) live-action cinema. Comic book film style therefore stands out more starkly in live-action films, which are overwhelmingly expected to obey certain laws governing film style (e.g., continuity editing)—not to mention the laws of physics, which animation flouts as a matter of routine. Moreover, the integration of comic book stylization (e.g., visualized onomatopoeic sound effects, motion or "stink" lines, etc.) are already much more common in animated fare, such that they don't disrupt the verisimilitude of the representation in the same way that they might in predominantly photographic worlds.

While historians of comics and film will continue to debate the precise date of their respective births, comics and film came into being at roughly the same time, eventually became two of modernity's defining mass media, and led to the creation of many seminal and even canonical works of American art in the twentieth and twenty-first centuries. Contemporary Hollywood cinema is awash with superhero films and comic book adaptations, but it's not just film narratives that have been influenced by comics. Contrary to popular belief, comic book film style is not the product of "incorrect" or overly "literal" adaptation; it is a deliberate hybridization of distinct and often oppositional forms of representation. Similarly, comic book film style is not a failure to adhere to classical continuity principles; rather, it is a provocative and deliberate abandonment of classicism's invisible approach to narration in favor of self-conscious mediation. Above all, comic book film style is a distinctively cinematic embodiment of the creative and representational richness that the comic book medium offers, and it deserves to be understood in all of its intermedial complexity. This book represents a first step toward granting the remediation of comic books its proper status: at the vanguard of stylistic experimentation in contemporary Hollywood cinema.

CHAPTER 1

THE SIX MODES OF INTERACTION BETWEEN COMICS AND FILM

In 2010, ten years into the "Golden Age of Comic Book Filmmaking,"[1] Hollywood released no fewer than six blockbuster (or would-be blockbuster) comic book adaptations: *Kick-Ass*, *The Losers*, *Iron Man 2*, *Jonah Hex*, *Scott Pilgrim vs. the World*, and *RED*.[2] Though the comic book film and the superhero film are often conflated in mainstream discourse, the offerings from 2010 forcefully demonstrate what a misconception this is: if anything, *Iron Man 2* is the odd one out in this list, representing the sole entry in an established cinematic superhero franchise that year. Rather than superheroes, the comic book films of 2010 were dominated by underdogs, ranging from the Canadian slackers of *Scott Pilgrim*, the powerless superhero wannabes of *Kick-Ass*, the retired secret agents of *RED*, to the presumed-dead special forces team taking on a corrupt CIA operative in *The Losers*. *Jonah Hex* might even be considered an underdog film for its failed attempt to incorporate the dormant western genre into the current wave of comic book filmmaking. (*Cowboys and Aliens* would try something similar the following year.) Generically speaking, however, these films are quite diverse: while *Kick-Ass* joins *Iron Man 2* as a superhero film, it is equally a parodic satire of the genre; *The Losers* and *RED* are both comedic action pictures; *Scott Pilgrim* combines a variety of genres but is simply a romantic comedy at heart. Though all of these films are based on comic books and can thereby be classified as comic book films in a general sense, any attempt to group these six films together into a single generic category based on their narrative content is doomed to fail.

What these film share—though, again, *Iron Man 2* may be the exception—is an intermedial interest in comic books. In this chapter, I propose a means of understanding the comic book film that is based entirely on the concrete, demonstrable ways in which they interact with comics, both in a micro sense (i.e., through the adaptation of individual texts or textual elements) and a macro sense (i.e., through the remediation of the medium itself), with a strong emphasis on the latter. While adaptation tends to dominate how most people conceive of the comic book film, remediation is more salient to the present discussion of comic book film style, which is the comic book film's primary contribution to contemporary filmmaking practice. In looking at comic book films closely, we can determine six distinct ways in which these films negotiate the differences between the comic book medium and cinema. Briefly articulated, these six strategies are:

1) *Diegetic intertextuality*: the presence of characters, narrative, settings, and other content from particular comics' diegetic worlds;

2) *Compositional intertextuality*: moments in a comic book film in which the arrangement of mise-en-scène elements directly recalls a specific comic book panel, similar to a *tableau vivant*;

3) *Explicit intermediality*: the incorporation of actual comics or comics art into a film;

4) *Expressive intermediality*: the presence of conventions associated with comics, both visual (e.g., caricature, particular uses of line and color) and narrative (e.g., text captions, speech or thought balloons, onomatopoeias, motion lines), in a film;

5) *Formal intermediality*: the use of comics' formal system—sequential images, arranged spatially and available for simultaneous view—in a film, often through split screen;

6) *Figural intermediality*: attempts at bridging the phenomenological experience of reading comics and watching films by mimicking comics' elastic temporality and staccato rhythm.

These categories provide the conceptual framework that will be used throughout this book. Readers satisfied with this cursory understanding of these six categories and anxious to find out how specific films negotiate the key sites of struggle or ontological difference between film and comics may want to skip forward to chapter 2. But rather than wield these terms like blunt instruments in later chapters, I want to first refine and nuance precisely how these six aesthetic strategies function cinematically and the myriad ways in which they manifest in specific textual circumstances, while also identifying the unique effects they have on the viewer's experience and understanding of a given film.

While later chapters will draw on a wider array of filmic examples that demonstrate the breadth of variation possible within each category, here I focus on a single film to lend greater cohesion to my explanation of these six strategies. For a variety of reasons, I have chosen *The Losers* as that case study. To a much greater extent than the superhero films that are more commonly held up as illustrative of the comic book film, *The Losers* is a comprehensive and heretofore underanalyzed example of comic book film style that allows us to confront the multiple levels on which cinema can remediate the form and conventions of comics, in addition to adapting the narrative content of a particular comics text. Using a single film throughout the chapter also allows me to clearly define and illustrate how each of the above-mentioned strategies of intertextuality and intermediality manifest and work together in the comic book film.

Stylistically, *The Losers* is also of a piece with trends in contemporary cinema generally and the action genre more specifically that have been defined by David Bordwell and Steven Shaviro as "intensified continuity" and "post-continuity" respectively.[3] This allows us to understand comic book film style as an intervention within broader debates over the historical poetics of contemporary Hollywood. For instance, Bordwell identifies "a fast cutting rate, the bipolar extremes of lens lengths, a reliance on tight singles, and the free-ranging camera" as the salient stylistic features of intensified continuity, concluding that these tendencies bend but don't break the rules of classical continuity filmmaking;[4] all of the qualities he mentions are on display in *The Losers*, and, as Bordwell would expect, the film remains coherent as a piece of mainstream narrative filmmaking at all times despite moments of stylistic extravagance. Observing the nearly avant-garde extremity of style in films by the likes of Tony Scott, Michael Bay, and Neveldine/Taylor, however, Shaviro counters that contemporary Hollywood action cinema has now reached an "absurd, hyperbolic point" that doesn't so much bend the rules of continuity as it radically undermines them. In this new post-continuity paradigm, Shaviro writes, "a preoccupation with immediate effects trumps any concern for broader continuity—whether on the immediate shot-by-shot level, or on that of the overall narrative."[5] *The Losers*' regular abandonment of photographic imagery in favor of drawings (or even the appearance of comics themselves), the integration of text as a non-diegetic visual element, the occasional use of self-conscious compositional choices that create frames within the frame, and a refusal to restrict its playback speed to a uniform temporal flow can all be understood as the kinds of "immediate effects" that could potentially undermine continuity.

Though it may seem somewhat contradictory, I believe that a film like *The Losers* can thus be productively understood as an example of both intensified continuity *and* post-continuity simultaneously, largely through its incorporation of the six aforementioned strategies into its broader stylistic program. All of the aforementioned effects exceed the demands of narrative and thereby draw attention to style as an extra-narrative force. This happens at the expense of *continuity*—understood as the set of rules or principles that create the "invisible style" associated with classical filmmaking—but not at the expense of *coherence*. While such aesthetically hybrid effects may complicate strict shot-to-shot continuity, they nevertheless remain coherent as intermedial gestures toward comics and become comprehensible in these terms. In other words, these moments are intelligible to the viewer not as contributions to the narrative but rather as manifestations of the film's intertextual and intermedial relationship to comics. Indeed, what becomes evident in such moments is the considerable influence that the comic book medium has exerted on contemporary film culture as part of the broader category that Shaviro refers to as "the excessive, overgrown post-cinematic mediasphere."[6] Chapter 5 explores the consequences of this influence in greater detail, but for now we will turn to *The Losers* more closely in order to understand precisely what these six modes of interaction entail.

Diegetic Intertextuality: Adapting Comics' Storyworlds

Of the six types of interaction between comics and film, we must begin with the most general, which refers to the importation of the characters, narratives, dialogue, settings, and other diegetic material from comic books into cinematic texts: in other words, what we generally refer to as adaptation. As already discussed in the introduction, it is this paradigm that has dominated the discourse about comic book films to date, and understandably so, given the long history of adaptation studies and fans' overwhelming desire to understand any film adapted from a previous work in terms of its allegiances to and divergences from that original text. Diegetic intertextuality refers entirely to content, not style; as a concept, it merely acknowledges that a character, narrative, setting, or other diegetic element in a film previously appeared in another medium. For this reason, it's the least crucial category to understanding comic book film style. Hypothetically, a film could adapt a comic book very closely in terms of its narrative content, but present that content in such a way that its comic book origins would be totally obscured. David Cronenberg's *A History of Violence* (2005) comes to mind, which the director made based on a screenplay he was unaware was adapted from a graphic novel.[7] This also seems to be the goal with many recent superhero films; the "house styles" adopted by Marvel Studios (as seen, for instance, in *Iron Man* [2008]) and Warner Bros. (as exemplified by *Batman v Superman: Dawn of Justice* [2016]) largely attempt to create verisimilitudinous storyworlds that privilege photographic reality (even when it's computer-generated) over the self-conscious artifice and overt stylization associated with comic books and comic book film style. Occasional stylistic flourishes do sneak into these films—and some will be singled out in later chapters—but, generally speaking, these are not particularly rich sources of comic book film style.

While diegetic intertextuality is the dominant mode through which these films interact with comics, it is merely the opening salvo of *The Losers'* engagement with the medium. Like *A History of Violence* and the Marvel and DC superhero films, *The Losers* features characters, settings, and narrative events that had been previously depicted, suggested, or alluded to in the Vertigo comics series written by Andy Diggle and drawn by Jock: in other words, it is an adaptation thereof. Therefore, loosely following George Bluestone's suggested reading strategy in his pioneering work *Novels into Film*, I could watch *The Losers* film with the trade paperback of *The Losers* comics in my lap and compare the two versions, noting the differences and similarities between them and systematically cataloguing the relationship between the two versions.[8] Based on this direct juxtaposition, I might observe that the film begins many months before the comic, narrating in the present tense events that are presented as flashbacks in the comic; that the film increases the sexual tension between Clay and Aisha; or that Roque's betrayal of his teammates is pushed to much later in the narrative, from only the third issue of the thirty-two-issue comics series to the climax of the film. I could then account for why these changes might have been made and what effects they have on the narrative. While such a reading would undoubtedly be of interest to many viewers—who, according to Liam Burke's survey of comic book film audiences, are often invested in the idea of textual fidelity as a marker of quality even if they haven't read the original comics[9]—such issues of diegetic intertextuality are, at best, peripheral to questions concerning comic book film style.

As we'll see in later chapters, a great many comic book films don't have any basis in the diegetic material of comics, but they nevertheless draw on the aesthetic resources of the comic book medium. In the case of *The Losers*, however, diegetic intertextuality provides the ostensible motivation and rationale for the film's stylistic incorporation of comics throughout; infusions of comic book film style should suggest, even to viewers unaware of the film's status as an adaptation, that *The Losers* is either based on or inspired by comics, which might then call to mind a set of generic or narrative expectations that the film may or may not satisfy. In other cases, however, such direct intertextual linkages are not present despite the presence of comic book–inspired aestheticization, further demonstrating that adaptation need not be central to understanding the comic book film's contribution to contemporary film style. That said, the next intertextual strategy is also limited to films based specifically on comics.

Compositional Intertextuality: Panel as Storyboard, Film as *Tableau Vivant*

Whereas diegetic intertextuality refers to the presence of narrative content from comics, it doesn't speak at all to the specifics of that content's representation. Unlike most novels, comics already feature visual depictions of their storyworlds that are ripe for cinematic appropriation, suggesting certain camera angles, compositions, lighting, uses of color, and so on. Through a practice I call "compositional mimesis," filmmakers like *The Losers*' director, Sylvain White, treat specific comic book panels as storyboards during shooting, resulting in shots that closely resemble images from particular comics while also differing from them in significant ways.[10] By re-creating the compositions of the comic book, such films not only recall particular graphic intertexts but also foster a similarity to the artistic tradition in which live performers engage in reenactments of still images before a live audience: the *tableau vivant*. The key differences between compositional mimesis and the *tableau vivant* are the addition of movement to the composition and the mediation of the film screen. In a traditional *tableau vivant*, the performers appear in the same space as the audience, often on a stage, while in the comic book film's mimetic compositions, the performers are only present to the camera; the "liveness" of the actors is thus replaced with a photographic trace of their presence. Despite these differences, the similarities between the two practices are striking, especially insofar as they seem to be judged based on the same criterion: their faithfulness or deference to an original.[11] While comics fans generally consider such compositions as important markers of textual fidelity, it's counterproductive to focus entirely on similarities when the differences between the two media involved in the intertextual exchange fundamentally alter the context in which a given composition is reproduced and read. Burke has the right idea when he proposes that "instances of fidelity/infidelity" should be treated "not [as] the end of an investigation, but rather [as] a good place to start digging."[12]

This kind of intertextual play is much more specific and directed than most instances of diegetic intertextuality, which indicates a process of adaptation but not necessarily one that would be considered "faithful" (not that there's an objective standard by which fidelity could be assessed). For instance, while the title characters in comic book adaptations like *Steel* (1997) or *Catwoman* (2004) don't closely resemble their print counterparts in either appearance or behavior, the mere presence of these characters and their associated storyworlds—even if drastically altered—satisfies the basic criterion of diegetic borrowing. It's therefore not surprising that fans and critics often understand comic book adaptations that feature mimetic compositions as automatically more "faithful" compared to those that don't.[13] The Internet is replete with websites devoted to side-by-side comparisons between comic book panels and film shots that ostensibly testify to various films' fidelity.[14] When discussing compositional mimesis, we should recognize that while filmmakers' intentions may be to produce faithful adaptations, and fans of the source material may value such visual gestures as markers of fidelity, such interpretations tend to privilege similarity over difference and risk erasing the processes of remediation that necessarily occur in compositionally mimetic shots. Whether the panel being referenced is obvious or obscure, these shots create a superficial visual connection to a particular intertext and, more significantly, a complex relationship between two media with two fundamentally different formal systems, one of which is based primarily on drawing and the other of which is based largely (though increasingly less) on photography. It is through these moments of allusion that the differences and similarities between the modes of representation available to these two media are laid bare, and moments of aesthetic compromise are achieved through remediation.

With this in mind, let's now turn to *The Losers* to see how compositional intertextuality functions. As an example, I focus on one of the most iconic moments of both versions: Aisha's sudden reappearance during the climactic action set piece, bazooka in hand.[15] Given the narrative similarities in play here, this is undoubtedly an instance of diegetic intertextuality; a close comparison of the two compositions, however, reveals a number of differences that result from the shift in medium. In the comic, Aisha is shown from a low angle and occupies most of the frame; the portrait dimensions of the comic book page accommodate the character's entire body and emphasize the forward movement of the bazooka blast as it moves toward the top of the page.

FIGURE 1.1. Page from *The Losers* #4

FIGURE 1.2. Still from *The Losers*

In the film version, the content is similar but the composition is altered drastically: the angle is now straight on, and Aisha is shown in a long shot on the right side of the screen, occupying a comparatively small amount of the image due to the much wider aspect ratio of the film.

The bazooka blast now moves from the right to the left of the screen, instead of from the middle to the top of the page, also as a result of the different dimensions of the image and the established spatial relations of the mise-en-scène. Further differences could also be noted: whereas the comic version included only a blue sky as a background, the film shot is replete with additional visual details in the background; the lighting and color values are much darker with an increased emphasis on shading in the comic compared to the film; and so on. In citing the differences between the two versions, we interrogate the kinds of compositional and aesthetic choices available to each medium rather than simply guess at the filmmaker's intentions (e.g., to please fans by creating a faithful adaptation).

Though discourse around mimetic compositions tends to emphasize fidelity to their original comic book referents, analyzing such intertextual moments always reveals productive divergences between the two versions. In *The Losers*, another excellent example is found in a scene in which Jensen is caught stealing information in a high-rise office building.[16] Jensen is backed against a wall of windows by a series of security guards, with the team's sniper, Cougar, positioned in an adjacent building. Communicating with his teammate wirelessly, Jensen feigns telekinesis by "shooting" a series of security guards with his fingers; Cougar's perfectly timed shots complete the illusion. The penultimate shot of this gag is a mimetic composition that incorporates a six-panel sequence from the comics: Jensen makes an *O* with his thumb and forefinger, through which we see the bullet holes in the window; with each subsequent panel, we get a closer view of the adjacent building until Cougar and his smoking gun are revealed.

The six panels are equal in size and panoramic in shape, reminiscent of a cinematic widescreen. Unlike the previous example, then, the film version here doesn't need to alter the composition to accommodate a different frame

FIGURE 1.3. Page from
The Losers #3

shape. The fundamental difference between the two versions here is that the comic sequence occupies a full page containing six discrete images, whereas the film version conveys the same information in what appears to be (by virtue of digital animation and compositing) a single zoom shot.

Based on this, the temptation may be to interpret the film version as the telos of the comics sequence that inspired it: while comics can only suggest movement and the passage of time through a series of representative still images, the shot gives us the event itself as it occurs in real time. The film might therefore be read as improving upon the comic version, as fulfilling the promise of the comic, or refashioning it in the name of "the real," as Bolter and Grusin might have it. According to this logic, comics become a mere precursor to or imitation of cinema rather than an autonomous medium that produces distinct aesthetic effects. Even if this sequence is itself remediating a cinematic zoom, which is entirely likely and not uncommon in comics, we should always consider how comics have transformed the technique by subsuming it into its own formal structure and expressing it in a particular way. Addressing this need, Thierry Groensteen has termed this phenomenon "optical progressivity," a particular panel-to-panel relationship that "gradually brings us closer or further away from a given subject," as a zoom lens does; crucially, however, he also describes the rhythmic pattern that is in play and that creates visual relationships between the panels across a page.[17] The co-presence of these panels is an effect that simply has no equivalent in the cinematic remediation thereof; while the comic book reader's point-of-view essentially moves in two directions at once—forward in diegetic space and downward across the page—the spectator's point-of-view moves forward only. The cinematic remediation reconstructs the sense of fluid spatial continuity that is not present or possible in the comics version.

Even in a mimetic composition such as this one, then, it is never a simple or direct "translation" from one medium to the other: there is always addition, loss, and alteration as a result of the necessary transitions from drawn to live action, from panel(s) to frame(s), from stasis to movement. It is therefore the processes and results of remediation that should be interrogated rather than the fidelity with which a mimetic shot replicates its source. Compositional intertextuality will be further discussed and complicated with regard to issues of movement and temporality in chapter 4.

FIGURES 1.4, 1.5, 1.6, AND 1.7. Stills from *The Losers*

Explicit Intermediality: Drawing in and on Film

When a comic book film incorporates actual pieces of art from (or in the style of) comics, it is drawing on the mode of explicit intermediality. This remediation strategy can usually be found in predictable locations: in and before opening or closing credits sequences,[18] at the beginning of scenes, or elsewhere in the opening moments of a film. In adaptations, the use of comics art in such moments functions as a declarative statement, effectively announcing to the viewer that the film is aware of the original comics, that the filmmakers have not ignored the source material, and accordingly that the film will not displease fans of the original. Because of these implications, explicit intermediality can be a valuable marketing tool. There is a reason why the advertising materials for comic book superhero films tend to employ the iconic logos of the characters, often to the exclusion of all advertising copy, including the title of the film. The Superman crest has such cultural currency that, coupled with a release date at the bottom of the poster, it may be all that is required to sell a film to audiences. The same is true of Batman's insignia, Iron Man's helmet, Spider-Man's mask, and Wolverine's claws. Indeed, the initial teaser posters for *Superman Returns* (2006), *Batman*, *Iron Man*, *Spider-Man* (2002)/(2006), and *X-Men 3: The Last Stand* take precisely this approach. None of these images are dependent on the visage of a particular actor, which inevitably stray from the nonphotographic images of the comics. Indeed, nowadays it is unlikely that these promotional images are even produced photographically; rather, they are produced in the same way comics images are: with pencils, paints, and pixels. As such, they provide an aesthetic entryway from the original comics into the film that may be reassuring to fans. Despite *The Losers* being based on a lesser-known comics series, its marketing materials make explicit intermedial connections to the original text, including a poster drawn by Jock that depicts the cast of the film in a style similar to his comics art.[19]

Explicit intermediality might also serve a narrative purpose within the films themselves, as it can serve to orient the comics reader within the film version. Such intermedial associations are present from the very first moments of *The Losers*. As the film opens, the Warner Bros. logo is presented in a drawn, graphic style, and is encased within a comic book panel, surrounded by other panels. The (virtual) camera whip pans to the right, showing a flurry of panels before settling on the next company logo, which is also contained within a panel on a comic book page. The art throughout is rendered in a dynamic way, with layered elements, ink splashes, and light animation added. The way the film transitions from these pseudo-comics pages to the live-action diegesis of the film proper creates the impression that the narrative to follow is not merely a *filmed version* of a comic book, but rather that the camera has somehow penetrated the diegesis of a comic and brought it to life before our eyes: that the film itself is, figuratively speaking, a comic book. Opening the film in this way is analogous to a similar moment in *Citizen Kane* (1941), wherein a close-up scanning the text of Thatcher's memoirs dissolves into the scene that those words narrate, the implication being that the scene that follows is a visual representation of the subjective memoir. These brief opening moments—totaling only twenty-three seconds of screen time—gesture toward and embrace the inherent hybridity of comic book film style, framing *The Losers* not just as an adaptation of a comic book but as a remediation of the comic book medium itself. We are mere seconds into the film, but the viewer's attention is already attuned to the stylistic appropriation of comics that will recur throughout in various ways.

The film continues to draw on the resources of explicit intermediality in its opening scenes in ways that reinforce its status as a remediation. Readers of *The Losers* are already well familiar with the appearance of each member of the ex-CIA team as drawn by Jock, but they may not recognize Clay as embodied by Jeffrey Dean Morgan or Jensen as played by Chris Evans. Helpfully, the filmmakers morph from the live-action footage to Jock's art— along with a title card detailing each character's name and his role in the team—as each new character is introduced in the film. This is both a stylish way of providing quick introductions to the central players and an explicit incorporation of comics art. The drawings, produced specifically for the film, occupy the aesthetic space between the photographic actors and the somewhat more caricatured or iconic comic book depictions of these characters from the comics themselves.

By employing this visual shorthand, the film is effectively smoothing over differences and setting up a correspondence between the two versions: Morgan's Clay = Jock's Clay, and more broadly, Warner Bros.' *The Losers* film = DC/Vertigo's *The Losers* comics. Again, what is at issue here is the suggested equivalence not just of the two texts but of the two media. Such visual gestures will be meaningful to viewers totally unfamiliar with the comics, and even to those unaware of the film's status as an adaptation: the presence of comics art explicitly brings the medium of sequential art to mind without requiring any prior knowledge of the property.

FIGURES 1.8 AND 1.9. Stills from *The Losers*

Ultimately, what does it mean to read a film as if it was a comic book? What does it mean for a film to stake its identity as a cinematic comic book, as a comic book come to life? Explicit intermediality is loaded with this kind of figurative value: allusions to comics in a film's paratextual marketing materials might create a tacit "fidelity contract" between the filmmakers and comics fans,[20] but the use of comics art in the film itself creates a more complex set of expectations that would vary from viewer to viewer, depending on both their knowledge of the original comics being adapted (if applicable) and their associations with the comics medium more generally. A film viewer with a limited experience of comics might wrongly, but understandably, hypothesize that *The Losers* will follow the narrative trajectory of a superhero film based on the way that it incorporates comics in its opening moments. Another viewer might interpret these explicit allusions to sequential art as indicators of an aesthetic approach that will hybridize cinematic style with the formal qualities of comics throughout its running time, resulting in a film that infuses standard intensified continuity style with extra-diegetic techniques that exceed the demands of the narrative. The latter viewer would be rewarded with a film whose every stylistic choice is potentially charged with intermedial significance: the composition of elements in the frame may be an allusion to a particular comics panel; the frame itself may abandon its fixed dimensions in favor of the flexibility of the comics panel; photographic images may be augmented with drawings and illustrations via compositing, digital animation, and other assorted post-production manipulations; and slow motion and other cinematic techniques may become loaded with figurative significance. In short, explicit interme-diality (like diegetic intertextuality) cues the viewer to be attentive to other strategies of remediation that may also be in play.

Expressive Intermediality: Blurring Boundaries

The fourth mode of interaction in the comic book film focuses on the dif-ference—and sometimes lack thereof—between cartoon/drawn images and live-action cinematography. This is achieved by incorporating conven-tions associated with the comic book medium into an otherwise live-action film: things like simplified, caricatured, or cartoonlike characters, props, or mise-en-scène; unnatural or painterly uses of color; motion lines; and the treatment of text as image, often including the manifestation of sound as visible text (e.g., onomatopoeias, dialogue balloons, thought clouds). These are the aesthetic markers that most comics rely on to tell their stories and to produce the kind of imagery that we overwhelmingly associate with the medium, even if they aren't necessary or constitutive features of comics. Though there are certainly photographic comics, colorless comics, and wordless comics that eschew some of the above conventions, comics readers are not surprised when characters are not naturalistically depicted, when color and light are used expressionistically, when movement is represented through a static flurry of lines, and when words are graphically depicted as key components of a particular image. In contemporary mainstream cinema, however, none of these devices are common enough that they would pass by viewers unnoticed; rather, all of them represent overt and self-conscious attempts at stylization that would call attention to the artificiality of the film. For many critics of comic book films, it is the very *absence* of these markers that signals a "successful" adaptation: by stripping away these markers of "comic book–ness" and replacing them with a more conven-tional (read: invisible) cinematic style, the content of the comic book, sup-posedly, is elevated, or at the very least brought in line with a traditionally cinematic mode of representation. As Neil Rae and Jonathan Gray found in audience surveys performed after comic book film screenings, non–comic book readers specifically "seemed to see realism as something that good filmmakers *added* to the stories, almost working against the inherent 'unbelievability' of 'totally outrageous' comics."[21] According to these critics and fans, good comic book films should take what is cartoonish on the page and make it realistic, imbue caricatures with the complexity of humanity, and transfigure the implausible into the plausible. Film adaptations that instead choose to retain the medium-specific markers of the comic book—and all the baggage that comes along with them—despite the content's migration into another medium go against expectations and standard adaptation practice. Comic book films that take this tack self-consciously foreground their artifice and undermine any claim to realism they may have gained by virtue of film's (seeming) basis in photography.

Expressive intermediality thus tackles Pascal Lefèvre's third "adaptation problem" plaguing the comic book film head on, which is "the dilemma of translating drawings to photography."[22] According to Lefèvre, "A photographic image has, by its optic nature alone, a quite different visual ontology [than a drawn image]. Viewers do not react in the same way to a drawing as to a photographic image. Although photos can also be manipulated by using special software such as Photoshop, generally the viewer still accords more realism to a photo than to a stylized drawing."[23] Lefèvre's understanding of photographic ontology seems heavily indebted to André Bazin's influential article "Ontology of the Photographic Image," in which the French film critic argued that photography, in contrast to painting, produces its images "automatically, without creative human intervention, following a strict determinism. The photographer's personality is at work only in the selection, orientation and pedagogical approach to the phenomenon."[24] In the comic book film, though, a highly artificial mise-en-scène, expressive cinematography, and (digital) visual effects can combine to produce photographic images with an "aesthetic of artifice," as Michael Cohen puts it in his article on *Dick Tracy* (1990);[25] in such cases, the image's basis in reality and "documentary value"[26] is less central to the way we read or experience the film. Instead of objectively and automatically reproducing whatever is placed before the camera, as Bazin claimed, we're often dealing with images that are suppler and more elastic in their representational capabilities, freely combining live action with computer-generated and drawn images. Nevertheless, these images are ultimately incorporated into and subsumed by the live-action photographic flow, accruing a certain "residual realism" from their contiguity to photographic images; that is, even when the image in question is ontologically identical to a (computer-) animated cartoon, when images look photographic, we tend to respond to them similarly to photographic images proper. Thus if a heavily stylized comic book film has a greater "reality effect" than comics themselves, it is more a result of this residual realism and the addition of movement and synchronized sound than of its total commitment to a photographic ontology or classically realist aesthetic.

Three factors are in play here, all of which contribute to bridging the gap between the diametrically opposed categories of "pure drawing" (associated with absolute artifice) and "pure photography" (associated with absolute realism) that Lefèvre reductively associates with each respective medium: namely, *what* is being photographed (mise-en-scène), *how* it is being photographed (cinematographic technique), and how the photograph is *manipulated* after the instant of capture (digital/visual effects). As Stephen Prince correctly notes, visual effects can "open pathways for the attainment of realist designs just as they afford ways of designing fantasy worlds and situations that are patently unrealistic,"[27] and indeed this is most often how they're used in Hollywood films. So just as photography doesn't necessarily entail realism (if what's being photographed is itself artificial, or is captured in a stylized way), the use of digital visual effects doesn't necessarily entail artifice (if what's being digitally created is something that appears to be natural).

While *The Losers* is heavily stylized in many ways—see the previous section on explicit intermediality for ample evidence—its mise-en-scène and use of digital visual effects largely attempt to maintain the reality of the diegesis in the way Prince describes. While the film features a deliberately limited palette, its use of color never undermines the photographic reality of the settings, as in films like *Sin City* or *300*; similarly, the character designs are closely inspired by the comics—from Jensen's spiky hair to Roque's facial scar—but they never approach *Dick Tracy* levels of abstraction. On these grounds, I would conclude that expressive intermediality is not central to its particular application of comic book film style. Indeed, the film only draws on intermediality in its expressive mode in the establishing shots that signal shifts in narrative location: for instance, at 2:23 an extreme long shot of a forest features the text BOLIVIA on top of the foliage, encased within a box that resembles a comic book caption. In such a moment, the film is literally superimposing a visual convention of comics onto the otherwise photographically represented world. While textual elements such as these are perfectly common within globetrotting action-adventure films, where they keep viewers abreast of shifts in locale, *The Losers* presents them in a specifically stylized way that invokes a representational convention of comics: the caption box. Such uses of onscreen text, which recur throughout the film, work in concert with explicit intermediality to create the impression that *The Losers* is not simply a photographic representation of the world, but rather a comic book remediated by the cinema. Other comic book films certainly go further in their cinematic appropriation of comics' visual conventions than *The Losers*: examples that come to mind include *Batman: The Movie*'s use of textual onomatopoeias and the incorporation of word balloons in lieu of traditional subtitles in *Kick-Ass 2* (2013), to name just two. Both of these sacrifice cinema's claim to photographic realism to varying degrees in favor of aestheticized representations that either "cartoon" the diegetic world or pepper an otherwise photographic world with nondiegetic conventions ripped from the comic book page. Readers particularly interested in these issues will find them more fully explored in chapter 2.

Formal Intermediality: Panels within the Frame

While expressive intermediality concerns the cinematic remediation of conventions associated with comics, formal intermediality refers to the appropriation of comics' unique formal structure in a film, which hinges on the visual and narrative relationships between juxtaposed images. Unlike the conventions discussed in the previous section, Groensteen asserts that it is a "necessary, if not sufficient, condition" of the comics medium to contain multiple images that are "correlated in some fashion."[28] In comics, each panel has its own designated space; there is no competition for room or attention, as each discrete visual block will be read in turn. In the comic book film, however, panels actively compete with each other to occupy the same (time-) space. Lev Manovich has identified a similar tendency within digital cinema more generally, which he calls "spatial montage," in which several discrete shots or images occupy the screen simultaneously. This editing strategy, he writes, "represents an alternative to traditional cinematic temporal montage, replacing its traditional sequential mode with a spatial one."[29] While the lack of sequential order certainly applies to other new media, like the desktop computer, Manovich perhaps overstates the degree to which this increased spatial complexity displaces sequentiality in digital cinema. There is still a linear viewing logic in place insofar as individual frames appear sequentially in a preordained order and remain onscreen for a predetermined duration;

what has changed is that the minimal unit of screen space has been atomized from the shot to the shot within the shot, or subshot, which comes to function much like panels that coexist on the comics page. When the film frame contains two or more subshots simultaneously, each one then assumes a status similar to a panel, effectively transforming the screen into an ersatz comic book page, or hyperframe, composed of several panels that are to be read in dialogue—if not necessarily in sequence—rather than in isolation.

In cinema, this effect is most obviously achieved using split screen, though this technique is actually fairly rare in comic book films: exceptions include heavily stylized films like *Hulk*, *Scott Pilgrim vs. the World*, and *The Green Hornet*. At various points in these films, the frame's traditional function as a single "window" onto the filmic world is shattered, creating individual windows within the larger frame that each provide a unique and distinct vantage point on the diegesis. Like expressive intermediality, the use of split screen can come at the expense of narrative immersion. As Lefèvre puts it,

> Since multiple-frame imagery is still quite unusual—especially when the split-screens themselves are moving on the screen as in *Hulk*—it tends to surprise the viewer and to make him or her more aware of the filmic code of framing. It then functions as a self-referential technique. Though multiple-frame imagery is closer to comics, it breaks the usual cinematographic illusion.[30]

The use of this technique in these films will be discussed at much greater length in chapters 3 and 5.

There are, however, other ways in which film is "catching up on the formal potentialities of the comic book page," as Jochen Ecke puts it.[31] *The Losers* approaches formal intermediality in a less literal way than the films mentioned above, avoiding split screen and instead evoking a paneled aesthetic in certain shots by dividing the frame with diegetic objects contained within the mise-en-scène. The integrity of the frame is thus maintained and a subtle (if superficial) allusion to the aesthetics (though not the function) of the comic book page is created. For instance, in one shot Jensen is shown entering a lobby: the screen is divided down the center by the wall of the building, with the left half of the screen showing the outside area and the right side showing the interior space.

The perfectly symmetrical composition is certainly striking and unusual, but not to such an extent that it "breaks the usual cinematographic illusion" as a proper split screen would. Instead, the barrier merely bifurcates the space and makes clear the spatial relationship between the two areas by displaying them simultaneously. There's even a weak sense of sequentiality in play in the shot by virtue of Jensen's movement from the left of the screen to the right, which also echoes the left-to-right reading pattern of North American comics. If we consider each half of the screen in this shot as its own ersatz panel, the similarity to the form and function of a comic book page becomes evident: like comics, we read them in sequence but can also oversee the whole composition outside of narrative sequentiality. Even so, a shot like this wouldn't likely call comics to mind if not for the other appeals to the medium made throughout the film, and certainly such a shot wouldn't be considered an example of comic book film style without other instances of remediation present to lend credence to such an interpretation.

A second example is more stylistically overt but ultimately produces a similar effect. After discovering that she withheld information from them, the Losers (except Clay, who is in bed) hold Aisha at gunpoint. Outnumbered, she creates a diversion by shooting a mirror mounted on the ceiling, raining shards of reflective glass upon the group. As the glass falls, the playback speed ramps into slow motion and, amid the chaos, Aisha leaps into the bathroom for protection from the ensuing gunfire. The film then cuts to a slightly out-of-focus shot of Clay getting out of bed; as glass shards fall in elegant slow motion in the foreground of the shot, the focus racks to one large shard in particular, which shows Aisha in the offscreen space directly behind the camera, continuing her evasive maneuver from the previous shot.

Like the wall in the previous example, the shard here functions as an ersatz panel that isolates Aisha within the shot, displaying her in a separate view of the diegetic space. Though the actions take place simultaneously, the shifting focus draws the viewer's attention from Clay's movement on the right side of the screen toward Aisha on the left in a linear manner, implying a sequential relation between the shot and the subshot within it. Thus in both of these examples from *The Losers*, the tension between simultaneity and sequentiality, which is always present on the comic book page, is maintained, albeit expressed in a more linear and temporally inflexible way. Despite the use of slow motion and the ersatz split screen, both of which are stylistic contrivances that call attention to themselves, spatial continuity is maintained from shot to shot because of Aisha's consistent placement within the frame. This brief shot thus combines the multiple simultaneous views of the comics page with the linear progression and spatial continuity of cinema

FIGURES 1.10 AND 1.11. Stills from *The Losers*

in a fairly complex way that most analyses of split screens (whether diegetic or nondiegetic) in comic book films don't recognize. Chapter 3 addresses these shortcomings and theorizes in far greater depth about the various forms that the remediation of the comic book page has taken. The use of slow motion in this second example, however, provides an appropriate segue to the final mode of intermediality.

Figural Intermediality: Panel Time

Another fundamental difference between film and comic books is that watching a film is simply a different process and a different kind of experience than reading a comic book. The medium of comics requires readers to combine text with other kinds of visual information and to actively create the narrative by linking sequential panels together. Arguably, the most significant difference between comics and film is not related to visual ontology or narrative style but rather lies in the difference between the internalized, rhythmically variable, and potentially nonlinear experience of reading comics and the temporally (if not narratively) linear momentum of watching a film. As Jared Gardner puts it, comics is "a form that depends on an active and imaginative reader capable of filling in the gaps in time. As a form that works with traditionally incommensurate systems of meaning—text and image—to tell its story, it also requires its readers at every turn to make active decisions as to how to read the two in relationship to a larger narrative."[32] For this reason, Scott McCloud claims that "No other artform [*sic*] gives so much to its audience while asking so much from them as well."[33] A comic, consisting of a series of still images that are only rendered coherent by the extrapolation and intervention of an active reading process, allows its reader the freedom to linger on certain images as he or she sees fit, and also encourages him or her to contemplate each image for its aesthetic qualities in addition to its function within the narrative. By comparison, a film's rigid temporality (standardized at 24 frames per second since the introduction of sound) determines and standardizes the viewing experience for all viewers to a far greater extent. Within this stricter framework, the viewer is of course free to independently scan the image, but outside of the pause function afforded by home viewing, opportunities to savor individual compositions for an extended period of time are generally not determined by the viewer's whim but rather by the rate of cutting, which is especially rapid in the intensified continuity era. While the differences between the two media seem particularly stark with regard to their representations of time, comic book films have developed a means of remediating what Martyn Pedler has described as comics' "elastic temporality":[34] by using selective speed ramping and other temporal interventions—including freezing the frame or even removing selected frames—comic book films can create a staccato rhythm that allows them to escape the tyranny of "real time." Speed ramping in particular functions to slow certain images down almost to the point of stasis, resulting in "panel moments" that allow for prolonged aesthetic contemplation of those compositions, as in a comic book. Figural intermediality refers to this and other such manipulations of film style, all of which visualize the elastic temporality of comics and negotiate between the privileged instants of comic book panels and the narrative information that is representationally lost in the gaps between them.

In *Understanding Comics*, McCloud explains how the space in between each panel in a comic book—known as the gutter—becomes the locus of the reader's creative intervention in the production of the narrative. Since the static images of comics necessarily provide incomplete representations of whatever they depict, it falls to the reader to fill in the temporal gaps between each image in order to coherently synthesize each panel within the larger sequence. McCloud calls this process "closure."[35] In *The Aesthetics of Comics*, David Carrier evocatively describes the results thusly: "We construct a jumpy narrative, like a movie shown with the projector not quite in sync. Just as, when seeing a representation, we form and test some hypothesis about what is depicted, so, with comics, we construct and check a narrative that makes sense of the scenes."[36] This process of narrative construction occurs internally and usually unconsciously; if readers had to consciously formulate and test individual hypotheses for each and every panel transition, comics reading would likely be an incredibly time-consuming and perhaps even arduous and unpleasant activity. Groensteen has argued, contrary to McCloud, that this process is invisible and to some extent automatic—the comics equivalent of classical Hollywood's seamless and unobtrusive style—resulting in a sense of immediacy rather than estrangement: "Every comics reader knows that, from the instant where he is projected into the fiction (the diegetic universe), he forgets, up to a certain point, the fragmented character and discontinuity of the enunciation."[37] The comics-literate reader thus becomes a largely *unconscious* collaborator in the construction of the narrative, with closure occurring automatically. The story is, by the nature of the medium, "full of holes, but it projects me into a world that is portrayed as consistent, and it is the continuity attributed to the fictional world that allows me to effortlessly fill in the gaps of the narration."[38] Like most comics conventions, however, what operates invisibly in its native medium becomes a hypervisible stylistic device when remediated into a live-action film.

In a comic book, each panel is available indefinitely for the reader's contemplation; in a film, by contrast, each frame has exactly one twenty-fourth of a second and each shot has a predetermined duration to make an impression on the viewer. Figural intermediality refers to any stylistic intervention that approximates the irregular temporality of comics by divorcing representational duration from diegetic time. A specific trope I call the "panel moment" goes even further than this, using selective speed ramping to visually remediate the process of closure described above. The aesthetic effect can certainly be described as an elastic treatment of time, as a single instant is stretched far beyond its diegetic duration and thereby treated as a privileged instant within the flow of images. In such cases, the playback speed is expanded like a rubber band, becoming slower as its stretches before snapping back to its natural state: the slow-motion portion of the shot represents the comic book panel, while the footage surrounding the slow motion represents closure, that is, the connective tissue intuited by the reader in transitioning from one panel to the next. By remediating this process cinematically, comic book films turn this invisible, unconscious process into a stylized effect. Unlike closure, panel moments don't contribute to the construction of the diegetic world or enable the viewer to better understand the narrative; rather, they function specifically to aestheticize the representation, putting the process of mediation on self-conscious display.

To better understand the panel moment and other evocations of panel time, however, we need to differentiate between their denotative and connotative functions. Despite vastly different representational abilities and strategies, the connotation of images in both comics and film is the same: that the events depicted are occurring in real time, despite their fragmentary representation by either medium. The panel moment allows film to denote this in a way more similar to comics: that is, through a series of (nearly) static images that represent, but whose representation does not take place in, real time. In the film, however, the images are not separated from each other in the same way they are in comics; rather than being partitioned by gutters, these moments are given to us onscreen in a consistent space, providing a more complete representation that includes both the static images (the panel moments, presented in slow motion) *and* what the comic book reader otherwise contributes internally (presented more normally). Cinematic panel time thus divorces the film from the literal representation of time, instead offering a *figural* representation of time as mediated by comics and its unique reading process. The panel moment closely resembles Carrier's description of closure quoted above: a "jumpy narrative" produced by a seemingly defective film projector.

Undoubtedly, panel moments are most closely associated with the films of Zack Snyder, including *300* and *Watchmen*,[39] though they also appear in *Sin City*, *The Incredible Hulk* (2008), *Wanted*, and *The Amazing Spider-Man 2* (2014), to name just a few. In all of these films, the technique could easily be mistaken for "bullet time," the aesthetic trope pioneered and popularized by *The Matrix* (1999).[40] Though both rely on increased shooting speeds (i.e., more frames per second) to extend or halt representational time with slow-motion effects, there are key differences between them. Firstly, proper bullet time is not slow-motion cinematography at all, but rather is produced by digitally combining still photographs taken from a variety of cameras from different vantage points into a single image capturing a 360-degree space, allowing filmmakers to make virtual camera movements (which necessarily have a duration and occur over time) within a single, seemingly frozen instant of time.[41] Due to its method of production, instances of bullet time must be planned in the découpage stage, prior to shooting. Panel moments rely instead on speed ramping, which is a postproduction effect that can be added to any shot during editing as long as it was originally shot at a high frame rate. These differences in methods imply a difference in form, namely that bullet time is a fundamentally *spatial* effect while panel moments are essentially *temporal*. Bullet time halts *diegetic* time, giving the camera freedom to explore a space untethered to time's arrow and a character more time to dodge an attack, whereas panel moments slow *representational* time, using slow motion to emphasize a movement or pose without any implied change to the flow of time within the storyworld itself. Put another way, bullet time is a literal effect, while panel moments are figurative. In most cases, bullet time represents the experiences of characters with enhanced sensory capabilities (e.g., the representation of "spider-sense" in the original *Spider-Man* trilogy [2002, 2004, 2007]) or the supernatural ability to bend time to their whim (e.g., *The Matrix*). Panel moments, on the other hand, do not signify anything about the diegesis or the characters' experiences thereof, but rather something about the intermedial aims of the film; panel moments indicate a formal debt to comic books and represent a stylistic means of paying that debt. To demonstrate this with concrete examples, I will turn once more to *The Losers*, a film that makes ample and varied use of figural intermediality.

Panel moments abound in the film, punctuating action scenes and other narratively significant moments with selective speed ramping. The first such instance occurs when Clay throws all of the Losers' dog tags into a fire, which effectively fakes their deaths for the CIA. The gravity of the moment is emphasized by a panel moment that appears to defy gravity, as the dog tags hang suspended in the air for an extended period of time before finally descending into the fire smoldering in the foreground.

This single shot, like all panel moments, can be divided into three distinct phases: (1) the beginning of the action; (2) the iconic panel moment, visually emphasized by its near stasis; and (3) the end of the action. The extreme slow motion in the middle phase approaches (but never reaches) the stasis of a comic book panel, allowing for extended contemplation of the composition and privileging it within the linear flow of images, while the moments that bookend it assume the ephemeral quality of the gutter. This time-stretching effect recurs throughout the film, emphasizing key narrative turns and assorted "Wow!" moments, including the bazooka shot mentioned earlier in the section on compositional intertextuality (see fig. 1.2) and the second ersatz split-screen shot analyzed in the section on formal intermediality (see fig. 1.11). As these examples suggest, temporal manipulations are often combined with other modes of intermediality in ways that more obviously call attention to the comic book medium: in these cases, the former example uses speed ramping to extend a moment that recalls a specific panel in the original comic book, while the latter allows the viewer more time to take in a shot that juxtaposes two distinct views of the diegesis within the same frame, much like a comic book page. The presentation of the film's title functions similarly, combining the figural and explicit modes of intermediality. After tossing the dog tags into the fire, the five Losers stand in formation, looking directly toward the camera with *tableau vivant*–like stillness; instead of ramping back to regular playback speed, this panel moment suddenly dissolves into a drawing by Jock that replicates the composition precisely, literalizing the slow motion's evocation of the panel with an explicit incorporation of comics art. The title card, which recalls the logo from the original comics, is then superimposed over the five drawn figures. The image suddenly shatters like glass, sending jagged image fragments flying toward the viewer. At this point, the playback rhythm slows again to near stasis, allowing the pieces to hang suspended for another panel moment before giving way to the next scene. All of these stylistic gestures are essentially nonnarrative in their motivation: they don't advance the viewer's knowledge of the diegetic world but instead contribute to the film text's intermedial relationship with comics and that medium's specific mode of representation. Panel moments, especially when combined with other intermedial techniques as in this example, forge a hybridized mode of expression that not only bears a superficial visual similarity to comics' drawn and static images but also visualizes the internal process of interpreting those images, of turning them into a coherent narrative. They impose a readerly experience of time—*panel time*—on the film viewer that, quite unlike bullet time, is alien to the characters and to the diegesis itself. It is time as experienced by the comic book reader.

Panel moments, however, are not the only way that *The Losers* conjures panel time. Like slow motion, freeze frames are not exclusive to the comic book film, but they can assume an enhanced significance within it. For example, while the freeze frame that famously ends *The 400 Blows* (1959) can be read in several different ways (e.g., as a statement about the character's uncertain future after the film, as a Brechtian entreaty to the viewer, etc.), the film offers no reason to interpret it as an intermedial appeal to the medium of

FIGURE 1.12. Still from *The Losers*

comic books; in *The Losers*, however, such a moment could legitimately be interpreted in this way, because there are other markers of remediation that make such a reading plausible. One early action scene uses freeze frames, combined with a slight zoom effect, to punctuate Cougar's kill shots and lend the scene an unpredictable staccato rhythm that remediates the panel time of comics.[42] These brief moments in which time is temporarily suspended retain a sense of forward momentum as a result of the zoom-in effects. The shots are thus simultaneously static *and* dynamic, remediating how the stasis of comics imagery contrasts with the movement imagined by the reader. Likewise, a brief scene in which Aisha and Clay simply walk down a set of stairs is imbued with comic book style in yet another way.[43] Here, panel time is evoked by removing small chunks of frames at seemingly random intervals, resulting in a stuttered editing rhythm that adds momentum to the action by intermittently jumping forward in time in fits and starts. Though less jarring than proper jump cuts, this technique remediates what McCloud has referred to as comics' "jagged, staccato rhythm,"[44] again without any ostensible narrative purpose.

Whether jagged and staccato or loose and elastic, what all of these instances of figural intermediality have in common is the unnatural manipulation of time in ways that filter comics' form through cinematic style. Panel time divorces diegetic time from representational duration, often in ways that evoke the reader's experience of comics or at least superficially resemble comics' static yet dynamic images. In arguing that comics and film are ontologically irreconcilable, Lefèvre asserts that a "viewer of a still image will always be reminded of the fragmented and frozen time," whereas a moving image gives a "greater impression of realism."[45] But while comics are restricted to using still images, cinema is not restricted to moving images in the same way: film is equally capable of bending, fragmenting, or freezing time in ways that can estrange the viewer from duration as usually experienced. All of the techniques described above complicate cinema's linearity by appealing to the looser experience of panel time, where past, present, and future can coexist and iconic moments can linger in the reader's perception. Panel time and comic book temporality more generally will be discussed at greater length in chapter 4.

Conclusions

Based on the above analyses, we could conclude that *The Losers'* stylistic system is largely dominated by its remediation of comics, and by explicit and figural intermediality in particular, with each of the other modes used more sporadically in ways that support and are enabled by the film's intertextual association with comics. Certainly the film functions as an adaptation of Diggle and Jock's comics series, constructing its narrative using characters and events depicted throughout its thirty-two-issue run, but the film also does considerably more than that in terms of its relationship with comics. It's clear from the first frames that the aesthetics of comics will be crucial to the film in ways that go beyond the narrative content being adapted. Indeed, comic book film style is largely deployed in ways that don't contribute to the film's narrative at all, but rather serve only to aestheticize its live-action representation of a comic book storyworld. *The Losers* is, as much as any other comic book film yet made, a comic book come to life through its complex and multifaceted remediation of the content, style, and form of comics.

The six modes of remediation defined in this chapter can be used to categorize the various means that the comic book film has at its disposal to forge intertextual and intermedial links with comics. This includes not only the adaptation of specific texts (diegetic intertextuality) and particular visual moments within those texts (compositional intertextuality) but also the transformation of various attributes of the medium itself, namely, the use of actual comics art (explicit intermediality), the juxtaposition of multiple images within a frame (formal intermediality), the appropriation of conventions associated with comics (expressive intermediality), and an elastic or otherwise unnatural representation of temporality that approximates a readerly experience of time (figural intermediality). Obviously not all of these modes of interaction between comics and film are equal in status: while diegetic and compositional intertextuality are certainly the most common ways for films to poach from comics texts, the four modes of intermediality are far richer sources for new stylistic utterances that rearticulate elements from comics in uniquely cinematic terms. Different comic book films employ different combinations of these strategies: some remediate on multiple levels simultaneously, while others never venture beyond the most superficial engagement with comics. As we'll see throughout the remainder of this book, comic book film style offers no shortage of opportunities for creative filmmakers to play in the margins between these two media, sometimes even pushing film style into unexplored aesthetic territory and often going against the grain of stylistic norms. The remediation of the ways in which comic books hybridize text and image offers just such a case, and it is to this subject that we now turn.

CHAPTER 2

VANDALIZING THE FOURTH WALL

WORD-IMAGE HYBRIDITY AND A COMIC BOOK
CINEMA OF ATTRACTIONS

As a print medium, comics began without access to the resources of sound and, unlike film, never sought to gain them through technological advances. Instead, comics developed and refined a series of medium-specific conventions to indicate different kinds of narrative information to the reader through text: balloons for dialogue and thoughts, which can easily be attributed to specific characters; caption boxes for voiceover or "voice of god"–style narration; and onomatopoeias, graphically depicted, for all manner of sound effects—the more cacophonous the better. These are among comics' most immediately recognizable conventions and are deeply associated with the medium across the world. For instance, David Carrier identified the speech balloon as the medium's "defining element . . . because it establishes a word/image unity that distinguishes comics from pictures illustrating a text."[1] In contrast to the definition offered by Scott McCloud, Carrier claims that to "reduce the comic to mere words—or, conversely, to treat it as merely a sequence of images—leaves aside what defines this art form, the integration of words with picture."[2] Carrier is certainly not alone in his emphasis on word-image hybridity as the medium's defining characteristic. For instance, in Italy comics are known as *fumetti* (puffs of smoke), which refers to the appearance of speech balloons—a much more evocative and accurate designation than the North American designation of "comics," which refers not to any distinctive medium-specific attribute but rather to the comedic genre. Similarly, in 1989 a group of eleven international comics experts decided that the birth of comics occurred in 1896, not with the first Yellow Kid strip but rather with the Yellow Kid strip that first introduced the speech balloon.[3] Implicitly, strips of sequential art that preceded this innovation were thereby relegated to the status of protocomics. Comics historians will continue to disagree about when the medium was truly "born"—McCloud famously describes the Bayoux Tapestry, which dates back to the eleventh century, as comics,[4] and Thierry Groensteen has argued that the medium is "impossible" to exhaustively define[5]—but the kind of word-image hybridity represented by the balloon is clearly central to the medium's distinctive character and how it tells stories.

While comics have always relied on the creative combination of text and image, cinema adopted a synchronized soundtrack as soon as it was technologically feasible, giving birth to the talking picture and largely usurping the role of the text-based expository intertitles that were necessary in the silent era. Despite the fact that sound is not a defining feature of cinema—indeed, the medium was already more than three decades old when the "talkie" was born with the release of *The Jazz Singer* (1927)—the absence or presence of sound has been cited as an irreconcilable ontological difference between comics and film, and therefore an "adaptation problem" that films based on comics must reckon with.[6] Pascal Lefèvre writes that, unlike film,

> comics do not have a sound track: music, voices, and noises can only be suggested by stilled and visible signs (text, ideograms, balloons . . .) printed on paper. It is possible to use similar techniques in film, but they do not function well. Except for tongue-in-cheek approaches as in the *Batman* television series (1966–68), onomatopoeia in a cinematographic context looks rather strange.[7]

Certainly the textual visualization of dialogue, narration, and even sound effects didn't appear strange in the silent era, but it does today. There are two reasons why this might be so. First, the film soundtrack seems to render the visualization of sound in textual form either redundant or unnecessary. In a sound film context, text-based narration may appear antiquated at best and "uncinematic" at worst. Second, comic book conventions like the balloon, caption box, and graphic onomatopoeia are not commonly used in film and therefore stand out as self-conscious stylistic interventions. While classical film style's mode of narration is designed to be as unobtrusive as possible, avoiding whenever possible the kinds of direct address and self-conscious artifice that these conventions represent, comic book film style instead puts the processes of mediation and remediation on deliberate display.

It's easy to see superficial similarities between comics and silent film, since both rely on discursive textual interventions to narrate, contextualize, and give "voice" to their images and the storyworlds they represent. In this chapter, I demonstrate how the remediation of comics' distinctive word-image hybridity harkens back not just to the silent era but more specifically to a *preclassical* era of film style, which Tom Gunning has influentially defined as a "cinema of attractions." More than merely providing narrative information via text, as intertitles do, caption boxes, word (speech or thought) balloons, and graphic onomatopoeias call attention to themselves as intermedial intrusions in the representational space of cinema, resulting in the kind of obtrusive style and direct address that classical film style expressly avoids.

Though Lefèvre claims that text, ideograms, and balloons "do not function well" in film, implying that they're entirely superfluous stylistic gestures, he simultaneously (though perhaps inadvertently) suggests what their greater value might be. Comics' use of text in general and the speech balloon in particular is remarkably intuitive, transmitting "the impression of sound so that a child can perceive it."[8] As Carrier notes, "the seemingly complex conventions associated with word balloons were, without any explanation, mastered rather quickly by everyone who read them."[9] In their native medium, they serve their intended function in an exemplary manner. Film sound has a similarly immediate appeal. As Carrier reminds us,

> At the movies, seeing the characters on the screen as speaking is only an illusion—I know that these voices come from the speakers on the wall. I hear voices, but imagine them coming from the actors. If, forgetting the libretto, I read the supertitles at the opera, I *see* in English translation the words I *hear* sung in the original language without supposing that the translated words I read are being sung. When reading comics, I see the depicted words as spoken by the depicted figures. That is a different illusion—I look at words and imagine them to be spoken.[10]

It's important to recognize that both synchronized film sound and comics' word balloons are artistic (and artificial) devices, not natural features of their respective media but conventions that have become accepted over time.

Lefèvre is correct in that comics conventions such as these *do* appear strange when remediated by the cinema; but more than that, they *make strange* in the Russian formalist sense. They have a defamiliarizing effect in line with Bertolt Brecht's *Verfremdungseffekt* or Victor Shklovsky's *ostranenie*, enstranging the viewer from the fictional storyworld by calling attention to the text's surface, its form, and its artificiality.

Dialogue on a film soundtrack generally doesn't call attention to itself in this way, instead presenting itself as a natural part of the projected onscreen world, as Carrier suggests; the same is true of a speech balloon in a comic book, not because it's a natural part of the diegesis—it isn't—but because its use over time has made it the conventionalized means of representing spoken dialogue in the medium. But the presence of a speech balloon *in a film* doesn't disappear into the representation in the same way precisely because of its novelty, its *strangeness*. As in a comic book, the speech balloon cannot be interpreted as a natural part of the represented world; but unlike comics, it is not an accepted convention for communicating dialogue in this medium. The speech balloon is thereby enstranged, to use Shklovsky's term; it becomes an object of fascination in itself rather than merely a means of communicating narrative content. "By 'enstranging' objects and complicating form," writes Shklovsky, "the device of art makes perception long and 'laborious'" rather than automatic and immediate.[11] The presence of comics conventions in a film—and, moreover, their seeming lack of utility in a medium that has access to realistic, audible sound—calls attention to themselves in precisely this way, prompting the viewer to reflect on how they function and create meaning differently in these contrasting contexts.

This is all in direct opposition to the goal of classical Hollywood style, which is primarily oriented toward concealing "its artifice through techniques of continuity and 'invisible' storytelling."[12] For Jared Gardner, this is the central difference between comics and film, both of which relished in gaps, discontinuity, and fragmentation up to the point where classical Hollywood style became codified and standardized. As cinema moved toward long-form storytelling and away from the kinds of "discontinuous serial narratives" associated with comic strips, Gardner writes, the film industry

> trained audiences to privilege continuity, resolution, and closure—and to reject as "bad film" the fragments, the gaps, the illogical connections of early film. The gutter that film and comics shared for their first decade was dissolved, so that film might become a very different kind of product,

one that offers more easily regulated pleasures. After 1910, with the exception of the newly emerging field of animation and the serial, American film moved increasingly from the logic of the comic strip serial in favor of the self-contained narrative, where the fragments are, in Lyotard's terms, put to productive, "procreative" work.[13]

While the movement inherent in cinema allowed for the possibility of fluidity through editing practices that would deemphasize the gaps between shots or views, comics have gaps built into their formal architecture on a fundamental level: "in the passage from one frame to the next, the gutter intervenes, and the message is transformed in countless ways by the syndicated act of millions of readers filling in the gaps between."[14] The rejection of these gaps in favor of continuity is tantamount to a rejection of comics in favor of classical cinema. The remediation of comic book text, then, has the potential to disrupt classical film style in three distinct ways: (1) by calling attention to the artificiality of the cinematic representation; (2) by integrating conventions from a separate medium that doesn't prioritize continuity in the same way as cinema; and (3) by prompting the viewer to consider the impact that different media have on the way narratives are shaped and experienced.

Prior to the advent of synchronized sound, narrative cinema—even as it otherwise adhered to the principles of narrative causality and continuity editing—necessarily succumbed to diegetic and representational gaps in the form of intertitles. As Michel Chion writes,

> The intertitle had an inherent limitation: it interrupted the images, it implied the conspicuous presence in the film of a foreign body, an impurity. At the same time it allowed great narrative flexibility, since title cards could be used to establish the story's setting, to sum up a part of the action, to issue a judgment about the characters, and of course, to give a free transcription of the spoken dialogues. In general the text merely summarizes what was being said, it made no pretense to exhaustiveness. Dialogue could be presented in direct discourse or indirect discourse ("she explains to him that"). In short, the silent film had the entire narrative arsenal of the novel at its disposal.[15]

Similar in purpose to the "desperation device"[16] that is the comic book speech balloon, the silent film intertitle represents a "narrational intrusion"[17] into the representation, conveying necessary exposition and dialogue but interrupting the viewer's access to the projected storyworld in doing so. Though widely adopted for their ability to help clarify narrative action, intertitles were considered to be an unnatural addition to the medium, and many filmmakers sought to limit their use as much as possible, if not to eliminate them entirely. As Kristin Thompson writes, "Scriptwriters seemed to assume that every title in a film betrayed a weak point where its author had failed to convey the situation properly through the images. In 1913, Famous Players' president Adolph Zukor was reported to be working toward eliminating titles from his company's films: 'We are trying to let the story tell itself so far as possible.'"[18] Though strategies were developed that minimized the self-consciousness of intertitles' onscreen presence—for instance, by cutting to a dialogue intertitle only after a character's lips had begun to move—the device nevertheless "breaks the film's visual continuity."[19] The introduction of sound allowed for the elimination of the gaps caused by intertitles and smoothed over other kinds of visual discontinuities with aural continuity.[20] In this brave new world of synchronized sound, intertitles were cast aside like a vestigial limb, an expressive device whose usefulness had been relegated to the newly audiovisual medium's silent past.

For good reason, silent film intertitles have been compared to comic book captions. In his article "Beyond Remediation: Comic Book Captions and Silent Film Intertitles as the Same Genre," Jeffrey S. J. Kirchoff argues that 1940s comic book captions remediate silent-era intertitles based on overwhelming similarities in form, style, and narrative purpose.[21] While his points are largely well taken, I think his thesis overreaches somewhat. It can be difficult, if not outright impossible, to measure influence in this way, but the historical presence of captions in comics (and protocomics) prior to the existence of cinema suggests that films may have looked to the comics caption as an influence for the intertitle rather than vice versa.[22] In any case, the influence is much more likely to be mutual and dialogic rather than simply monodirectional. Moreover, Kirchoff's argument overlooks a key difference between how they are deployed in their respective media. While they may be stylized in different ways—or even expressively animated, as in F. W. Murnau's *Sunrise* (1927)—film intertitles don't share the frame with the diegetic world; instead, intertitles *interrupt* our access to the diegetic world in order to advance or clarify the narrative. In comics, by contrast, captions, balloons, and onomatopoeic sound effects all appear as graphic elements within the panel, sharing space with the diegesis as part of the total composition. These conventions are located "neither entirely within the picture space nor outside it," representing "a cumbersome alien body in the book."[23] In *Making Comics*, McCloud puts it perfectly: "Balloons don't exist in the same plane of reality as these pictures, yet here they are, floating about like physical objects!"[24] In terms of sound, then, comics are not exactly like silent film or sound film, but are somewhere between the two: comics "sound" is represented synchronously with the images but still manifests textually rather than sonically.

Despite their inherent differences, certain experimental uses of onscreen text in the silent era emphasize the potential parallels between comics and film to a greater extent than intertitles. Nowhere is this clearer than in the work of Edwin S. Porter, which represents an ongoing conversation between the two media. Not only did he direct adaptations of serialized strips like Richard F. Outcault's *Buster Brown* (*Pranks of Buster Brown and His Dog Tige*, 1904) and Winsor McCay's *Dream of the Rarebit Fiend* (*Dream of a Rarebit Fiend*, 1906), but he also experimented with alternatives to intertitles that synchronized the textual appearance of dialogue with its articulation within the diegesis, thereby turning the screen into a heterogeneous, lexico-visual space in which words and images interact in dynamic ways. In such films, literal images of the storyworld appear alongside figurative, textual representations of the world's sonic features. Porter's *College Chums* (1907) is exemplary in this regard, as a telephone conversation between two lovers is conveyed by words dancing across the screen from one interlocutor to the other. As Rick Altman details, other attempts at overcoming intertitles' limitations were even more directly evocative of comics:

> In mid-1911, the Horsley Co. began distributing the Nestor Film Co.'s productions of "Mutt and Jeff Talking Pictures." Based on familiar comic-strip characters, these films offered an unexpected solution to the dialogue problem, simply inserting speech balloons like those found in the contemporary funny papers. These experiments culminated in a bizarre 1917 patent for producing filmed cartoons without resorting to animation or drawings. Charles F. Pidgin's process called for each actor to inflate, at the appropriate moment, a balloon carrying the words to be spoken. As Pidgin put it, "the words constituting the speech of the actors or characters are placed on balloons of oblong shape adapted to be inflated to a relatively large size and normally occupying a comparatively small space with the words entirely visible."[25]

Had this "bizarre" idea been implemented in live-action films, it would undoubtedly qualify as a direct remediation (and literalization!) of the speech balloon. I suspect that its failure was due to the extreme self-consciousness involved in displaying dialogue in this way, which would not have fit with the developing classical style. Though Pidgin claims that the process would "add to the realism of the picture by the words appearing to come from the mouth of the players,"[26] it is difficult to imagine what kind of spectator—in 1917 or today—would accept an actor inflating a balloon as a *realistic* depiction of the act of speaking. Nevertheless, this does seem somewhat in line with more contemporary attempts at remediating comic book sound, which also disrupt the reality (and realism) of the film with self-conscious style that is often superfluous to the narration as such.

In this way, I would suggest that remediating comic books' word-image hybridity represents a return to a preclassical approach to film style, wherein filmmakers had to overcome the technological limitations of the nascent medium with different effects that read to us today as stylized. Gunning's concept of the "cinema of attractions," which coalesces certain tendencies of pre-1908 cinema into a theory of direct spectatorial address, effectively elucidates the kinds of remediation effects that I'm exploring here.

FIGURE 2.1. Still from
College Chums

While contemporary blockbuster cinema is often understood as a return to spectacle at the expense of narrative, comic book film style offers a particularly striking example that better fits Gunning's original definition of the term. Special effects may certainly be spectacular, and they often represent an interruption in the narrative's development, but in the vast majority of cases—including *The Matrix*'s "bullet time" effects[27] and the computer-generated imagery (CGI) that brings superheroes to life in live action—these so-called "attractions" are strictly kept within the bounds of the diegetic world. As Dick Tomasovic writes with regard to Sam Raimi's *Spider-Man*,

> This kind of cinema attracts the spectator to the spectacle of its technology, but, at the same time, aims at the fantastic element and transfers the attraction of the technology toward the diegetic. This is particularly evident in the sequences shot with the so-called "spider-cam" which is constantly showing its own virtuosity while being completely subjected to the recording of the extraordinary acrobatics of the hero. The technological device exhibits itself while highlighting, above all, the extraordinary action of the diegesis offering throughout these bewildering moments a double attraction (the attraction of the film and the attraction of the *dispositif*).[28]

By contrast, the original cinema of attractions was comparatively unconcerned with neatly integrating its effects into a self-contained diegesis. While many attractions did exist within the bounds of a loose narrative— for instance, the various trick shots that constitute *A Trip to the Moon* (1902) or the gunshot at the camera that closes *The Great Train Robbery* (1903)[29]—others were bound only by the logic of the variety show. In all cases, Gunning defines attractions primarily by their willingness to address the spectator directly: "This is a cinema that displays its visibility, willing to rupture a self-enclosed fictional world for a chance to solicit the attention of the spectator."[30] Movies like *The Matrix* and *Spider-Man* certainly display their visibility, but they don't rupture the fourth wall that separates the diegetic and nondiegetic worlds while doing so. Despite their spectacular nature, these films' stylistic systems remain primarily devoted to integrating spectacular visuals into the diegesis via classically constructed narration; ultimately, they address their audiences in a way that allows them to experience the pleasures of spectacle within an overarching logic of narrative absorption. The comic book cinema of attractions is not defined by an interest in action sequences, in spectacular stunt choreography, or in superlative comput-er-generated visual effects, but rather in the interplay between a live-action diegesis and nondiegetic conventions associated specifically with comics' style of narration. This interplay *itself* is the attraction: rather than tran-scending or challenging the ontology of cinema, such intermedial attrac-tions flout the restrictions of classical film style and demonstrate the medi-um's true ontological range. They treat film's representational flexibility as a spectacle in its own right, embodying a sense of intermedial play and sty-listic experimentation.

When remediated by the cinema, the balloon, the text caption, and graphic onomatopoeia manifest within the film frame as nondiegetic visual elements, rupturing the reality of the film with a burst of self-conscious expressive intermediality. In a much more direct way than *Spider-Man*'s "spi-der-cam," for instance, expressive intermediality presents the medium itself as an attraction—or, rather, the *media themselves*, since film and comics are dialogically hybridized and thereby exhibited simultaneously. As Gunning reminds us, "Early audiences went to exhibitions to see machines demon-strated . . . rather than to view" specific films,[31] evincing an interest in the apparatus irrespective of the content being displayed. In remediating com-ics' conventions, comic book film style puts both media on display and cre-ates opportunities for comparing and contrasting the ways in which they communicate. These attractions are generally not integrated into the sto-ryworld, instead demonstrating an interest in "exhibitionist confrontation rather than diegetic absorption"; these films presume that the comic book's intermedial relation to film is "of interest in itself."[32]

A lexico-visual medium like comics, in contrast to an audiovisual medium like cinema, relies on text to a much greater extent for its narration: it must represent sound visually or not at all, resulting in images that are populated by diegetic elements and visual manifestations of the sonic landscape simul-taneously. As my comments about *Spider-Man* suggest, however, not every comic book adaptation betrays a stylistic interest in the comics medium in addition to its interest in the narrative content of particular texts. It's an even smaller subset of comic book films that remediate the word balloon or other text-based conventions of comics. But for those that do, we can determine a set of questions that will guide our inquiry: Does the film adapt or realize the sounds of comic books using its soundtrack only? Or does it also remedi-ate comic book text's inherent visibility, making significant sounds textually legible on screen? If the latter, how is the text integrated into the visuals, and what is its relationship to the diegesis? Is the text rendered narratively redundant by the soundtrack, or does it make a novel contribution to the narration or meaning of the film? Over the following pages, I analyze the remediation of onomatopoeias in *Batman: The Movie* and *Super* and word balloons in *American Splendor* and *Kick-Ass 2*, indicating the ways in which these films hybridize words and images in a specifically comics-inspired mode.[33] In so doing, all of these films draw attention to the fourth wall that separates the diegetic world from the spectatorial space, thereby emphasizing the "gaps, discontinuities, and the visibility of the representational apparatus"[34] that comics share with the preclassical cinema of attractions.

Snikt! Thwip! Bamf! Realizing and Remediating Graphic Onomatopoeias

Far and away the most common approach to adapting the text-based "sounds" of comic books for the cinema is to replace the visual dimension of balloons, captions, and onomatopoeias with a properly and exclusively sonic one. I dub this approach *realization*, which, in contrast to remediation, attempts to represent the graphically rendered sounds of comics in a cinematically verisimilitudinous way. This is antithetical to a comic book cinema of attractions insofar as it merely adapts the *content* of comics to a cinematic paradigm and does not engage with the specificity of the medium's form. For instance, the balloon as an artistic device is not *remediated* whenever a film actor speaks words that happened to have once been contained within a balloon in the original comics; this merely *realizes* the words expressed within the balloon in an audiovisual format, and ignores the play between diegetic and non-diegetic graphic forms that defines comic book sound. In the terminology introduced in the previous chapter, this is more aptly described as diegetic intertextuality than expressive intermediality. As Marina Warner articulates with regard to film sound,

> Diegetic sound can be and is frequently introduced as artificially as non-diegetic, but in thrall to the gods of verisimilitude, it conceals its simulation. Film remains haunted by vacancy and the vacancy has to be supplied for it to become enfleshed. Actual fizzles might be just fizzles, a kiss is just a kiss, but footfalls are footfalls, and like shadows they show us that the image on the screen belongs to someone—someone with a material body if not a soul.[35]

Sound is much less important in comics than it is in film, which relies on an ever-present soundtrack to provide ambiance, mood, narration, and affect, while also giving weight and credibility to the world depicted onscreen. Foley work, sound montage, on-set recording, and postproduction looping combine on the film soundtrack to provide a much more comprehensive aural reality than we ever experience in comics. By contrast, comics only explicitly articulate narratively significant sounds and forgo ambiance for the most part.

The realization of graphic onomatopoeia is worth exploring in some detail before moving on to the different strategies for remediation, since it is by far the most common approach in comic book adaptations. Certain comic book characters are so closely identified with specific sound effects—the "snikt!" of Wolverine's claws, the "thwip!" of Spider-Man's webbing, the "bamf!" of Nightcrawler's teleportation—that film sound designers take great care in developing sonic analogs that will be both realistic and satisfying to those familiar with the text-based articulation. In the context of comic book–derived video games, Jennifer Rowsell, Isabel Pedersen, and Douglas Trueman identify such significant sounds as "touchpoints" between different articulations of transmedial characters such as these:

> Touchpoints can both reflect canonical worlds *and* they can signal ways of deviating from established story worlds. For example, when Wolverine extends his adamantium claws in the comics, the action is always accompanied by the word "snikt," a visual onomatopoeic construction that serves to illustrate the sound of metal scraping against metal. Because video games are multimodal, the developers can choose to replace the visual representation with a sound effect or further illustrate this touchstone with the word appearing on-screen. Much like there is no way to truly express the auditory representation of a musical note in any other medium, there is no true way to literally translate "snikt" to an aural medium or vice versa. Developers, then, must do the best with the resources they have available.[36]

Since film is similarly multimodal, these comments apply equally to comic book films. The specificity of these onomatopoeias, as intermedial touchpoints, becomes a crucial marker of fidelity for some viewers. But with regard to their "translation" from text to sound and the question of fidelity, I think it's important to revisit the definition of onomatopoeia: these are not *sounds* per se, but rather words that are derived from and are meant to approximate or embody sounds. As onomatopoeias, "snikt!" and "thwip!" are not of value in themselves, but are instead valued for their ability to communicate their real-world referent. The sonic versions of these onomatopoeias, whether in film or video games, function as indexical signs that point back to the (nonexistent) original sounds that inspired them in the first place: rather than a faithful or unfaithful "translation" of the comic book onomatopoeia, the comic book "thwip!" and the filmic "thwip!" should be understood as equal insofar as both are merely simulacra—that is, simulations of something that has no real-world referent[37]—of the imaginary sound Stan Lee had in mind when he first wrote the sound effect in *Amazing Spider-Man* #36 (May 1966). For this reason, I think that assessing these sound effects in terms of their "fidelity" to the sound evoked by the comic book onomatopoeias is somewhat misguided. More important is how these sound effects are integrated—whether by a logic of realization or remediation—into a given film's stylistic system.

Though most comic book filmmakers don't put onomatopoeias on the screen in explicitly graphic form, they often emphasize these sounds in other ways that don't break the reality of the film. The close-up insert shot, which can be seen in movies like *Spider-Man* and *X-Men Origins: Wolverine* (2009), is the most common strategy. In both of these cases, the films cut to close-ups of the titular superheroes' hands as their CGI-enabled superpowers are put on display. Through what Chion dubs the "audiovisual contract"[38]—referring to the myriad ways that film sound conditions our experience of the image, and vice versa—these close-up inserts function also as auditory close-ups, directing the viewer's attention to the sound effect through visual cues. Alternatively, in *X2: X-Men United* (2003), Nightcrawler's "bamf!" sound effect is accompanied by visible puffs of smoke (*fumetti?*) that transform the nondiegetic visuality of comic book onomatopoeia into a *diegetic* visual effect.

But what of those films that turn comic book onomatopoeias into *nondiegetic* visual effects? As Warner argues, onomatopoeia occupies a similar position as the balloon in terms of its importance to the medium's unique visual identity:

Since Popeye first landed his fist to a resounding "Splat!" or Batman and Captain America laid about them to accompanying sound effects, visualizing noises has become a defining feature of this storytelling medium, unique as far as I know and original to the form. Its closest analogues—not that close, though—would be the Mayan glyph, which as a single sign dynamically combines word and picture. Egyptian hieroglyphics are different again, being ideographic and combining elements alphabetically, but neither of these ideographic scripts is precisely ideophonic, or acoustic—in quite the same way as the visual sound pictures of the cartoon—what one might call the sonics of comics.[39]

Given the device's extreme importance and close association with comics, it makes sense that some filmmakers would want to make use of the specific visual effect achieved by onomatopoeia, even if the film soundtrack renders its use ostensibly redundant. *Batman: The Movie* employs this device most famously in the climactic battle royal on the deck of the Penguin's submarine. As Batman and Robin fight through a parade of supervillains and anonymous goons, graphic onomatopoeias appear to punctuate certain attacks.[40] Unlike many instances of onomatopoeia in the television series from which the film derived, these colorful chunks of text share the frame with the photographic action rather than appearing as autonomous intertitles, turning

FIGURE 2.2. Still from
Spider-Man

FIGURE 2.3. Still from
X2: X-Men United

the film frame into a more heterogeneous zone of representation that combines not only photographic and drawn elements, but diegetic and nondiegetic ones as well.

Though superficially this seems very similar to how comic book onomatopoeias operate, it's crucial to consider how this artistic device is transformed through the process of remediation. In his article on text-image hybridity in comics, Thomas E. Wartenberg describes how onomatopoeias typically function:

> When we see a word such as "Pow!" in a comic, it indicates the presence of an event, such as someone hitting someone else. So although comics cannot directly present the passing of time since they lack duration—something that films have the capacity [to do] because of their nature as temporally extended objects—they have developed a unique representational scheme for presenting temporal events in a less direct manner than verbally representing them with a phrase such as "and then." Through an interesting use of visual signs, but primarily through the use of onomatopoetic words, comics are able to [represent] temporally-extended processes or events in a way that traditional visual mediums such as painting standardly do not, since they eschew such symbolic means of representation.[41]

Like the word balloon, comic book onomatopoeia might be considered a "desperation device," a symbolic lexico-visual element that compensates for certain of the medium's fundamental shortcomings: in this case, the lack of sound and movement. When transposed to a cinematic context, however, these shortcomings disappear and the device becomes unnecessary as a narrative tool. As Wartenberg notes—and as we'll discuss in greater detail in chapter 4—film is distinct from comics in that it has duration, meaning that it can show an event rather than merely evoke that event through a figurative device. To what end is onomatopoeia used, then, in this audiovisual moving image environment?

The most immediate difference is that cinematic onomatopoeia becomes a supplement to the sound and movement rather than a marker of and substitute for their absence. *Batman: The Movie* doesn't use onomatopoeias to replace the sound effects that one would expect to hear in a scene such as this; as usual for films, the blows are accompanied by sound effects, produced

FIGURE 2.4. Still from *Batman: The Movie*

by Foley artists in postproduction and added for the ostensible purpose of creating verisimilitude. As Chion astutely notes, "In real life a punch does not necessarily make noise, even if it hurts someone. In a cinematic or televisual audio-image, the sound of the impact is well-nigh obligatory. Otherwise no one would believe the punches, even if they had really been inflicted."[42] It seems somewhat counterintuitive to claim that an outlandish onomatopoeia like "URKKK!" could serve the same function, but this is precisely what Warner claims for comics, in which graphic sound effects express "the weight and substance, the capacity for pain and for sensation of their drawn characters."[43] This is because onomatopoeia has become a conventionalized storytelling device and is therefore expected as part of a comics-based representation; it doesn't undermine the verisimilitude of a comic book any more than Foley effects do in a film, as both are artificial means of imposing sound on a narrative event. It is precisely this artificiality that cinematic onomatopoeias reveal. It seems, then, that these devices serve similar functions in their respective media, which makes sense, given that they're medium-specific approaches to conveying the same thing: diegetic sound effects.

When remediated by film, however, the meaning of comic book onomatopoeia also changes. In a film like *Batman: The Movie*, rather than add to the believability and intensity of the fight, the nondiegetic intrusions represented by the onomatopoeias function in the opposite way, to undermine the verisimilitude of the action; aiding in this is the fact that in many cases the Foley sound effects are drowned out on the soundtrack by nondiegetic orchestra strings. The cartoonish and colorful onomatopoeias don't lend weight and substance to a cartoon world, as they might in a comic, but instead *detract* from the weight and substance of the live-action world by equating it with the flat, static imagery of the comic book page. This is because the comic book elements are not integrated organically into a photographic mode, but rather clash and collide with it whenever they appear; they're hybridized in such a manner that they remain deliberately heterogeneous. In short, *Batman: The Movie* uses hybridization in such a way that "one voice [ironizes] and [unmasks] the other."[44] The comic book aesthetics unmask the verisimilitude of live action, exposing the fraudulence of the medium's purported realism, while the live-action photography ironizes the comic book, exposing its supposed lack of aesthetic sophistication. In juxtaposing comics' visual and representational strategies against those of live-action cinema, *Batman: The Movie* parodies the comic book medium as a whole while also satirizing the superhero genre specifically.

Though most often discussed as an example of camp,[45] *Batman: The Movie*'s stylistics, I argue, are better understood as parody. Though it is among the earliest superhero films, the genre was already mature enough in comic books that its conventions were ripe for parody, even in a different medium. And while the film does parody the superhero genre—from the ludicrousness of double identities to the increasing improbability of the heroes' evasions of death—comics as a medium is also specifically targeted. The medium's very name in the English language—"comics" is a synonym for "funnies," as though the medium was meant for or restricted to this particular genre—itself functions to devalue it, or at least to undermine its aesthetic potential.[46] Indeed, until the final decades of the twentieth century, American culture had largely accepted "the [premise] that there is nothing worth looking at in comics,"[47] a misperception that *Batman: The Movie* reifies by parodying not just the superhero genre but also the larger idea that anything in comics could be worth investing in as a reader or viewer. According to Gérard Genette, merely imitating a style "of low repute" can function to parody the same,[48] which is *Batman*'s strategy here. By contrasting it against the live-action footage, *Batman: The Movie* engenders an ironic distance from the aesthetics of comics and depicts it as a cheap, garish, and unsophisticated medium.

The style also exceeds the needs of the narrative, creating meaning by breaking—though perhaps "vandalizing" is a more apt word—the fourth wall, implicitly asking viewers to consider the relationship between these two media and the differences between them. This is done in precisely the way outlined by Gunning with regard to the cinema of attractions of some sixty years earlier:

> This action, which is later perceived as spoiling the realistic illusion of the cinema, is here undertaken with brio, establishing contact with the audience. From comedians smirking at the camera, to the constant bowing and gesturing of the conjurors in magic films, this is a cinema that displays its visibility, willing to rupture a self-enclosed fictional world for a chance to solicit the attention of the spectator.[49]

In general, the film makes little attempt to create a "realistic illusion," opting instead to juxtapose photography and drawing, sound and text, cinema and comics, in ways that call attention to their differences, resulting in self-consciously heterogeneous imagery that the viewer must negotiate in ways similar to the comics reader. In *Batman: The Movie*, the comic book medium's subsumption by the cinematic apparatus is presented as an aesthetic novelty meant to solicit viewers' attention, as well as part of a larger visual strategy to undermine the photographic reality of film.

A much more recent film, *Super*, also uses comic book–style onomatopoeia as a nondiegetic visual effect. Like *Batman: The Movie*, *Super* assumes a satirical stance vis-à-vis comic book superheroes, portraying superhero vigilantism as the pastime of mentally unstable individuals.[50] Also similarly to *Batman: The Movie*, *Super* associates the superhero genre with the aesthetics of comic book conventions like onomatopoeia. But whereas the impact and realism of Batman and Robin's blows are deliberately undermined by the addition of onomatopoeias, in *Super* they function differently. While onomatopoeias are sparingly peppered throughout the film, most instances of this device are used during the film's climax, when protagonist Frank (in full superhero regalia as the Crimson Bolt) attempts to break up a drug deal and rescue his wife from a drug dealer named Jacques. As Frank takes out each of Jacques's bodyguards in decidedly R-rated fashion, the cinematic movement comes to a brief halt and the colorful, cartoonish onomatopoeias appear onscreen in the frozen frame.

FIGURE 2.5. Still from *Super*

Rather than transform acts of violence into harmless moments of cartoonish play, as the onomatopoeias do in *Batman: The Movie*, the contrast
between the realistic violence and the patent artifice of the onomatopoeias
heightens the impact of the violence through ironic juxtaposition. Similarly,
the freeze frame's artificial lack of movement doesn't merely strengthen the
image's similarity to a comic book panel: it also forces the viewer to linger on
the blood spray, which stands out more strongly against the orange impact
star[51] than it would against the dark background. By recontextualizing *Batman: The Movie*–style onomatopoeias within scenes of graphic violence,
Super confronts the viewer with a startling and deliberate contrast between
the brutal reality of Frank's actions and the playful artificiality of this comic
book convention.

    In both of these cases, it cannot be said that the onomatopoeias are redun-
dant, but rather that their use and potential meaning have been altered and
renewed by their new context. In a comic book, the "KA-POW!" and its
accompanying impact star seen in figure 2.5 would function as the primary
means through which this violent event would be represented and "felt"
by the reader. In both *Batman: The Movie* and *Super*, the presence of sound
and movement negates the device's original narrative purpose, but in the
vacuum thus created, new possibilities for meaning emerge. Moreover, the
very presence of onomatopoeia—a nondiegetic visual intrusion in the film
image—puts the artificiality of the representation on display and emphasizes

the film's intermedial connection to comic books. The presence of words on the screen implicitly recognizes the presence not just of a viewer but of a *reader*, and specifically the kind of active reader that can negotiate heterogeneous images and synthesize different kinds of representational codes. In displaying onomatopoeic sound graphically, these films solicit the attention of a film spectator who must act like a comic book reader.

Blowing Up Word Balloons: Reading Remediated Comics Text

Onomatopoeia, of course, is not the only text-based comics convention that has been appropriated by films. The varied remediation of balloons—that "defining element" of comics[52]—further demonstrates the potential utility of word-image hybridity in an audiovisual format. To an even greater extent than onomatopoeia, balloons occupy a privileged position in the comics medium, so it stands to reason that comic book films would want to draw on this strong intermedial association in order to clearly announce or reinforce their affiliation with comics. Speech and especially thought balloons have become quite common in animated cartoons, from *The Simpsons* (1989–) to *The Peanuts Movie* (2015); since they are not limited to text in terms of the visual content they can display, they're useful for displaying a character's thoughts through images. Balloons have been less common in live action, where common wisdom suggests that synchronized sound has rendered them useless; in the sound film, recorded dialogue or voiceover narration has usurped the balloon's ostensible function.

A notable exception, albeit a televisual one, can be found in Spider-Man's live-action appearances on *The Electric Company* (1971–1977). In these short segments, the action would be contained within a single comic book panel in the center of the screen, surrounded by static panels on the periphery of the image. Within this smaller frame, live action and drawn images intermingle in various ways: the actors seem to exist in a cartoon world of patently artificial backgrounds, and the camera will often cut to drawn static images to transition between scenes of live-action footage. But what's most interesting here is how Spider-Man's dialogue is presented. Instead of speaking out loud like all the other characters, the actor playing the superhero remains totally mute while a speech balloon appears adjacent to his head. To emphasize it, Spider-Man sometimes even turns his head to look directly at the speech balloon. Since this is a children's educational program, presumably the intent here is to force young viewers to read in order to follow the

FIGURE 2.6. Still from
The Electric Company

narrative, and using a well-known comic book character presents a natural opportunity to integrate onscreen text into the show via the balloon. Children would think it only natural that Spider-Man speak through text—after all, this is how he has always communicated in the comics. Moreover, this kind of implicit direct address and overtly stylized narration is an accepted convention of children's programming.[53]

The use of the balloon in shows like *The Electric Company*, similarly to the use of onomatopoeia in *Batman: The Movie*, seems to reify comics' cultural reputation as an immature, childish medium. Consequently, films that incorporate aesthetic effects and storytelling devices associated with a "low" medium like comics may be taken less seriously as works of art or be associated with camp (read: "bad" taste) or children's fare, rather than as works that critically interrogate and push against cinema's perceived limits of representation. Two live-action films for adult audiences that challenge these associations and assumptions directly are *American Splendor* and *Kick-Ass 2*. The former film, Robert Pulcini and Shari Springer Berman's adaptation of Harvey Pekar's long-running autobiographical comics series, makes use of a wide variety of comics devices, including thought balloons, as part of its larger ambition to self-reflexively trouble the authority and truth value of fictional and documentary forms by emphasizing the film's various strategies of mediation, and specifically its intermedial relationship to comics.[54] The latter film, Jeff Wadlow's satirical superhero sequel *Kick-Ass 2*, uses speech balloons as a form of nontraditional or creative subtitling that subverts the expectations of subtitles both in terms of context and execution. In creating these meanings, both films don't just transform the original use of the balloon by remediating it in an audiovisual context, they also eschew classical style in favor of a comic book cinema of attractions that makes its own artifice and stylization an essential characteristic and appeal of the representation.

American Splendor's interest in exploring the intersections between comics and cinema is inseparable from its interest in troubling the relationship between representation and truth.[55] From the very outset of the movie, Pulcini and Berman undermine the possibility that their film could offer anything resembling a truthful, authentic, or singular portrait of Pekar. Indeed, by the end of the opening credits, the viewer has seen no fewer than eight distinct representations of the film's subject (two actors and six different comic book versions).[56] This list will later grow with the addition of the "real" Pekar, appearing as himself in both documentary and archival footage, a play-within-the-film version of Pekar, and numerous animated renditions. Through this polyphony of representational styles, the film emphasizes difference, uncertainty, subjectivity, and self-reflexivity rather than the authoritative neutrality of classical style. As Matthew Bolton puts it in his article about the film, "By rendering their own role as mediators and interpreters visible, Berman and Pulcini invite their audience to not only engage with their text, but also to view their text as explicitly a repurposing of Pekar's comics," which are similarly interested in this kind of multiplicity.[57] The film calls attention to its own artificiality in a variety of ways: by juxtaposing its fictional representations against documentary footage (and emphasizing the contrivances inherent in both), by self-reflexively exposing and dramatizing the process of filmmaking (specifically in the footage of the real Pekar recording his voiceovers for the film), and most importantly for my purposes here, by turning the film frame into a heterogeneous space where the live-action diegesis is invaded by nondiegetic devices from comic books.

While comic book conventions and imagery appear regularly throughout the film, it is the film's use of thought balloons that I would like to focus on here. This convention features most prominently in the scene that re-creates Pekar and R. Crumb's comic short story "Standing Behind Old Jewish Ladies in Supermarket Lines" from *American Splendor* #3 (1978). As Pekar (played by Paul Giamatti) contemplates which checkout line to enter at the grocery store, the image freezes and a thought balloon appears, textually articulating his inner monologue. The thought balloon, clearly hand drawn and lettered in Crumb's style, has the visual texture of pulpy paper, and during the freeze frames this texture expands to the entire image as well. In these ways, the film hybridizes the original comic book text with its cinematic re-creation, simultaneously emphasizing and blurring the line between the contrasting materialities of film and comics. In these moments, the film also trades the sonics of cinema for the silence and visibility of comics, forgoing voiceover

FIGURE 2.7. Still from *American Splendor*

narration entirely in favor of text. As Drew Morton observes, "The filmmakers, instead of transposing the text into voice-over narration, acknowledge the mediation of the balloon in comics."[58]

More than this, though, replacing a "cinematic" voiceover with an "uncinematic" thought balloon simultaneously emphasizes the similarities and differences between the two devices. They are equivalent insofar as both are nondiegetic and present a direct address to the viewer/reader; but they are distinct insofar as the balloon occupies *visual space*, drawing attention to its presence in the film frame. The freeze frame reinforces the fact that while voiceovers exist in time and have duration, the thought balloon is temporally indeterminate: representational time must come to a halt for the viewer to read the contents of the balloon, but it has no diegetic duration per se. In this way, the balloon seems to overlap with the silent film intertitle, but the similarities don't extend much further than that. Intertitles don't just interrupt diegetic time but also interrupt our access to the diegesis itself; by contrast, the balloon is superimposed over the diegetic space, allowing viewers to maintain visual contact with the storyworld, albeit one that contains "a cumbersome alien body" in the form of the balloon.[59]

After two such balloons, however, the film changes its approach: in the third balloon, text is replaced by an animated representation of Crumb's Pekar, who speaks his dialogue aloud in a direct address to the camera. This drawn version of Pekar manifests in the scene specifically to "solicit the attention of the spectator," to use Gunning's words.[60] The film then changes things up once more, as the drawn Pekar intrudes onto the left side of the screen, separated from the diegesis proper by a traditional comics gutter. The thought balloon has now disappeared completely, and with it the direct address to the spectator; the cartoon Pekar now solicits the attention of the live-action Pekar, who suddenly seems aware of his imaginary double. After the camera cuts to a closer view of Giamatti, his animated doppelgänger appears over his left shoulder, having now transcended the gutter to infiltrate the diegetic space itself, albeit only within the protagonist's subjective fantasy. The integration of animation and live-action cinematography in this scene superficially recalls films like *Who Framed Roger Rabbit* (1988), but the two films are actually quite opposite in terms of the relationship they posit between these two representational modes. In the world of *Roger Rabbit*, animated figures exist within a hybridized diegesis, and interactions between the animated characters and their live-action surroundings lend credibility and verisimilitude to the animation. In *American Splendor*, the opposite is true: since the animation doesn't have any concrete existence within the storyworld, its presence in the live action not only reminds the viewer of its own artificiality but also reinforces Giamatti-as-Pekar's status as one representation of Pekar among many, none of which has a greater claim to authenticity than the others.

This is a much more complex remediation of comics text than we've seen in previous examples, which perhaps befits *American Splendor*'s status as an art house docudrama rather than a high-concept blockbuster. *Kick-Ass 2*, by contrast, is a film that seems to revel in its own immaturity, gleefully embracing and realizing the cartoon violence inherent in the superhero genre.[61] In terms of its comic book stylization, the film's remediation of the speech balloon is most relevant to the present discussion. In comics, the speech balloon serves multiple tasks simultaneously: the presence of a balloon automatically indicates that speech is taking place; the tail of the balloon points to the speaker, identifying the "I" of the speech; the words inside the balloon convey the precise content of the speech; variations in the lettering of the words contained in the balloon determine the manner of speech (using italics or bold for emphasis), and the size (larger text for louder speech, smaller text for quieter) indicates the speaker's volume.[62] For such an intuitive and economical convention, the speech balloon is rich with nuance. All of these functions, however, are rendered redundant in a typical sound film, where

FIGURES 2.8, 2.9, AND 2.10. Stills from *American Splendor*

the diegetic sound and images can convey all of this information and more to the viewer without resorting to nondiegetic interruptions like the intertitle—except, that is, in the case of foreign language dialogue, which necessitates the use of subtitles in order to become comprehensible to the viewer. In translating and transcribing spoken dialogue, subtitles—like the comic book speech balloon—make diegetic sound visually legible within the image in the form of synchronous, nondiegetic text.

According to Giorgio Hadi Curti, "Subtitles have been accused of pulling the spectator away 'from the bodily presence of the film' through their 'intrusion into the visual space of a film' . . . or faulted for 'despoiling the image and separating spectators from the beauty of the original.'"[63] Unlike intertitles, which interrupt our access to the diegetic world, subtitles are superimposed over the images. In this way, they are more similar to speech balloons. Despite existing on the same visual plane as the diegesis, both are meant to be as unobtrusive as possible: for subtitlers, "'invisibility,' and thus sameness, is often seen as a marker of good quality,"[64] while in comics "the audio code transmitted through the balloon passes largely unnoticed, unless attention is called to it through direct textual comment."[65] The fairly recent practice known as creative subtitling turns all of this on its head by drawing "inspiration from the stylistic characteristics" of the film in question, "utilising both the content and form of the subtitled text to provide visual information that goes further than simply providing a translation of spoken dialogue."[66] In the case of *Kick-Ass 2*, the creative subtitles specifically put two medium-specific conventions—subtitles and speech balloons—in direct conversation. In a scene where Kick-Ass and his superhero team ambush a group of Chinese gangsters during a poker game, the film uses speech balloons in place of traditional subtitles to translate and transcribe the non-English dialogue.[67] By aestheticizing the subtitle in this way, the film subverts the norms of subtitling practice by self-consciously emphasizing their visibility.

In the wake of films such as *Man on Fire* (2004) and *Night Watch* (2004), creative subtitling has proven controversial, with some theorists and practitioners claiming that it is amateurish in execution and uninformed in its rejection of subtitling conventions.[68] Defenders of the practice counter that it offers a much-needed aestheticized alternative to traditional subtitling: rather than adopt a "one-size-fits-all" approach to displaying translated dialogue on screen, creative subtitling allows for the necessary onscreen text to

FIGURE 2.11. Still from *Kick-Ass 2*

"creatively [respond] to the individual film text in terms of both language and style."[69] While traditional subtitles operate based on what Jan Pedersen calls the "contract of illusion"—whereby "viewers suspend their disbelief and accept that 'the subtitles are the dialogue, that what you read is actually what people say,' while subtitlers keep their end of the bargain by producing subtitles that are as unobtrusive as possible"[70]—creative subtitles lean into the inevitability that they will not only be read but also *seen* by aestheticizing them in a way that fits into the broader visual design of the film. They remain external to the diegetic world, but their aestheticization allows them to be better integrated into the style of the film.

In her article "In Support of Creative Subtitling," Rebecca McClarty remarks on the "appropriateness" of creative subtitling in the era of digital media, which has made inserting text into images easier and more commonplace, resulting in audiences that are increasingly sophisticated in their ability to synthesize text and image. This echoes D. N. Rodowick's observation about his early encounters with new media. When first faced with computer-generated moving images, he writes,

> It was impossible not to be astonished by how fluidly text was spatialized, thus losing its uniform contours, fixed spacing, and linear sense, and how precisely space was "textualized"; that is, how the Euclidian solidity of the image was fragmented, rendered discontinuous, divisible, and liable to recombination in the most precise ways. Suddenly the image was becoming articulable, indeed discursive, like never before.[71]

"Like never before," Rodowick writes—except, that is, in comic books, which have relied on discursive images, spatialized text, and various combinations thereof since the medium's inception. As Gardner puts it,

> That the contemporary graphic novel came of age in the late 1980s and 1990s in America, at precisely the same time as the rise of the personal computer, is no coincidence. Suddenly, the need to be able to read and navigate sequential text/image fields is more pressing (and less culturally devalued) than at any time in modern history. The comic, because of the unique way in which it brings together different signs (figural, textual, symbolic) into a crowded field where meaning is both collaborative and competitive (among different semiotic systems, between frames, between reader and writer) emerged as a preeminent form for those interested in developing and interrogating theories and methods of reading the everyday world.[72]

The creative subtitles in *Kick-Ass 2* make new media's debt to comics explicit, drawing on the resources available to digital cinema to imbue the film image with comics' specific brand of word-image hybridity. Naturally, the balloon loses much of what makes it unique in comics—its permanence, its place within a certain reading order, its phonostylistic attributes—but it fulfills the role usually held by traditional subtitles while also adding intermedial value through its resemblance to the comics' balloon.

Despite appearing "rather strange," in Lefèvre's parlance, *Batman: The Movie, Super, American Splendor*, and *Kick-Ass 2* all benefit—thematically, narratively, and aesthetically—from the addition of onscreen text in the form of onomatopoeias or balloons. Rather than being a redundant addition, these comics-specific devices are remediated in ways that add value, narrative or otherwise, to the films. Besides drawing explicit connections between the film and the comic book medium, the onscreen text deliberately estranges the viewer from the fictional world, directing his or her attention to the film's surface, to its artifice, and to the visibility of the apparatus and its myriad mediating effects. In addition to whatever other kinds of pleasures and spectacles individual films may provide, comic book film style treats the fourth wall as a transparent canvas to be scrawled upon, as an opportunity to hybridize the film image with text and other kinds of illustration. While the specific techniques used in these cases are remediated from comics and therefore seem "uncinematic" by definition, in fact they harken back to a preclassical cinema of attractions, which embraced the kinds of discontinuities and gaps, direct addresses to the viewer, and hybridizations of text and image that characterize comics to this day. From balloons to onomatopoeias, the use of comic book conventions in a cinematic context draws attention to itself, to stylization as an end in itself, and therefore to the varied abilities of the cinematographic apparatus.

If comics' particular approach to word-image hybridity defines the medium for Carrier and other like-minded theorists, it is the medium's juxtaposition of discrete images in sequence that defines it for others, including McCloud and Groensteen.[73] This formal characteristic is enabled by comics' division into *panels*, which makes each page legible as a series of discrete, but nevertheless connected, sequential images. And just as word-image hybridity can be remediated by appropriating—and necessarily transforming—the conventions through which this quality manifests in comics, so too can the panel be remediated in a variety of ways. Split screen is the most obvious manifestation of this, resulting in a superficial visual similarity between the film image and the comics panel, but it is not the only tack that comic book films have taken in their attempts to appropriate the dynamic interplay between images that transpires on the comics page. It is these different approaches to formal intermediality that will be explored in the next chapter.

CHAPTER 3

THESE PANELS HAVE BEEN FORMATTED TO FIT YOUR SCREEN

REMEDIATING THE COMICS PAGE THROUGH THE CINEMATIC FRAME

"This film has been formatted to fit your screen." So reads the disclaimer often preceding predigital televised or video-based transmissions of feature films. As a child, watching movies on either television broadcasts or VHS, I often wondered how the manufacturers knew how big *my* TV screen was. Surely televisions come in all manner of sizes, and there couldn't be a separate broadcast or video cassette for the 13-inch television upstairs and the 25-inch "big screen" in the basement. My confusion persisted until I saw a film that had *not* been formatted to fit my screen, a film presented on 4:3 televisions in its original widescreen aspect ratio, complete with the so-called "black bars" that maintained the rectangular dimensions of the image on the (nearly) square screen. As a video store employee at the height of DVD sales, I would later consider complaints regarding these very "black bars" the bane of my existence; as a child, they were a revelation. I suddenly understood that the "formatting" of the film image was not in terms of the screen's size, but rather of its shape or ratio: portions of the rectangular images were being excised to fit the different dimensions of home viewing screens. As the film critic Gene Siskel once put it, "It's as if the ends of a painting were chopped off because they didn't fit on your wall."[1]

Siskel's analogy between painting and cinema, apt though it may be, needs nuance. In cinema, the frame functions to isolate the representation from the rest of the world, both perceptually and materially. Per Jacques Aumont, the frame is "that which demarcates the closure of the image, its finiteness... its perceptible limit.... [It is] where the image ends, defining its field by separating it from what it is not."[2] In film, these functions are served by the edges of the screen, which both frame the image for presentation and demarcate its limits. The dimensions of the cinematic frame are fixed, static, consistent from a film's first frame to its last. After all, the surface that reflects these images is itself of fixed dimensions, be it the 4:3 (also known as 1.33:1, the "Academy ratio") dimensions of older televisions and classical Hollywood cinema screens, or the wider aspect ratios of contemporary televisions and cinema (1.85:1 or 2.35:1 being the most common). Of course, there are any number of ways that filmmakers may seemingly transcend the boundaries of the fixed frame without changing the size or dimensions of the screen itself: the iris shot, which was more common in the silent era than it is today, is but one example in which the size and shape of the film image differs from that of the film frame. Iris shots direct or narrow the viewer's focus within the frame by changing its perceptual limits, which simultaneously calls attention to both the plasticity of the image and the fixity of the frame. As Jean Mitry puts it, "The frame is no more part of the image than it is of the represented reality. Rather it is the other way around: the image is the product of the frame—at least as far as its compositional structure is concerned."[3]

As a child, I mistook the cinematic frame, a box of fixed proportions functioning as a window onto a cinematic world, for something more dynamic, for something that changes not only its size but also its shape based on the avenue of its exhibition and the nature of the content being displayed; I mistook it for something more akin to a comic book panel, a vehicle of representation with which my younger self was equally familiar. The mistake is not surprising, given the role each plays in its respective medium: the cinematic frame and the comic book panel both visually demarcate the boundaries between the represented diegetic world and the nondiegetic world of the viewer or reader, and both divide the diegesis into digestible pieces that are consumed in sequence. Of course, the obvious difference between the two is that every image in a film appears in succession in the same frame, one after another at a mechanically predetermined rate, while every image in a comic exists simultaneously in its own discrete panel, arrayed spatially across the pages of a book. Film offers us a frame, while comics offer us hyperframes (each page as a discrete unit) contained within a larger multiframe (the total sum of pages and the relations within them).[4] Even in films that literally show us entire pages of comic books on the screen—as in the prologue of *Superman*, the transitional sequences in *Creepshow*, or the opening credits of *American Splendor*, all of which are analyzed in this chapter—the duration of the page's appearance on the screen is not beholden to the viewer/reader, but is rather subject to the pacing choices of the film's editor. Though comics direct the reader's experience through the text using various visual cues, the film viewer's attention is more forcefully (though still not completely) controlled by the visual, sonic, and temporal cues of cinema, such as camera movement and editing.

It goes without saying, then, that comics and films are different in their deployment of framing, just as they are distinct in other ways. Indeed, the resemblances between the two media only make the differences between them starker. Roy T. Cook addresses this issue at length in his essay "Why Comics Are Not Films," wherein he lays bare the fundamental formal differences between the two media. According to Cook, a film adaptation of a comic could only maintain perfect fidelity to its source if "we project each entire page on to the screen, one at a time." On the same page, however, he undermines this claim, writing that "scenes in a film are projected—that is, their order and duration are controlled solely by the filmmakers (and perhaps the projectionist)—while panels in a comic can be perused in whatever order we decide."[5] This introduces a necessary and profound difference between the "identical" printed and projected versions that Cook imagines, however similar they may be in other respects. Naturally, these kinds of medium-specific differences should not be interpreted as signs of a "failed adaptation" any more than a pear should be interpreted as a failed apple. Remediation, after all, is not reproduction, and attempts to reproduce or replicate the effects of one medium in another should not be judged based on one medium's capacity (or productive failure, more often) to perfectly evoke another.[6] Indeed, my interest here lies not in the similarity or difference between two related texts or media, but rather in the creative combination and transformation that occurs through various processes of formal and stylistic interchange: in other words, comic book film style.

Given the impossibility of a perfect convergence between the cinematic frame and the comic book panel, then, what does it mean for a film to remediate this aspect of comics' formal system? What might it look like? Any self-conscious play with the framing of the image—like an iris shot or a split-screen composition—has the potential to make the viewer aware of the frame as a construct, as a mediating force that controls the viewer's access to the diegetic world. However, the cinematic frame is never merely a window onto a reality that exists external to it; rather, it precisely determines and conditions the viewer's position vis-à-vis that world, though it has traditionally sought to efface the processes through which it does so. Mitry argues that the conventional deployment of the film frame "presents reality objectively and makes each of us, the audience, attentive observers 'outside' the drama. It establishes a sort of alienation between the characters and us, an alienation accentuated by the impossibility of contact or communication."[7] What's distinctive about comics is that this sense of alienation between audience and diegesis is intensified, largely because the sense of continuity that enables the film frame's key representational illusion becomes impossible. If the constancy of the film frame allows for it to be perceived as a single "window on the world," the comic book page's hyperframe, which offers the reader a simultaneous view of different points in time and space, not only shatters the window but also the Cartesian sense of perspective that it creates. As Anne Friedberg writes, "A 'windowed' multiplicity of perspectives implies new laws of 'presence'—not only here and there, but also *then* and *now*."[8] Comics don't merely reveal this to the reader: they insist upon it.

Hollywood films overwhelmingly tend to limit themselves to moving images that fill the entire frame at all times; shots rarely coexist within the frame (except in hidden form, like composites and mattes), but rather follow each other sequentially. This single-image paradigm characterizes cinema's representational norm, and any deviation from it (with some notable exceptions that have become conventionalized, such as the dissolve or the wipe) tends to disrupt the transparency of cinematic style. By contrast, the comics page has more flexibility: it may feature a "splash page" containing only a single image, or it may be densely filled with panels; the size and arrangement of these panels may be consistent on every page or they may be considerably more complex, becoming a very active and noticeable part of the image construction. Like the film frame, the size of the pages doesn't change within a single comic book, but the arrangement of images across those pages tends to be more dynamic in comics than in film. Comic book films that remediate the dynamism of the hyperframe and the plasticity of the panel—giving viewers access to multiple, simultaneous views within the film (hyper)frame—thus trade the kind of alienation Mitry associates with the cinema for that associated with comics. He continues:

Alienation, the impression of nonreality, even of artifice, becomes more pronounced as the image becomes more complicated, as the effects of the framing become more convoluted, the more the aesthetic qualities take precedence over the immediate content. By the same token, directing and editing which are overelaborate or broken up, a kaleidoscopic vision of the world and its objects, also destroy the perceptual reality of the content. Unless, of course, these effects have some other *justification*. And, in my opinion, it is this *justification* which is the key to the problem of an aesthetic of the cinema, the condition of compositional qualities and stylistic system, of whatever kind.[9]

Critics that dismiss contemporary film aesthetics as artless perversions of classical norms, like Matthias Stork in his video essays on "chaos cinema," ignore or overlook intermediality as a possible motivating factor behind these stylistic choices.[10] In all the examples of remediation to follow in this chapter, any nontraditional or self-conscious deployment or manipulation of the film frame can be justified by the film's intermedial relationship with the comics medium. It follows, then, that attempts to remediate the panel or the comics hyperframe within the film frame would tend to draw the viewer's attention to the frame itself as a construct, and to the single-image paradigm as merely the dominant convention but not a necessary feature of cinema. In doing so, the comic book film appropriates some of comics' formal plasticity by interrogating, pushing, and possibly even transforming the notion that the film frame provides a single, fixed window onto the diegesis. As we'll see later in this chapter, the single-image paradigm may be directly challenged through the use of split-screen imagery; even though the film viewer will never have the same kind of autonomy that is granted to the comics reader, they are nevertheless able to read simultaneously presented images both in parallel and in sequence. The overt stylization and consequent deviation from the conventions of classical continuity (or intensified continuity, more often) style in these films thus becomes a substantive part of how these film texts create their meaning.

There has been some scholarly debate over whether the comic book panel is analogous to the cinematic frame, shot, or sequence. For instance, Henry John Pratt asserts that "panels and the transitions between them are to comics what shots and the transitions between them are to film."[11] This, however, is a somewhat reductive view that doesn't do justice to the expressive flexibility of either medium. A page from *Watchmen* #1 (September 1986), for instance, clearly reproduces the effect of a cinematic zoom-out, maintaining the perspective of a single (though mobile) shot across seven discrete panels, while a single panel from *The Amazing Spider-Man* #127 (December 1973) presents a "montage" sequence within the confines of a single panel. A page from *The Immortal Iron Fist* #3 (February 2007) presents a more marginal case that seems more akin to a single shot despite its division into nine panels. Iron Fist appears a total of seven times over the course of these nine sequential panels, which are read, unusually, in a reverse *S* pattern, as indicated by the character's trajectory across the page and the placement of captions. The hyperframe presents a single view on a space that is fractured into panels representing sequential moments as the martial arts superhero navigates his way through the grid. The reader is thus invited to simultaneously view the hyperframe both as a unified space *and* as nine discrete images that represent sequential instants in time. The continuity of space represented herein— unusual, but by no means rare in comics—is belied, however, by the lack of continuity in time. The conventions of comics dictate that sequential panels usually follow each other in time (if not in space), which results in the reappearance of Iron Fist in multiple panels, thus undermining the unity of the composition on the level of the hyperframe. Many instants, and many Iron Fists, exist simultaneously for the reader: the comic book thus represents time and space in a way quite distinct from how we experience them in the cinema or in our day-to-day lives, which is itself the basis for the alienation Mitry describes.

In its representational flexibility, then, we could more accurately say there is no consistent or necessary relationship between the panel and the shot. Thierry Groensteen offers a definitive counterpoint to Pratt: "The comics panel is not the comics equivalent of the *shot* in the cinematographic language. With regard to the length of time that it 'represents' and condenses, its loose status is intermediate between that of the shot and that of the photogram, sometimes bringing together the one and the other according to what occurs."[12] Thus we should understand an empty panel as a temporally indeterminate space whose duration will be collaboratively defined by its content (both visual and verbal), its context in a (narrative) sequence, and the time devoted to it by a reader.[13]

Since the prototypical comic book page features several images, each of which plays its part in advancing a visual (usually narrative) sequence, the

FIGURE 3.1. Page from *Watchmen* #1

FIGURE 3.2. Panel from *The Amazing Spider-Man* #127

film frame that remediates comics often functions less like a single panel and more like a page, or hyperframe. Each panel within a hyperframe is separated and demarcated by fixed and clear boundaries, often referred to in comics scholarship as the gutter. According to Scott McCloud, the gutter represents the space in which the reader performs the mental work required to connect one panel to the next in a process he calls closure.[14] In cinema, something resembling a gutter can only manifest visually when the single-image paradigm is subverted and the frame hosts multiple discrete images simultaneously. Some of the examples encountered later in this chapter do make use of split-screen effects in order to emulate the co-presence of panels within the delimited visual field of the page. But even when split screen is employed to this end, the relationship between the discrete segments of the screen tends to be distinct from what we see in comics. The cinematic gutter acts only as negative space organizing the array of images within the frame, similar to the "black bars" of letterboxed home video presentations, rather than as a productive space of readerly intervention.

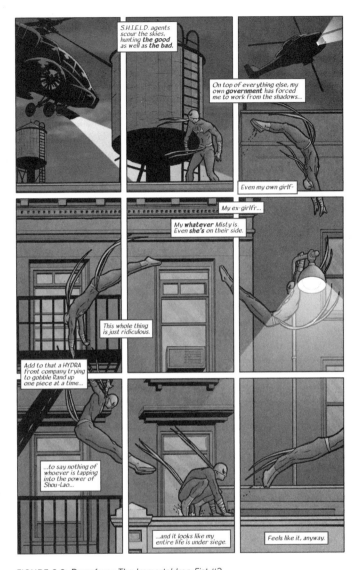

FIGURE 3.3. Page from *The Immortal Iron Fist* #3

When discussing the various ways in which filmmakers might potentially remediate the comics panel cinematically, we must start by asking questions. How and to what extent is the film evoking the comics page? Is the film playing with the size and shape of images within the frame in an attempt to transcend what Greg Smith refers to as the "aesthetic tyranny" of the fixed frame?[15] Is the frame being divided into two or more "panels" that coexist within the film frame? If so, are these "panels" diegetic or extra-diegetic? If the latter, how does this usage of split screen differ from its typical use in cinema? In comics, one image dominates the reader's attention at any given time, while others float around the periphery of his or her attention, waiting to play their part in the reading experience. This is the ontology of the hyperframe that makes up most comics pages. When films attempt to remediate this element of comics, they may vary the size and shape of the frame; they may introduce diegetic elements that partition the frame; they may even introduce an actual comic book as a framing device, through which cinematic style is interpreted as a surrogate for a comic book. Rarer but more visibly obvious attempts at remediation draw on the technique known as split screen; certain scenes from these films, viewed out of context, may equally resemble the sequential panels of a comic book or the coexisting windows of a new media object, like a computer's desktop. In fact, however, cinematic remediations of the hyperframe tend not to follow either the strict sequentiality of comics or the alinear simultaneity of the desktop, but nor do they merely follow the rules of traditional split-screen cinematic conventions. There is an increased sense of play, a more dynamic interaction between the "panels" that coexist onscreen. They stake out the territory between simultaneity and sequentiality, between continuity and discontinuity, between subjectivity and omniscience—in short, between comics' mode of narration and that typically associated with film.

The Frame Undivided: The "Holistic" Approach

Despite the emphasis on split-screen techniques above, more comic book films (as well as television shows) attempt to remediate the comics panel or page without dividing the screen into discrete images. One technique that is sometimes used is changing the aspect ratio of the film itself from shot to shot, just as different comics panels might vary in size and shape. Christopher Nolan's *The Dark Knight* and *The Dark Knight Rises* (2012) both employ this technique, switching between 1.43:1 IMAX (70mm) film and 2.35:1

widescreen (35mm) aspect ratios. In both films, the opening sequences are shot entirely in large-format IMAX, imparting a sense of scope and grandeur to the proceedings not unlike opening a comic book with a splash page. For the remainder of the films, the IMAX is used more sparingly, usually for establishing transitional shots (often of the Gotham City skyline) and some action scenes. In the former, the IMAX format briefly interrupts the widescreen presentation, jolting the viewer to attention through the drastic shift in scope (not to mention the increased amount of light given off by the projector or screen); as such, these shots also tend to function like splash pages, which command the reader's attention not only by the increased size of the panel but by virtue of their novelty. The final issue of *Watchmen* (#12, October 1987) is largely considered to contain some of the most effective splash pages of all time, their impressiveness owing largely to the complete dearth of splash pages throughout the previous eleven issues. The potency of splash pages is thus inversely associated with their frequency. As Groensteen puts it:

> Although any infringement of the regular pattern is significant, it is obvious that the more it departs from the norm, the more it will stand out. In this respect, the first six pages of the twelfth and last chapter of *Watchmen*, the only splash pages of the whole work, have a remarkable impact. The rhythm of the narration freezes, and time is suspended over these images of devastation, an effect underlined by the title of the film being shown at the Utopia Cinema: *The Day the Earth Stood Still*. Douglas Wolk has made the valid comment that the reader perceives these six outsize images like "six consecutive unexpected gongs of a clock."[16]

While many scenes in Nolan's latter two Dark Knight films are shot entirely in widescreen and are only punctuated at the beginning or end by these "splash shots," some scenes (particularly action set pieces, including chase scenes) relentlessly crosscut between widescreen and IMAX footage. This occurs in *The Dark Knight* in the sequence immediately preceding the destruction of Gotham General Hospital, for instance. The scene intercuts between segments taking place at the hospital, in Bruce Wayne's car, in his underground hideout, and in Commissioner Gordon's car. All of these are presented in 2.35:1 except interior shots of Wayne's car and select shots of its exterior. The sequence reaches its entirely IMAX climax as the Joker walks out of the hospital, detonates the bomb, and boards a school bus, which drives away as the hospital goes up in flames. In these sequences and others like it, Nolan uses IMAX footage selectively to increase the impact of certain shots within larger sequences and to give added emphasis to climactic moments of spectacle, not unlike how comics artists might size their panels differently to control pacing and emphasis on the page.

Danger: Diabolik (1968), an English-language Italian-French coproduction based on an Italian comics series (or *fumetti*), takes a different approach to remediating the comics page while also maintaining the unity of the film frame. Throughout the film, director Mario Bava uses internal framing devices—that is, objects within the diegesis that visually divide the space of the frame into smaller sections—in a way that evokes the fractured space of a comic book page. As Jochen Ecke writes, "The use of up to ten (!) additional frames that partition a given shot is clearly meant to draw attention to the screen's spatiality and imitate the paneling of a comic book page."[17] One example occurs in a scene where Diabolik and his partner, Eva, are staking out the location of their next heist. In a single shot from inside a car, we see the house where their robbery is to occur in the distance while a separate two-shot of Diabolik and Eva can be seen in the foregrounded rearview mirror, not dissimilar from the composition of figure 1.11. The placement, angle, and shape of the rearview mirror collectively point toward the home's turret, where the heist will take place specifically, while a lighted window adds visual emphasis to this section of the edifice against the (day-for-)night sky. The rearview image itself contains only the heads of Diabolik and Eva against a pitch-black background, cutting them off from their bodies while also abstracting them from their surroundings.

A few scenes later, Bava ups the ante on mise-en-scène-based internal framing devices when a group of criminals conspire to capture Diabolik. In this scene, Bava shoots the action through an empty bookshelf that divides the frame into several "panels" of varying rectangular dimensions. The shelves, acting superficially as gutters, isolate and emphasize the heads of the scene's key players while also "fragment[ing] and foreground[ing] the space of the screen."[18] I use the caveat "superficially" here because the shelving unit doesn't provide the opportunity for any kind of creative intervention on behalf of the viewer; there is no lost time to be filled in here between these "panels" because there is no sequential relationship between them, only a spatial one. In a comic book, the scene would be read both as a total composition *and* one panel at a time as a narrative sequence; in the film, by contrast, the frame is read only in its totality, while the "gutters" work to

FIGURE 3.4. Still from *Danger: Diabolik*

emphasize and visually demarcate certain areas of the screen. The doubled articulation seen in figure 3.3—wherein the hyperframe articulates a unified space while the gutters divide the space according to a temporal sequence—is absent here.

For Ecke, *Danger: Diabolik* is one example of how "mainstream cinema is catching up on the formal potentialities of the comic book page."[19] In my view, however, it's difficult to see much remediation here; indeed, the only difference between these shots and, say, something from the house-of-mirrors sequence in Orson Welles's *The Lady from Shanghai* (1947; in which each mirror functions as a frame within the larger film frame) or even one of Abbas Kiarostami's many two-shots of a car's front seat (in which the windshield acts as an internal framing device) is that *Diabolik* is based on a comic book, and the film's resultant relationship to comics encourages the viewer to read such shots intermedially rather than as merely ostentatious, economical, or visually dense framing choices. Such compositions are not uncommon in cinema: Gilles Deleuze claims that "the great directors have particular affinities with particular secondary, tertiary, etc. frames," including Griffith, Eisenstein, Dreyer, and Lang.[20] Ecke's claim that Bava "aims to reproduce the experience of reading a comic book page as, to again quote Groensteen, a 'synthetic global vision,' a space representing numerous simultaneous actions that the viewer can roam at will"[21] begs the question:

doesn't the film viewer *always* have the freedom to "roam [the screen] at will" as it presents "a space representing numerous simultaneous actions"? The fractured space of comics has a medium-specific function that is arguably superfluous to the mode of narration favored by the cinema. Moreover, the "synthetic global vision" that the comic book provides is not one of simultaneous *actions*, but more specifically of simultaneous *representation* of *sequential* actions. This fundamental difference between how these two media communicate is central to understanding cinema's diverse and varied remediations of the comics page.

As overt as *Danger: Diabolik*'s invocation of the comics page may seem, several films take such experiments in formal intermediality a step further by combining it with explicit intermediality. As we've already seen in *The Warriors* and *The Losers*, including actual comic book art—and, quite often, full comic book *pages*, similar to Cook's aforementioned conception of the "perfect fidelity" adaptation—in an otherwise live-action film can communicate to the viewer that the film being viewed is a cinematic representation of a comic book storyworld rather than a cinematic representation of "the real world." Put another way, such films take the world as already mediated by a comic and then *re*mediate it cinematically. One example of this phenomenon can be seen in the prologue of *Superman*. The film opens on a title card reading "June 1938," the month of Superman's first appearance in *Action Comics* #1. We then see said comic onscreen (albeit with a different cover than the real issue!). A child's hands turn the pages, which are not shown long enough or in sufficient detail to be read by the viewer; the camera tracks into a close-up on the final panel of a two-page spread, which dissolves into a live-action version of the same. The dissolve from cartoon to photograph is charged with the meaning outlined above, but the film doesn't return to this conceit—there is no bookend at the close of the film, wherein we dissolve back to the comic book, and see the child's hand close the book.[22] Once the dissolve is complete, the film fully adheres to a conventionally "invisible" cinematic style, and any traces of comics disappear (save for the diegetic intertextuality that necessarily runs throughout the film due to its use of comics characters and concepts).

Another example bears more fruit. George A. Romero's *Creepshow*, not an adaptation but rather a homage to the "New Trend" EC Comics of 1950–1954, adopts a similar strategy as *Superman* but expands on it in several ways. This film presents its opening credits over a montage of horrific comics-style images, culminating in an image of "The Creep," a surrogate for EC Comics'

FIGURE 3.5. Still from *Superman*

Cryptkeeper, the narrator of the series *Tales from the Crypt*. As the camera pans to the left, we realize that we are looking at the opening page of a comic book story entitled "Father's Day." The ghastly visage just offscreen narrates the text in a familiar, Cryptkeeper-esque parlance: "Heh, heh! Greetings, kiddies, and welcome to the first issue of *Creepshow*, the magazine that dares to answer the question, 'Who goes there?'" What was implicit in *Superman* becomes explicit here: *Creepshow*, the film, is now understood by the viewer as *Creepshow*, the fictional comic book magazine. The camera tracks downward to the opening panel of the story, which dissolves, as in *Superman*, into a live-action *tableau vivant* that shortly comes to life.

Unlike *Superman*, however, the film doesn't abandon its interest in comics at this point. Indeed, throughout the individual segments of this episodic film, the aesthetics of comics are brought to bear on the photographic world at various points. For instance, a shot from the concluding moments of the first segment mirrors the expressionistic way EC Comics images often abandon spatial context and continuity in order to produce subjective aesthetic effects. Not unlike the use of onscreen onomatopoeia in *Batman: The Movie* discussed in chapter 2, the jagged, dramatic red and black lines emanating from the character in figure 3.8 remediate an expressive tool often used in comics for the cinema.[23] The film uses this device to transition the viewer back from a cinematic aesthetic (albeit a heightened, giallo-esque one) to a comics aesthetic. The next shot returns to a *tableau vivant*, which dissolves into its comic book double. Thus where *Superman* abandons its framing device after the brief prologue, *Creepshow* maintains its commitment to being a cinematic comic book throughout. The camera tracks back, revealing a

FIGURES 3.6 AND 3.7. Stills from *Creepshow*

two-page spread with an advertisement on the right-hand page. The page then turns to the next two-page spread, which features the comic book's obligatory letter column on the left side and the beginning of the next story on the right. The camera pans across each page in isolation before settling on the first panel of the next story, which then dissolves into a live-action version, as in the previous story.

The film's ability to give aesthetic priority to the comic book despite its status as a film is noteworthy. Whereas *Diabolik*'s intermedial play with the spatiality of the frame merely produces some superficial visual similarities to the comic book page, *Creepshow*'s (and *Superman*'s, to a lesser extent) strategy treats the film frame as a cinematic surrogate for a comic book panel and the camera as the magical revealer of the comic book's diegetic reality. As a result, cinematic techniques can be read as equivalents for their comic book counterparts, regardless of the style of execution and how similar it may or may not be to a comic book. This is made clear in figure 3.10, in which a speech balloon manifests visually in the drawn image that was not present in the live-action *tableau*; a film may remediate comics' sound by including actual speech balloons in the image, but *Creepshow*'s framing strategy ensures that viewers understand that any dialogue on the soundtrack conveys the content of balloons without having to visually insert them into the live-action frame.

The strategies employed in *Superman* and *Creepshow* become more complicated still in the opening credits of *American Splendor*, wherein the frame is entirely occupied by the architecture of a comics page, whose panels contain a combination of live-action moving images, comics-style text, and static comics images. As the camera moves to focus on one panel, its image dissolves from a sepia-toned photograph into full-color movement; and just as

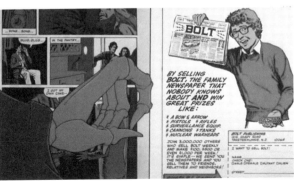

FIGURES 3.8, 3.9, 3.10, AND
3.11. Stills from *Creepshow*

the camera moves on to the next panel, the image arrests and dissolves back to sepia. Aside from the viewer's lack of autonomy over the pacing of the images (and inability to take in the entire two-page spread simultaneously), *American Splendor* arguably provides the closest cinematic approximation of the experience of reading a comic seen thus far; each panel represents a self-contained part of a larger narrative sequence, and only assumes its full meaning when read in conversation with those around it (rather than simultaneously or in isolation). In other words, the gutters here function just as they do in a comic book. Whereas *Danger: Diabolik* divided the image into a comics-like grid purely for its aesthetic effect, and *Creepshow* elided the problem entirely by dissolving in and out of the comics page, *American Splendor* combines the paneled architecture of comics with moving images in a way that still allows the images to be read *as comics*.[24] What this sequence visualizes is that each panel—whether its content is drawn or cinematic—is "activated" one at a time, though they all also exist simultaneously as interlocking visual elements on the page. When a panel is activated by the camera's attention, it has a set duration, contributes its part to the overall sequence, and then fades into the background as the reader forges ahead. While the camera in *Creepshow* functioned as a magical device, capable of penetrating comics so deeply as to reveal their underlying reality, here the camera simply functions as the eyes of a comics reader, scanning the page as a whole and stopping to read each panel in sequence. The jazz music underlying the entire sequence also provides a sense of aural continuity that smooths over the jumps between media that occur between panels.

All of these comic book films remediate the comics page, and often in a literal-minded way. Indeed, one might argue that *Superman, Creepshow,* and *American Splendor*'s explicit use of *actual* comics (i.e., explicit intermediality) doesn't evoke comics in a cinematic way so much as show the viewer actual comics on screen. While representing one medium in another *is* the very definition of remediation,[25] other films take greater stylistic risks and yield more complex dividends while negotiating the differences between the screen and the page, the panel and the frame. In the next section, I specifically focus on those comic book films that employ split screen as a means of getting at something conceptually similar to the films discussed above, but with markedly different results.

FIGURES 3.12 AND 3.13. Stills
from *American Splendor*

Splitting the Screen: The "Hyperframe" Approach

When one thinks of cinematic techniques that have the potential to evoke the comics page, split-screen photography is probably the first thing that comes to mind. As defined by David Bordwell and Kristin Thompson, split screen refers to when "two or more images, each with its own frame dimensions and shape, appear within the larger frame."[26] In short, it refers to cinematic frames in which the single-image paradigm is abandoned. The term "shot" no longer applies, given the multiplicity of coexisting shots—which I'll refer to as "subshots"—within the frame. The film frame ceases to function as a transparent "window on the world" with a singular perspective, instead offering an assortment of perspectives through multiple coexisting "windows" in a way that Friedberg associates with cubist painting's challenge to Renaissance perspective.[27] In film, Bordwell and Thompson associate the technique with the staging of telephone conversations—such as those in *Suspense* (1913) or *Bye Bye Birdie* (1963)—or with building tension and suspense without crosscutting between locations, as in *Sisters* (1973).[28] While the technique is arguably most commonly associated with the experimentation wrought by New Hollywood filmmakers—as evidenced in *Grand Prix* (1966), *The Thomas Crown Affair* (1968), *The Boston Strangler* (1968), *Woodstock* (1970), and several films by Brian De Palma—more recent projects like *Run Lola Run* (1998), *Timecode* (2000), *The Rules of Attraction* (2002), *Conversations with Other Women* (2005), and the television series *24* (2001–2010) have given renewed visibility to the technique. While still exceptional in cinema, the fragmentation of screen spaces has been completely normalized in other contexts as a result of our daily interactions with digital media: most notable are cable news networks' use of multiple windows and text crawls; multi-player video games, which split the screen horizontally down the center for two players and into quadrants for four; and the ubiquitous desktop computer with its multiple "windows."

The incorporation of new media aesthetics into filmmaking practice has given the subject of cinematic split screen some renewed urgency, as demonstrated by key works such as Friedberg's *The Virtual Window* and Lev Manovich's *The Language of New Media*, both of which historicize the multiple-frame screen associated with digital displays within a broader artistic history. These texts, however, notably fail to consider the impact that comics have had on the multiplication of perspective: while Manovich simply dismisses comics as "a minor form of Western culture,"[29] Friedberg doesn't even mention the medium. It's a conspicuous oversight, especially in her discussion of Edwin Porter's seamless use of split screen in *Dream of a Rarebit Fiend*, a short film based on Winsor McCay's comic strip.[30] Her claim that "aside from some notable historical anomalies, only in the last two decades—markedly with the advent of digital imaging technologies and new technologies of display—did the media 'window' [begin] to include multiple perspectives within a single frame"[31] would be radically undermined if she considered comics. Over a century of American comic strips and books can hardly be dismissed as a "historical anomaly," nor can the unique traditions of Franco-Belgian *bandes dessinées*, Japanese manga, and Italian *fumetti* be summarily dismissed as a "minor form of Western culture." The comics hyperframe represents a distinct application of multiple, sequential, and simultaneous image presentation, and like other formal elements of the comics medium, its influence can be directly felt in cinematic style. As we'll see in coming paragraphs, the novel use of split screen in films like Ang Lee's *Hulk* and Michel Gondry's *The Green Hornet* are best understood as remediations of the comics panel.

Due to its ostentatious embrace of artifice, *Hulk* is often used as a case study in comic book–influenced film style.[32] The film is rich with instances of formal intermediality, including onscreen text captions, freeze frames, split screens, and even a cinematic multiframe. While all of the split screens used in *Hulk* are nondiegetic—there are no objects within the mise-en-scène dividing the frame, as in *Danger: Diabolik*; rather, the divisions are imposed upon the images by an extra-diegetic force—we can nevertheless divide them into two distinct categories: "interlocking" and "discrete." Interlocking subshots fit together like puzzle pieces, forming a whole image that is made up of separate components that combine to fill the frame completely. In this mode of split screen, the visual similarity to the comic book page is obscured somewhat due to the lack of visual gutters between the separate image elements; the effect is closer to a collage. In *Hulk*, the seamless juxtaposition of images often creates a jarring effect as eyelines that we would expect to line up (based on the conventions of continuity editing) do not, drawing the viewer's attention to the independence of each component within the frame, to precisely how they *don't* fit perfectly together. Alternatively, discrete subshots function as autonomous "panels" that are experienced simultaneously but read separately; in other words, they don't intersect to form a single, composite image (though they may overlap, in some cases), and a visible negative space separates each subshot from the others. While it is tempting to read this space as functionally equivalent to the gutter, the similarities between them are again only superficial. The gutter only functions as such when there is both a sequential relationship between the panels that it divides as well as some action that is absent from, that exists in between, the represented image-instants. The negative space in the split-screen film, by contrast, functions no differently from the "black bars" produced by letterboxed presentations that I evoked at the beginning of this chapter; it's just unoccupied screen territory that allows the frame/subshots to assume their particular size and shape on a larger field.

From the opening moments of the film, the viewer is almost immediately put off guard by its unusual editing patterns; it immediately becomes clear that *Hulk* is not edited in a classical, invisible style but rather in what I would call a "comics montage" style, where panels converge, collide, and coexist within the frame in a dynamic play of images. Take, for instance, a short series of shots from the first scene after the credits. In the first shot, we see a close-up of Edith Banner on the right of the frame, standing in her kitchen, looking down-left. We cut to a medium shot of David Banner, standing in the same kitchen, in profile, occupying the right of the frame and facing downward as he pours a drink. At this point, the spatial relations between the two are not clear, though we can safely assume because of other visual and narrative cues that they are in the same room. Suddenly, the shot transitions, via two separate wipes that replace the left side of the frame with the close-up of Edith and the right side of the frame with a close-up of David, albeit from a different angle than before. As the wipes complete the transformation of the frame into a composite two-shot, Edith and David both turn to face each other; their eyelines, however, do not match, as Edith is seen in a three-quarter profile, facing right, while David is shot in full profile, facing left.[33] Between (and behind) them, a third panel intrudes into this matrix, this one a wide oval containing a close-up of Edith's face, upside-down and covered in sweat. As she screams, the oval panel swells in size, quickly overtaking the foregrounded panels and completing the transition to the new shot: a close-up of Edith's face as she gives birth to their son, Bruce.

Throughout this sequence of shots, and indeed throughout the film as a whole, *Hulk* relentlessly undermines the ontological unity of the shot. More like a comic book page than an individual panel, the intraframe editing here forces the viewer to read the film as an organized series of images that converge within the frame much as they would on a comics page. A film like *Hulk* effectively treats the film frame as a hyperframe—a space of fixed proportions that at any given time contains one or more "windows" and perspectives onto the diegesis. The key difference is that while the comics hyperframe is divided and subdivided a priori, the film frame is only fractured *as we experience it*; the panels are themselves mobile, demanding active engagement from spectators who are expected to assemble the diegesis from various views as it schisms before their very eyes. Thus, as dynamic as the hyperframe is in comics, such cinematic hyperframes are more dynamic still, presenting us with a fluid space in which one view may, at any moment, give way to several competing or complementary views on the diegesis.

In comics, each panel has its own designated space; there is no competition for room or attention, as each discrete visual block will be read in turn. In the comic book film, however, panels must actively compete with each other for the same space, forcing their way into the frame only by pushing others aside. Manovich has identified a similar tendency within digital cinema in general, which he calls "spatial montage," in which several discrete shots or images co-occupy the screen space. This editing strategy, he writes, "represents an alternative to traditional cinematic temporal montage, replacing its traditional sequential mode with a spatial one."[34] I want to stress that what I'm calling comics montage does not, as Manovich claims, *replace* sequentiality with increased spatial complexity. There is still a linear viewing logic in place, but the minimal unit of film grammar has shifted from the shot to the subshot; when the frame contains two or more shots, each subshot assumes the status of the panel, effectively transforming the frame into

FIGURES 3.14, 3.15, AND 3.16. Stills from *Hulk*

an ersatz comic book page composed of several panels that are to be read in dialogue (if not also in sequence) rather than in isolation. This is made explicit in *Hulk* in the moment after Talbot's death, when the virtual camera tracks *out of the diegesis itself*, revealing a multipanel matrix, organized like a comic book page. Though some films' stylistic systems are founded on this kind of rigid matrix (e.g., *Timecode* and *Conversations with Other Women*, both of which maintain consistent split-screen geometries throughout), *Hulk*'s is more fluid in its panel organization; therefore, the virtual camera selects and tracks into only one of the panels on display, which becomes the next narrative event. This "meta-shot" is a cinematic representation of the multiframe: the total comics work and all of the panel relations and hyperframes within it. As Groensteen writes, "In distinction to the hyperframe, the multiframe does not have stable borders, assigned a priori. Its borders are those of the entire work, whether it is an isolated strip or a story of two hundred pages. The multiframe is the sum of the frames that compose a given comic—that is, also, the sum of the hyperframes."[35] This moment in *Hulk* recognizes that, as in a comic (or a database), though each narrative unit exists concurrently, they are only *experienced* as narrative through their sequential organization within the hyperframe. The total sum of their relations (i.e., the total film, the total comic book, or the total database) composes a multiframe, a small portion of which we can glimpse in this moment. This is as close to the explicit intermediality of *Creepshow* and *Superman* as *Hulk* gets. As in those examples, the camera gives us a god's-eye view on the diegesis, from which vantage point it looks more like a comic than a film. Tracking out of one shot (a heavily stylized freeze frame, significantly), the frame becomes full of image-instants; as it swoops in to select the next shot proper, the chosen image begins to move. Here the camera fulfills a role in between what it does in *Creepshow* and *American Splendor*: while it scans around the narrative-encompassing multiframe like the eyes of a comic book reader (as in *American Splendor*), it also brings the images to life with its gaze (as in *Creepshow*). Furthermore, it affords the viewer a fleeting sense of the omnipotence that the comics reader enjoys. While the film doesn't give the viewer the same degree of choice and temporal freedom that comics do, it's nevertheless usually beyond the scope of a film to show past moments outside of narrative flashbacks, let alone a multiframe consisting of past and future moments alike.

Another way in which formal intermediality hybridizes film and comics is through the use of the freeze frame. Like onscreen text and split screens, freeze frames are not exclusive to the comic book film, but they assume an

FIGURE 3.17. Still from *Hulk*

enhanced significance within it. When the force of an explosion sends Talbot flying toward the camera, his movement is suddenly arrested and his body becomes surrounded by a thin white outline, a border separating his static shape from the flames still billowing behind him. This hyperframe contains two panels, or two discrete layers of action—the explosion (background, moving) and Talbot (foreground, static)—which are separated by a white outline. In juxtaposing these two images—one moving, one still—within the same frame, the film reveals something about comics' form: a comics panel, though static, does not usually represent a single instant of time. Unlike a photograph, a panel is capable of representing a duration of time, possibly containing both action *and* reaction, cause *and* effect, simultaneously. In arguing that comics and film images are ontologically irreconcilable, Pascal Lefèvre asserts that a "viewer of a still image will always be reminded of the fragmented and frozen time," whereas a moving image gives a "greater impression of realism."[36] On the contrary, the comics reader is presented with a composite image that collates events with a temporal duration. The Talbot shot in *Hulk* demonstrates that even in stasis, there can be movement and duration; while Talbot's image is arrested, the background lives on, indicating that time in the comic book has not stopped, even though the image may be still. This is not, then, an "empty" stylistic gesture whose significance ends with visual imitation or similarity; rather, it is a remediation of a mode of representation native to the comic book that demonstrates the unique

FIGURE 3.18. Still from *Hulk*

qualities of both media. In the following chapter, I explore issues related to time and movement in greater depth; for now, we'll return to *Hulk*'s use of split screen.

Comics are, as Jared Gardner puts it, "in many respects the most ineffi-cient" narrative form, because they depend "as much on what is left out as on what is included" as well as "an active and imaginative reader capable of fill-ing in the gaps in time."[37] While cinema is not inherently less "gappy" than comics, continuity filmmaking gives it the appearance of being so. Though already more efficient than comics—because its soundtrack is heard rather than read, its actions are presented fluidly to the viewer's consciousness rather than actively deduced from a series of incomplete stills, and so on—cinematic split screens are typically used to *further* increase film's efficiency by simultaneously cramming more unique information onto the screen at once. For example, a scene taking place simultaneously at two locations would typically have to be crosscut, leaving the viewer to reconstitute the spatiotemporal relationship between the two settings; using split screen, both settings can co-occupy a frame for the entire duration of a scene, elimi-nating the need for much of this mental work. This is a fairly typical deploy-ment of split-screen cinematography. For instance, an early scene in *The Boston Strangler* takes place in two locations simultaneously; the right side of the screen shows us two tenants in the hallway of an apartment building, talking about their mutual neighbor, whose door is visible; the right side of the screen shows us the other side of that door, including part of the tenant's lifeless body. Dramatic irony and suspense effects are thereby produced without any cutting, and the spatiotemporal relations between the two subshots is always clear (especially toward the end of the scene when the neighbors open the door, at which point they can be seen on both sides of the screen from different angles). Likewise, montage sequences can be denser, communicating more information to the viewer in less time.

Paradoxically, then, split screen fosters a superficial visual similarity between the comics page and the film frame while getting further away from comics' narrative inefficiency; as form converges, function diverges. Those who have attempted to understand *Hulk*'s remediation of the comic book frame have tended to either focus on the supposed "failures" of the film to match the comic book in both form and function or to equate all use of split screen with a "comic book" aesthetic a priori. Drew Morton, for instance, ultimately judges the film's attempt at remediation to be a "media specific ... compromise,"[38] while Michael Cohen argues "that the use of split-screen in the cinematic *Hulk* is part of a conscious effort to re-create the aesthetic of the comic inside the film."[39] Liam Burke gets closer to the heart of the matter when he writes that the film's "overt transitions moved the film away from continuity editing, thereby reminding the spectator of the artifice of cinema," though he also throws in a qualitative judgment that such techniques were "unnecessary" and "failed to utilize cinema's means of expression or effectively recreate the experience of a comic book."[40]

Morton also claims that the film merely "[provides] us with an embellished use of the split screen,"[41] but there is actually a tangible difference between how conventional films use split screen and how it is employed at various moments in *Hulk*. He is perfectly correct in his assertion that using split screen to present multiple perspectives at the same moment in time is the conventional way the technique is used and does not mirror the way comics typically employ their hyperframe.[42] Indeed, the film features several telephone conversations, usually between Betty and her father, General Ross, that use split screen in lieu of crosscutting—in other words, in the prototypical, efficiency-promoting way described by Bordwell and Thompson. However, the film also flouts this standard implementation of split-screen with some regularity. Indeed, in many cases, the film actually uses split screen to reproduce the visual dynamics of the comics hyperframe at the *expense* of narrative efficiency, showing the viewer more information than he or she requires or, often, redundant information given simultaneously from multiple perspectives. Andreas Rauscher claims that such redundant compositions are "meant to be reminiscent of the way in which panels are arranged in comic books," which misses the fact that comics' narrative inefficiency doesn't come from a surplus of visual information but rather from a deficiency thereof.[43] Rather, this redundancy is a specifically *cinematic* product that results from the remediation of the comics page. Figure 3.19, for example, is a frame containing two subshots that Morton singles out as an "illusory" hyperframe, "at least with regard to how it functions spatiotemporally in the narrative." He continues:

> Rather than giving us two images portraying separate instances of time (or space) as a comic book would, Lee gives us two images of space . . . that are taking place simultaneously. . . . Essentially, Lee is not drawing upon the unique aspect of the comic panel, "encapsulation," in which each panel represents a separate moment in time to which the [hyperframe] provides the structure.[44]

In this image, David Banner can be seen activating a countdown timer from two different perspectives. As Morton notes, this isn't how a comic book would present this information, but neither is it a typical use of cinematic split screen. Lee is both invoking the comics hyperframe in a superficial way (i.e., through visual similarity) and also in a more complex way by sacrificing film's claim to greater narrative efficiency.[45] We see something similar in figure 3.20, in which a helicopter convoy carries Bruce Banner to a military installation for testing. Throughout this sequence, "panels" appear hither and thither in the frame, each containing different views on the same action, none of which provides unique or crucial narrative information. Indeed, the redundancy of these images is itself the point; rather than guide the reader through a series of sequential image-events, as it does in comics, here the cinematic hyperframe functions to undermine the tendency of split screen to increase cinema's narrative efficiency. It's also quite possible that a more efficient use of split screen—one more in line with what one tends to encounter in comics—would risk becoming borderline illegible to viewers. The redundancy of the various subshots in these examples provides viewers with a multiplicity of perspectives without multiplying the number of narrative

FIGURES 3.19 AND
3.20. Stills from *Hulk*

events contained within them. Thus *Hulk* gains the superficial resemblance
to the comics page afforded by split screen while also dragging its narrative
economy closer to that of comics. Rather than read such moments as failed
attempts to capture what's unique about comics in film, I interpret them
as productive dialectics between the two media. The remediation of one
medium in another often results in the formation of new expressive tools
that are inspired by medium-specific conventions (e.g., the hyperframe, the
gutter, the cinematic split screen) but that also differ from them significantly.

The film is also incredibly complex in terms of its treatment of sequentiality versus simultaneity. As Malte Hagener notes in his article on split
screen and remediation,

> In a scene when the Hulk is transferred to a secret underground research
> centre under heavy security measures, this trip is shown in multiple
> windowed shots overlapping spatially (within the visible frame, but also

within the filmic space represented) and temporally (they emerge and vanish at different moments, while also depicting overlapping timespans). Constantly changing in size and position, the shots are presented in rough chronological order yet nevertheless sometimes overlap temporally, creating an impression similar to scratching in music. This effect, which is not easily detectable on first viewing, points out the basically arbitrary and manipulable nature of the filmic images.[46]

Figure 3.21 displays what seems at first glance to be two simultaneous views of the helicopter convoy, but closer inspection reveals that the helicopters in the upper subshot have some ropes dangling from them that aren't present in the lower image. The upper subshot therefore occurs chronologically later than the one below it. As the scene continues, the lower subshot dissolves to reveal more of the diegesis at the later moment that the upper subshot depicts; when the dissolve is complete, the small strip of negative space disappears and the unity of the frame is reestablished. The inconsistent treatment of simultaneity in this sequence is itself a departure from conventional usage of split-screen cinematography, but there is another element that must also be addressed: the sheer dynamism of how the subshots appear, disappear, interact, overlap, and generally compete for screen space, or what Jim Bizzocchi calls the "visual flow" of the graphic elements in play.[47] In most cases throughout the film, the "panels" don't appear onscreen at the same moment, but rather are introduced *sequentially*. It's decidedly unlike turning a page in a comic book: the panels don't all exist at the beginning of a scene and remain static for its duration. Regardless of whether the action in each of the subshots *occurs* simultaneously, the viewer is nevertheless encouraged to *read* them both sequentially and as part of the larger hyperframe due to how they appear on the screen.

A three-way telephone conversation between General Ross, a national security advisor, and the American president should further demonstrate how the complex sequencing of "panels" transcends their simultaneity. The scene begins with conventional full-frame shots, cutting between Ross, the president, and the advisor. As the scene cuts back to Ross, who announces that "'Angry Man' is unsecure," an inset "panel" with a digital map readout appears in the upper-right corner of the screen. Unlike conventional subshots, however, the panel begins to move downward on a diagonal slope toward offscreen right as Ross talks, guiding the viewer's attention in that

FIGURE 3.21. Still from *Hulk*

direction. When the full-frame shot cuts, the panel begins to fade away. As if a comics reader had turned a page with the cut, a new panel has appeared in the upper-left corner, in which the advisor chastises Ross for what she interprets as a blasé attitude toward civilian casualties. It too fades away just as a circular inset panel appears with another military computer readout of the Hulk's location. Immediately following the appearance of this round panel, the president appears in the scene's final rectangular panel at the bottom right of the screen. The final panel finally expands to fill the whole screen, bookending the scene with full-frame images. The subshots in this scene have been carefully sequenced to follow a particular reading logic, knowing that the film viewer—like the comic book reader—can focus on a particular panel while also taking in the whole of the hyperframe that contextualizes it. The viewer's eye movements are carefully choreographed by the appearance, movement, and disappearance of subshots, much as they would be across a comics page by the arrangement of panels, dialogue balloons, captions, and other visual cues.

There are two additional instances of split screen in the film that warrant special attention. The first occurs during Hulk's rampage through the military facility, immediately preceding the multiframe discussed earlier. Ross's men are spraying Hulk with quick-drying foam that is meant to hold him in place long enough for Talbot to extract a blood sample. The scene features

FIGURES 3.22, 3.23, 3.24,
AND 3.25. Stills from *Hulk*

a dynamic array of subshots, similar to the three-way telephone conversation analyzed above. A few frames in particular, however, feature one subtle effect that is common in comics but is usually not available in cinema. In figure 3.26, we see the foam stream from the central panel extending beyond its own borders, intruding into the next panel. Typically, the boundaries of the film image are also the boundaries of the screen, precluding the possibility that the images might spill over. In comics, the boundaries of the individual panel are always contained within that of the larger hyperframe, allowing such breaches to occur with some regularity (as in figure 3.3, for example). The fact that the foam stream is a digital element facilitates this, as the animators have the same freedom as the comics artist to color within or outside of the lines.[48]

Similarly, in figure 3.27, we see Hulk jump across three panels that exist independently but that collectively form a coherent chunk of diegetic space. They appear on the screen sequentially, sliding in from offscreen left (with the exception of the final panel, which slides in from above) one at a time as

FIGURES 3.26 AND 3.27.
Stills from *Hulk*

the Hulk jumps through them from right to left. As these subshots slide into place, the background fades to black, leaving only the three panels framed against negative space. The fact that this reverses the usual reading order of a comic doesn't negate this hyperframe's status as a remediation thereof. (As figure 3.3 demonstrates, the reading order of panels is determined by a combination of convention and the specific layout of elements within a given hyperframe, which guide the reader through the array.) Comics often divide a coherent space into panels in order to present a passage of time; the result is a "panning" effect as the reader moves through both the space and time of the scene together. In Lee's remediation of this technique, the panning effect occurs—as it does in comics—not through camera movement but rather through the viewer's eyes as he or she scans the screen, following the Hulk from right to left.

In concluding this chapter, I'd like to move from one emerald outlaw to another, namely, the Green Hornet. The Green Hornet and his partner, Kato, made their first appearance, on the radio, in 1936, before making the transition to film serials in 1940 (in *The Green Hornet* and *The Green Hornet Strikes Again!*). The character is perhaps best known for the television series starring Bruce Lee (1966–1967), which was contemporaneous with *Batman* (1966–1968); the two franchises even crossed paths in two notable episodes of *Batman*'s second season. The Green Hornet has also made appearances in several comics since 1940. The print rights to the character are currently owned by Dynamite Entertainment, which has published several miniseries, including one that serves as a transmedial prequel to Michel Gondry's film. Though the character did not originate in a comic book, the presence of formal intermediality in the film's closing credits suggests a greater engagement with comics than many of the other media in which the character has appeared. In this sequence, the film's cast and crew are presented within captions and balloons; for instance, the name of the creator of the radio series (and therefore of the characters and the storyworld in general), George W. Trendle, appears in a jagged speech balloon, such as would be used in a comic to denote speech coming from an electronic device such as a radio. Significantly, this is not a cinematic remediation of radio but rather a remediation of how *comics* represent radio broadcasts, neatly condensing the character's transmedia history within a single image. Aside from the film's frequent use of expressive slow motion in its fight scenes,[49] the film's tour de force split-screen sequence stands out as the most notable integration of

FIGURES 3.28, 3.29, AND 3.30. Stills from *The Green Hornet*

comics into its stylistic system. The sequence begins with a single criminal, a subordinate of the crime lord Chudnofsky, who passes his boss's instructions to kill the Green Hornet along to two women. As soon as they are given their marching orders, lines of negative space intrude into the image, dividing the frame into three subshots, each of which continues as its own autonomous shot, as if the camera spontaneously trifurcated, like cells dividing under a microscope. Each character continues along their own individual trajectory until they encounter another character, at which point their subshot divides again. This continues until there are, at its most complicated, thirteen sub-shots on screen simultaneously, many of which—if you watch closely—have proceeded without a cut since the beginning of the original shot.[50]

Just as *Hulk*'s use of split screen was more complicated than the technique's typical cinematic use due to the influence of comics, so too is *The Green Hornet*'s, but in a different way. While Lee's film explores the dialectic between simultaneity and sequentiality associated with comics and film, respectively, Gondry's film demonstrates an interest in the related dialectic of continuity versus discontinuity. Groensteen summarizes the typical role of each in both media thusly:

> Unlike those in a film, comics images do not create the illusion that the events are taking place as we read. Several factors work against this—in particular: the visible discontinuity of the sequential flow of the narrative; the fact that readers cannot forget the physical, concrete situation in which they find themselves, that of having a book in their hands (or in front of them), and turning the pages, at a rhythm that is not imposed but under their control; finally, the fact that each new image does not obliterate the previous one, does not take its place, but is added to it on the mode of accumulation, collection, with the totality of images remaining easily accessible at any time. For all these reasons, graphic monstration, in contrast with filmic monstration, does not create the impression of a story unfolding before our eyes.[51]

Much of narrative cinema's expressive potential emerges out of the continuity created between subsequent images, both on the level of the shot (allowing discrete still images to be seen by viewers as continuous moving images) and between shots (allowing individual shots to be read in conversation with each other, creating a coherent diegesis). In comics, by contrast, it is precisely the evocative discontinuity between images wherein the medium's expressive potential lies. Per Groensteen, "The discontinuity that is the basis of the language of comics forces the reader to make inferences in order to interpret each new image appropriately, that is to say to ensure that it correlates with the previous one and to the wider context of the whole text within which it occurs."[52] In the sequence in question, the line is thoroughly blurred between the varieties of continuity and discontinuity typically offered by these media. The images do not replace each other sequentially but rather accumulate on the screen, remaining accessible for the entirety of the sequence, as they do on the pages of the comic book; and yet despite the fractured, discontinuous nature of the screen space, the images are inextricably connected because of a lasting sense of continuity that pervades from the first shot to many of the thirteen subshots that occupy the hyperframe at its most complex. Thus *The Green Hornet*'s remediation of comics—like those offered by *Hulk*, *American Splendor*, and the other films held up for analysis in this chapter—assimilates one element of comics' form, including the sense of alienation thereby produced, but without replicating its medium-specific function, instead offering something that is atypical of *either* medium.

The cinematic frame is quite distinct from the comics page, but both can be host to multiple shots or panels simultaneously, creating various dynamics between the component parts that constitute the total image. It's through the accretion of these instants and events—whether within a fixed frame or on sequential pages—that both media create the image sequences that constitute their narratives. The similarities between the two are such that it may be tempting to overstate their equivalence, but the various attempts and strategies at remediating the panel and its context within the comics hyperframe discussed in this chapter tend instead to emphasize the differences between them. At the most basic level, stylistic norms for each medium dictate that a comic book page with multiple, simultaneous panels is perfectly conventional and demands no special notice from the reader, while a film frame featuring multiple, simultaneous images is an oddity that draws the viewer's attention with its ostentatious and obtrusive deployment of cinematic style. The invisibility of continuity editing is effectively thrown out the window; the film instead asks the viewer to consider the film's intermedial relationship to comics with stylistic choices that evoke—but do not simply reproduce—comics' formal system.

Ultimately, however, a crucial distinction between the comics panel and the film frame is that one contains images that *move* while the other contains images that remain still. The consequence of this crucial difference certainly contributes to many of the distinctions between the comic book films discussed above and comics themselves. Could the complex array of split screens in *The Green Hornet*—wherein each subshot presents a constantly moving camera, roaming from location to location—be as effectively or concisely articulated in comics? The fact that the images move means that each individual segment of the film screen has the potential to convey more information than a single comics panel, but more importantly that the two media produce different *experiences* of movement, based either in perception or in cognition. This leads us to another key issue at the heart of comic book film style, which is the relationship between the stasis of the comic book and the movement inherent in cinema. Films that remediate comics contend in various ways with this issue, which begs a similar set of questions as those that concerned us throughout this chapter: How do comic book films remediate comics' relationship to time and representations of movement? What kind of temporalities are produced when still images from comics are restaged in a cinematic (moving image) context? Is the film appropriating comics' conventions for representing motion? Is the film manipulating the flow of images and playback speed in a way that suggests the elastic temporality of comics? How do these strategies reconcile with the stylistic norms that overwhelmingly govern contemporary mainstream cinema? It is to these questions that we now turn.

CHAPTER 4

THE PRIVILEGED INSTANT

REMEDIATING STASIS AS MOVEMENT

Douglas Wolk opens his book *Reading Comics: How Graphic Novels Work and What They Mean* with a discussion of *Showcase* #4 (October 1956), the "Silver Age"–inaugurating comic book in which Barry Allen/The Flash makes his first appearance.[1] Wolk describes the comic's famous cover illustration thusly: "Its cover shows a strip of film, with a superhero called the Flash racing along each of its frames and bursting bodily through the last one."[2] He struggles, however, with the meaning of this image beyond obvious signifiers like the Comics Code Authority logo in the upper-right corner. Pondering its possibilities, he asks:

> Is this comic a showcase for art, as in a museum? A series of frozen representations of reality or representations of something so unreal that a body moving at high speed leaves parallel lines of ink behind it? A movie that isn't really a movie, made out of individual images that the eye can see in or out of sequence or at the same time? Something that breaks destructively out of attempts to fix it in place?[3]

At the time of its release, readers probably wouldn't have had such semantic crises: the superhero genre was already well established, as were the stylistic conventions of the comic book as a medium. Readers implicitly understood its differences from film and other narrative media, and certainly from the kinds of works that would be found in a museum. (A more likely response would be confusion: "Why is he bursting out of a film strip? Is this a character I should know from the movies?") At its most basic, the cover provides a striking and dynamic introduction to a new character, conveying his defining characteristic—superspeed—via a series of well-understood and oft-used visual conventions: most notably "motion lines" (the "parallel lines of ink" to which Wolk refers), which indicate a trajectory of movement and simulate photographic motion blur without distorting the subject, as well as the slanted green type that announces the character's name, which seems to burst forth from the whirlwind created in the Flash's wake; in the bottom-right corner, the text "Whirlwind adventures of the fastest man alive!" reinforces the image's content and generic context.

But what are we to make of *Showcase* #4's evocation of cinema? Wolk is correct to note that the image may be commenting on the relationship between the two media, but it's perhaps even more complicated than he realizes. The represented filmstrip, which implies duration by depicting the Flash at various instants, owes more to the protocinematic motion studies of Eadweard Muybridge than to cinema as we actually experience it. Using a series of deliberately positioned individual camera setups, Muybridge captured subjects in motion via a series of discrete images, which could then be studied independently as instants—for instance, revealing the moment at which all four hooves of a running horse are off the ground at once—or reconstituted as moving pictures via zoopraxiscope projection. Scott Bukatman has compared the early comics of Winsor McCay to Muybridge's chronophotography, noting that they produce "visual continuity, dynamic flow, and, importantly, credible naturalistic detail" in similar ways, and that the left-to-right reading procedure and "graph-like configuration" of panels allows readers to interpret a strip's discrete images "as stages in a single movement, as in a chronophotograph."[4] He continues, engaging with scholar Marta Braun and chronophotographer Étienne-Jules Marey:

> Braun emphasizes the difference between Marey's scientism and Muybridge's formalism: "Muybridge's concern [was] with narration, not with movement" (p. 249). For Braun, Muybridge's use of multiple, spatially organized cameras, as well as his characteristic array of discretely bounded, pleasingly composed images, privileged a sense of time as divisible and discrete. Contained parcels of space become analogous to

FIGURE 4.1. Cover of *Showcase* #4

contained parcels of time. Marey's single plates, by contrast, emphasized a temporal continuum, with the chronophotograph capturing instants along the axis of time's arrow.[5]

While comics occasionally dole out time on an instant-to-instant basis in a way that recalls Muybridge's sequential images, more often each panel represents a longer duration, leaving larger temporal gaps in the representation. In either case, however, the images are arranged in such a way that they relate to each other both sequentially (as a narrative unfolding over time) and spatially (as images on a page). If anything, however, comics are even more concerned with narration and less concerned with time than Muybridge was. Most comics panels represent what we might call an "image-event"—a chunk of narration rather than an instant of time—whose "duration" is not fixed (e.g., one twenty-fourth of a second, as in conventional film projection) but is rather a combination of two variables: the diegetic length of the event narrated (including action, dialogue, narration, etc.) and the nondiegetic time devoted to it by the reader. In the McCay comics that evoke Muybridge's chronophotography, each panel's image-event represents an instant of a greater movement, but this is not typical of comics.[6] Nevertheless, it's true that "comics more clearly resemble what Muybridge produced than what the Edison Company and the Lumières followed it with," at least in terms of their spatial juxtaposition of static images.[7]

With this context in mind, let's take another look at *Showcase* #4. Implying movement, the Flash's position changes slightly in each frame of the film-strip, just as in Muybridge's photos. At its most basic level, the implied reference to chronophotography suggests that something about the Flash's movement is worthy of scientific study, a subtle reinforcement of his superhuman status that also creates optical interest in his unique powers. It also suggests, however, that the Flash's speed is beyond the capacity of normal human perception, that, like the aforementioned horse's gallop, it requires mechanical eyes to view clearly. In the final frame, however, the "real" and "present" Flash (as opposed to the "photographed" and therefore "past" representations) bursts through the celluloid, suggesting the failure of even this technology to represent and contain him. The Flash's movement is ultimately *too* fast—faster, certainly, than a camera shutter—which prevents his movement from being captured photographically.[8] This image thus conveys the speed and dynamism of the newly rebooted superhero,[9] as well as a somewhat counterintuitive commentary on comics and film: because the Flash's

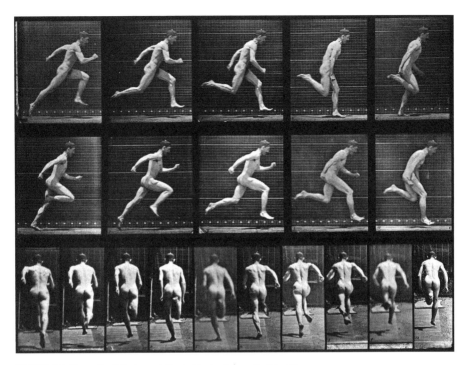

FIGURE 4.2. Example of Eadweard Muybridge's chronophotography

extreme speed exceeds the representational limits of cinema's fixed number of frames per second, his exploits might be better represented through the static images of comics and its unregimented relationship to time. As Liam Burke puts it, "The Scarlet Speedster's emergence from the celluloid is a giddy riposte to those who fail to recognize comics' possibilities and extol 'motion' pictures."[10] How can we account for this? To start, Rudolf Arnheim notes that "motion, like any other kind of change, is perceivable only within a limited range of speed. The sun and the moon travel so slowly that they seem to stand still; *a flash of lightning is so fast that its entire course appears simultaneously as a line.*"[11] Comic books always represent movement in this way: everything on the continuum from the perfect stasis of the inanimate object to the imperceptible quickness of the lightning bolt is represented using still images and appears to the reader's perception as such. In this context, the lightning bolt adorning the Flash's chest becomes quite evocative, simultaneously representing both his own superspeed and the stasis of the medium in which he appears.

And yet, somewhat contradictorily, the stasis of comics' imagery has the potential to produce an incredible sense of movement and dynamism. Angela Ndalianis pins down comics' relationship to movement thusly:

> To a certain extent, yes, the comic book is a static medium: comics do not succumb to the phenomenon of the persistence of vision [*sic*] that typify media like praxinoscopes or film animations, despite the fact that all three forms are famous for favouring the drawn image . . . [The] ontology of the comic book (and comic strip) is quite different to that of media such as live action and animated films, which rely more literally on the illusion of motion. However, . . . the comic book form is anything but static. The panels that litter its pages are riddled with a dynamism and motion that present their own unique articulation of time and space. Certainly, some of the narrative action represented within a comic book panel can "freeze" time, but other panels—while remaining visually static as still images on a page—open up complex depictions of time and space that create modes of perception that are particular to comics. The contradiction, of course, is that the comic represents the animated flux of time and space through stasis.[12]

The "dynamism, kineticism and energy"[13] associated with superheroes make them excellent representatives of comics' formal potential; but as Martyn Pedler has pointed out, "speedsters" like the Flash are superlative in this regard. In an inversion of Arnheim's description above, the Flash moves so quickly that to him all human endeavor moves as slowly as the sun and the moon—in other words, the world around him appears as static as a comic book panel.[14] The static images of comics therefore also convey the character's unique subjectivity.

Pedler writes, "Superheroes are born into a medium that appears to consist of static images. Without the ability to show literal movement, superheroes like the Flash are instead animated by the powerful techniques employed by comic book artists to create time and motion across the page."[15] Motion lines are one such technique that suggest movement (and therefore duration) within a single static image; another is the visualization of multiple instants within the same panel, whereby a subject is seen at different stages of movement simultaneously. The most basic representation of movement in comics, however, relies instead on the imagination of the reader, who synthesizes B (*movement*) from the given visualizations of A (*static image 1*) and C (*static image 2*) in a process known as closure. For Mary Ann Doane, "The positions of the figures were too far apart" in Muybridge's photographs, making it "often impossible to determine how the figure moved from one position to the next. Too much time was lost."[16] Closure thus has some historical precedent in chronophotography. But it is fundamentally in their relationship to this "lost" or unrepresented time that comics and cinema make a radical break from each other, with the former medium widening the gap between Muybridge's instants while the latter narrows it. As Bukatman puts it, "Cinema reconstituted the movement that one could infer from [Muybridge's] sequence[s] of still images, while comics retained the synchronous spatiotemporal array ... but both media were fundamentally bound to the explorations of time, rhythm and tempo so characteristic of modernity."[17]

Indeed, the relationships of comics and film to time and modernity warrant further exploration, as they represent a key point of distinction between the two media. Doane writes that the "emergence of mechanical reproduction is accompanied by modernity's increasing understanding of temporality as assault, acceleration, speed. There is too much, too fast. From Georg Simmel to Walter Benjamin, modernity is conceptualized as an increase in the speed and intensity of stimuli."[18] It is this experience of the world that necessitates Muybridge's chronophotography, and ultimately cinema, which captures segments of time and organizes them, often according to aesthetic rules meant to ensure their coherence. Additionally, however, "Modernity was characterized by the impulse to *wear* time, to append it to the body so that the watch became a kind of prosthetic device extending the capacity of the body to measure time. The acceleration of events specific to city life was inseparable from the effects of new technologies and a machine culture made possible by developments in modern science."[19] At a rigid 60 seconds per minute and 24 frames per second, the watch and cinema both embody a similar technological determinism with regard to time's division into discrete (and arguably arbitrary) units. While the construction of a particular film might play fast and loose with narrative chronology—perhaps best embodied in the comic book film by Superman's reversal of Earth's rotation, and thereby time, in *Superman*—cinema is essentially a linear medium; just as the hands of an operational timepiece move only in one direction, so too does the filmstrip travel through the projector in one direction only, irrespective of how a given film organizes its narrative events. Superman's reversal of Earth's rotation reverses diegetic time, but the linear momentum of the film representing this event continues to move forward all the same; this is to say that while film narratives (diegetic time) have the potential to be nonlinear, *film itself* (screen time) is necessarily linear. In direct opposition to the inelastic, linear, and unstoppable temporality of the watch and the film projector, however, comics might be considered as a means of asserting one's agency over time, of controlling the duration of represented events oneself: comics' time (as opposed to cinematic time) is not determined by an apparatus or the text alone, but rather by the collaboration of the text and the reader, and is thereby a closer relative to premodern media such as literature, painting, and drawing. In its "elastic temporality"[20] we find some resistance to time's standardization, mechanization, industrialization, and rationalization in modernity. Jared Gardner argues that the cinema of attractions—the exhibitionistic tendency of cinema prior to the conventionalization of what would become the rules of narrative and continuity style identified by Tom Gunning—didn't abide by these rules and was thus "relegated to the form's primitive past" while "Comics, always rooted in the narrative structure of shocks, fragments, and discontinuities, found itself increasingly defined as primitive and childish."[21]

It's clear, then, that comics and film have distinct relationships to movement, time, and duration, having pursued opposite agendas in the wake of Muybridge that resulted in the establishment of different representational conventions. The primary interest of this chapter is in how those differences are negotiated when comics' representational norms are remediated by the cinema. How do comic book films remediate comics' relationship to time and representations of movement? How do they transform comics' paradoxically kinetic stasis into (the cinematic illusion of) movement proper? Because comics' panel-to-panel and page-to-page relationship to temporality is mercurial, films remediating comics' treatment of time do so in a variety of ways, with a variety of results. Doane reminds us that

> for the most part, visible time in the cinema is equal to "real time," and any manipulation or troping of time takes place in the invisible realms of off-screen space or the interstices between shots. (Fast motion, slow motion, the freeze frame, and other distortions of time become, precisely, *special* effects, relegated to the marginal status of the heavily coded—and rare—moments.)[22]

It is largely through these kinds of special effects that the remediation of comics' time occurs, resulting in heavily coded, stylistically overdetermined moments. Whereas the remediation of the panel and hyperframe discussed in the previous chapter largely drew on the categories of explicit and formal intermediality for its effects, the remediation of movement primarily employs a different set of categories, namely, compositional intertextuality, expressive intermediality, and figural intermediality. As before, we will see that the use of such aesthetic strategies brings film further away from the immediacy of photographic representation and the invisibility of classical "continuity" style and closer to the hypermediacy of comics, in this case often by disrupting the uniformity of cinema's temporal flow in some way, thus drawing the viewer's attention to cinematic time as a construct.

Any discussion of movement in cinema is incomplete without some reference to Gilles Deleuze, as well as to the work of Henri Bergson that inspired him. The Deleuzian concepts that are particularly relevant here are the "privileged instant" and the "any-instant-whatever," which embody two distinct means of representing movement. The privileged instant refers to the division of movement into discrete and significant images, between which the actual movement occurs. As Deleuze writes, "Movement, conceived in this way, will thus be the regulated transition from one form to another, that is, an order of *poses* or privileged instants."[23] It's easy to see how we might conceive of the comic book in this way, given how each panel provides an instant that is literally privileged over all other narrative instants simply by virtue of its inclusion in the representation (not to mention how the "instant" represented in the panel may be a composite image representing a span of time: i.e., an *image-event* rather than a discrete moment in time). The process of closure represents the "regulated transition" (though comics are perhaps defined by a *lack* of regularity here) between poses. The any-instant-whatever, conversely, considers each individual image as a part that collectively reconstitutes a whole; no single image is privileged over any other and, furthermore, each functions as one cog in a mechanical process that relies on their equidistance from each other in a machine, such as a film projector. For this reason, Deleuze considers film to be the medium most exemplary of the any-instant-whatever: "Cinema is the system which reproduces movement as a function of any-instant-whatever, that is, as a function of equidistant instants, selected so as to create an impression of continuity."[24] He adds, however, that the cinema properly thrives on both, using any-instant-whatevers to produce privileged instants. However, the "privilege" here exists not on the level of form—all snapshots are equidistant and play an equal role in the production of the movement—but rather on the level of perception: for example, though it doesn't stand out formally, the frame in which Muybridge's horse's hooves are all off the ground simultaneously would be considered a privileged instant because of its significant content. The two strategies discussed in the following pages both represent a subversion of cinema's any-instant-whatever in favor of the privileged instant of comics; the any-instant-whatever doesn't disappear in either case, but is rather redeployed to create images (often poses, as in a choreographed dance) that stand out within the temporal flow. More specifically, mimetic compositions create privileged instants by virtue of their indexical relation to a previously existing and familiar comic book image, while the panel moment manipulates the ebb and flow of time, obliging the viewer's attention to linger on certain images in the temporal flow. Other heavily coded uses of film style to remediate comics' time—whether through slow motion or the appropriation of motion lines into a cinematographic context—are also analyzed here. We'll begin, however, with the least explicitly coded instances of temporal remediation, which use compositional mimesis—those explicitly intertextual moments in the comic book film in which the composition of the film frame directly mirrors or recalls a particular panel from a comic book—for its effect.

Mimetic Compositions: Indices of Memory

Aside from the borrowing of narrative content from comics (e.g., characters, settings, storylines, etc.), compositional intertextuality may be the most commonplace interaction between the two media in the comic book film. It's not at all unusual for comic book films' marketing materials to court fans' approval by prominently featuring compositions that mimic those found in the source texts they value so highly. *Spider-Man 2*'s trailer, for instance, lingers on a shot that directly recalls the infamous "Spider-Man No More" moment from *The Amazing Spider-Man #50* (July 1967), earning widespread fan approval and anticipation for the film; by contrast, the April 2015 online reveals of Jared Leto as the Joker in *Suicide Squad* (2016), which echo famous compositions from the seminal graphic novel *Batman: The Killing Joke* (1988), employed the same strategy but nevertheless proved controversial with fans.[25] Both of these examples are ostensibly meant as indicators of "fidelity" to and respect for their source material and as demonstrations of bona fides though the citation of key works. Mimetic compositions are thus a direct and unambiguous way to point at and pay homage to the "original" text, regardless of how many creative departures are otherwise made from it.

This phenomenon is defined as intertextual rather than intermedial because it relies on the relationship between a film and a *particular text* rather than the medium of comics and its form in general. Within that relationship, however, content is not merely appropriated or adapted but is utterly transformed by its new formal context. What is most interesting about these moments is not how they restage a familiar image in live action, nor how they animate those compositions—movement is often kept to a minimum to call attention to the image's similarity to one from the comics—but rather how they reproduce a memory image of the comic book version in the viewer's mind. By means of demonstration, let's look more closely at the aforementioned shot from *Spider-Man 2*. In both the comic and the film, the composition functions as the culmination of a storyline resulting in Peter Parker's decision to give up fighting crime as Spider-Man in order to better fulfill his civilian duties, like improving his grades at school and taking care of his Aunt May. The significance of both the panel and the shot within their respective works is indicated by their formal qualities: the panel occupies its entire page, expressing the magnitude of Peter's decision through form, while the importance of the shot in the film is indicated by its longer-than-average duration (twenty seconds) and its privileged position at the end of the scene, marked by a fade to black. Despite some differences between the two versions, there is no question that the shot is a mimetic composition. In terms of mise-en-scène, the essential elements are the same in both versions: they both take place on stormy nights, in tight and darkly lit New York City alleyways; in the foreground on the right, we see a metal garbage can with the Spider-Man costume draped over it; in the middle ground just left of center, Peter is seen from behind as he walks away from the costume, out of the claustrophobic alley and toward the light of the street. In both versions, the costume (and the mask, in particular) is the main focus: in the film version, the eyes of the mask, hanging upside down over the rim of the garbage can, remain illuminated for a moment after the rest of the mise-en-scène has faded to black, drawing our attention there even though movement is happening elsewhere in the frame.

The differences between the two versions are the result of the specific ways in which the film remediates the comic. For instance, the "portrait" dimensions of a comic book page beg a different approach to spatial organization than the "landscape" dimensions of a widescreen film frame; while the comic book version emphasizes height and verticality, the film version emphasizes width and horizontality. In the comics image, Peter seems boxed in by his surroundings: going clockwise, an overhead fire escape, the

costume-stuffed trash can, a dark shadow, and a brick wall are graphic features that surround and trap him within the image. Furthermore, the costume itself is given primacy in the composition, occupying about two-thirds of the image's height, overwhelming Peter's comparatively diminutive frame. The glove of the costume lies on the ground, seeming to stretch out longingly toward Peter's feet. The vertical composition allows for a greater sense of scope to the setting: we can see from the ground of the alley, below the base of the garbage can, to the buildings of a New York City street, all in sharp focus. By comparison, the film version stretches the composition out laterally and imbues it with a far greater sense of depth. Whereas in the comic the glove of the Spider-Man suit almost seems to touch Peter's feet, in the film version he seems to be at least a few meters away from the garbage can; furthermore, he is actively walking away from it, moving farther into the background with each step. The filmic alleyway seems much less claustrophobic in the foreground, but becomes increasingly tight as the walls recede toward the vanishing point. While the graphic elements of the comic page trap and diminish Peter's body, his receding into the claustrophobic (and out-of-focus) background in the film version suggests the uncertainty of his future and his reduced status without Spider-Man. The shot's lingering on the eyes of the mask after the rest of the image has faded to black further indicates the costume's continuing importance to Peter's ultimate destiny. Each version suggests, albeit in different ways, that Peter's problems will not be solved by retiring his superheroic alter ego.

Clearly, the meaning of the film shot is enhanced by its association with the comics version of the same. This is only a slightly modified articulation of the tendency toward cinematic allusionism that Noël Carroll associates with New Hollywood directors' obsession with film history: in both cases, a revered earlier work is invoked in a new context, in order to both "[project] and [reinforce] the themes and the emotive and aesthetic qualities of the new films," while also benefiting from the cultural capital associated with canonical works.[26] While *The Amazing Spider-Man #50* is hardly a canonized work of literature, it nevertheless holds a great deal of currency within fan circles, for whom the reference is both loaded and meaningful. This practice thus invokes what Carroll calls a "two-tiered system of communication which sends an action/drama/fantasy-packed message to one segment of the audience"—those who appreciate the film solely as a self-contained narrative—"and an additional hermetic, camouflaged, and recondite one to another"—those who seek out and understand these kinds of intertextual references and whose experience of the film is significantly enhanced by the supplemental meanings they invoke.[27] Allusionism may also flatter the fan because it "affords the opportunity to adopt the role of guardian of specialized knowledge."[28] For comic book fans, each new comic book film provides new opportunities to put their encyclopedic visual memories to the test.

Mimetic compositions also serve an indexical function, implicitly pointing to the previous text. Since indexicality is a concept that is so often misunderstood in film studies, it may not be immediately apparent how the relationship between the mimetic composition and its comic book source is indexical in nature. As defined by Charles Sanders Peirce, signs are "how we come to know things about the world by representing it," be they verbal or visual in nature.[29] Indexical signs—the index refers to the finger used for pointing—point toward something and are also existentially connected to the thing they represent. The concept of "existential connection," however, is not merely causal in nature: pronouns like "that" or "this" are indices of whatever they stand in for, and a person's first name is an index of that person. Most film scholars understand photographs as indexical because of how light imprints itself on celluloid, causing the image to come into being, similar to an inked fingerprint pressing against paper. Through the lasting influence of Bazin, Kracauer, Barthes, Cavell, and others, indexicality has become the photograph's—and therefore live-action cinema's—defining characteristic and the guarantor of its veracity. The shift to digital imaging practices, whether alongside or to the exclusion of emulsion-based photography, has been conceptualized by many as a loss of the image's direct relationship to the world. For many, this represents a crisis because "digital imaging operates according to a different ontology than do indexical photographs."[30] Lev Manovich has perhaps stated this most boldly in his pronouncement that "cinema can no longer be clearly distinguished from animation. It is no longer an indexical media technology but, rather, a subgenre of painting."[31] The problem with this logic is that painting *is itself also indexical*, just in a different way: the brushstrokes function as an index of the painter's movements, and a representational painting is also existentially related to its subject through the painter.[32] Computer-generated images, as we see in much contemporary cinema, are existentially connected to the digital artists who worked on them at various stages, as well as the programmers who created the applications used, the computers on which the images were created and refined, and so on. Manovich's claim is symptomatic of a widespread misunderstanding of indexicality as a narrower category than it is. Indeed, it makes little sense to say that a representational digital photograph is less indexical than a pointing finger, which is the index's namesake! In short, "An index represents an object by virtue of its real, existential connection with it. It makes no difference whether the connection is natural, or artificial, or merely mental."[33]

Compositional mimesis, however, represents a slightly more complex process than this. When a shot in a comic book film makes the viewer conscious of a particular panel from a comic book, it functions indexically because the shot depends on the prior existence of the panel, not in the sense of direct causation, but nevertheless the shot's composition wouldn't exist as such without the panel. However, this connection between the two images—one filmic, one drawn—is only recognizable to the viewer by virtue of their mutual resemblance or visual similarity: in other words, the film shot also bears an *iconic* relationship to the comics panel, and it is through this iconicity that we recognize the index. This is distinct from the pointing finger or the pronoun but *not* from the photograph, whose indexicality we also recognize by virtue of (and whose documentary value depends on) its likeness to that which it represents: the comics panel is to the mimetic composition as profilmic reality is to the photograph. In other words, the film version *represents* the comics panel just as a photograph represents whatever was in front of the camera.

What happens when a mimetic composition appears in a comic book film? If the viewer doesn't recognize the reference, then the shot recedes into the flow of images like any other. As we'll see later in this section, mimetic compositions are often granted privileged status in the narrative, serving as act break markers or coming at the beginning or ending of a film. If the viewer intuits the added significance of these images without knowledge of their intertextual status, it can potentially be attributed to their narrative import. Alternatively, additional stylistic interventions (such as slow motion) may also seem to "insist" that the viewer give added consideration to a particular composition. However, if the viewer *does* recognize it, a perceptual combination occurs, resulting in the creation of a hybrid image in which the film composition offered to the viewer's consciousness is combined and contrasted with one stored in memory. Bergson's understanding of how memory affects perception is appropriate here: "In concrete perception, memory intervenes, and the subjectivity of sensible qualities is due precisely to the fact that our consciousness, which begins by being only memory, prolongs a plurality of moments into each other, contracting them into a single intuition."[34] The image originally experienced within the comic book, as well as its context therein and the feelings associated with it, are suddenly brought to bear on the film image. This is a fairly complicated process that necessitates close readings of both versions to fully explicate.

Let's look, then, at some specific examples and how they function. Mark Steven Johnson's *Daredevil* is a film based on the blind Marvel Comics superhero, and it's arguably among the most reverent comic book films with regard to its source material. The story, as is often the case in superhero films, is not an adaptation of a particular work but is rather a hodgepodge of visual and narrative elements taken from decades' worth of serialized comic books, including the accident that robs the adolescent Matt Murdock of his sight but also imbues him with a superhuman "radar" sense, allowing him to assume the costumed alter ego of Daredevil; the murder of his father, boxer Jack Murdock;[35] Daredevil's first encounter with Elektra;[36] and Elektra's death at the hands of Bullseye.[37] More general elements from the comics are also incorporated, including the narrative's setting (Hell's Kitchen); Murdock's day job (lawyer), religion (Catholic), general lack of luck with romantic relationships, and playful banter with his friend and fellow lawyer Franklin "Foggy" Nelson; reporter Ben Urich's pursuit of the truth behind the Daredevil vigilante; and Kingpin as the hero's archnemesis. Additionally, a bevy of minor characters are named after key creative personnel spanning the history of the superhero, including Kirby (for artist Jack Kirby), Quesada (for artist Joe Quesada),[38] Father Everett (for Daredevil cocreator Bill Everett), and boxers Colan (for artist Gene Colan), Romita (for artists John Romita Sr. and Jr.), Mack (for artist David Mack), Bendis (for writer Brian Michael Bendis), and Miller (for writer/artist/Elektra creator Frank Miller, who also appears in a cameo role as one of Bullseye's victims). Daredevil cocreator Stan Lee also makes a cameo, as he does in most films featuring Marvel characters.[39] All of these could be described as diegetic intertextuality (or metatextuality, in some cases), and thus make the importance of the comic book texts perfectly clear to those familiar with both, while passing by undetected by those unfamiliar with the references. The film is also loaded with lines of dialogue taken verbatim from the speech balloons of comics and of compositions that refer to specific comics panels. Obviously, it is the latter that interests me here.

I will limit my analysis to three of the film's key moments: the opening and closing shots and the moment of Elektra's death, all of which are already privileged moments in the narrative whose impact is further heightened by their appeal to the privileged instants represented in comic book panels. The compositions for the opening[40] and closing shots are both taken from Kevin Smith and Joe Quesada's "Guardian Devil" story arc; specifically, they refer to the cover images of *Daredevil* #3 (January 1999) and #1 (November 1998), respectively. The images that appear on the covers of comics are often particularly iconic in that they exist outside of the narrative but must embody it or the character's identity as a whole; it is their job to attract customers' eyes to the book and, hopefully, get would-be readers—not only existing fans of the character but also neophytes who may be randomly browsing—to purchase it. It's not hyperbole to state that among the many privileged instants represented in a comic book, the cover image is the most privileged by virtue of its placement at the beginning of the book and its relative isolation from other images. A movie's poster or "one-sheet" may arguably serve a similar function, but whereas comics readers necessarily interact with the cover as a component of the comic book text itself, a movie poster is a marketing paratext that remains materially separated from the film it's selling.[41] It's perfectly plausible to imagine someone watching a movie without having seen its poster, but it's difficult to imagine a comic book reader reading an issue without poring over its cover. In terms of similarities, however, both comics covers and movie posters provide extra-diegetic spaces in which characters appear in particularly striking poses that don't require narrative justification—they're often surrounded by nondiegetic copy detailing the title of the comic or film, a tagline hinting at the plot, etc.—and whose primary purpose is to attract an audience to the comic or film itself.

The comic book cover is also roughly equivalent to the opening or closing shot of a film in terms of its significance. It comes as no surprise, then, that *Daredevil* would begin and end with mimetic compositions that reference such visually striking covers as these. The film begins in medias res, near the chronological end of the narrative before flashing back to Murdock's youth and proceeding chronologically from there; we see Daredevil, clearly hurt and grasping onto the crucifix at the spire of a Catholic church. The juxtaposition of a man in a red devil costume and the explicitly Catholic imagery is obviously intended to grab viewers' interest; for comics readers, however, the image is also the first of many indications that the film is fully engaged with the history of the character. Smith and Quesada's eight issues are hardly as revered by fans as Miller's "Born Again" arc or his *Man Without Fear* miniseries,[42] but these cover images rival anything in Miller's books in terms of sheer distinctiveness. The transition from drawing to live

FIGURES 4.5 AND 4.6.
Stills from *Daredevil*

FIGURE 4.7. Cover of *Daredevil* #3

FIGURE 4.8. Cover of *Daredevil* #1

action, however, necessarily results in some differences: reformatting from a vertical rectangular image to a horizontal rectangle means that Daredevil is considerably smaller in the film frame than in the comic (though the camera movement and a helicopter searchlight emphasize him in the shot) and he is centered; the camera angle frames the crucifix against the moon and clouds, while the cover image uses a mass of industrial buildings and steam as its backdrop; and most notably, almost all of the color has been drained from the image, resulting in a shadowy black figure (we only see the red of his costume when the searchlight hits him) against a shadowy black night sky.

The most significant difference is not aesthetic, however, but narrative. The cover image of *Daredevil* #3 is essentially nondiegetic; it doesn't advance or contribute to the issue's narrative in any way (other than perhaps thematically), and indeed doesn't reappear within the narrative proper. It falls to the film version, then, to insert the image of Daredevil grasping the crucifix atop the church into a narrative context. On the issue's cover, Daredevil appears to be monitoring the area below; the church roof presumably offers him an ideal vantage point. This, of course, is speculation, since the image exists outside of the book's narrative. In the film, Daredevil is beaten and bleeding; he holds onto the crucifix to support him before falling through the roof, landing in front of the pews in the church's main hall. It's totally unclear, however, when in the film's narrative this event occurs; it cannot be after defeating Bullseye, because the villain is shown leaping away from the scene; it cannot be after defeating Kingpin, because Daredevil loses his mask in the skirmish. To some extent, then, it seems that we're meant to read this image as both inside and outside of the narrative simultaneously, almost as a "cover image" that represents something about the character without fitting neatly into the narrative of the film. Christopher Nolan's Dark Knight trilogy regularly engages in a similar practice, using spectacular helicopter shots of Batman overlooking Gotham City from the peak of a tall tower or skyscraper as transitional images between scenes. Taken in the "Gosh, wow!" spirit they're given—ultimately these shots halt the narrative in order to impress the viewer visually—they present no problem, functioning as iconic moments that resemble cover images from comic books.[43] Narratively, however, these shots make little sense: How did he climb so high? How does he intend to get down? What's he looking at from up there? However, such narratively incongruous shots within comic book films may be understood as intermedial gestures to the aesthetics and function of the comic book cover, whose purpose is not to advance the narrative, or even to participate in it, but rather to provide a striking, iconic image that establishes characters, content, or themes from within a *quasi-diegetic* space, attracting attention based largely on its aesthetic qualities.

The closing shot of *Daredevil* offers another mimetic composition that cites an even more abstract image in terms of its narrative associations. *Daredevil* #1's cover, also drawn by Quesada, is part of a long tradition of comic book covers that don't provide even the slightest hint of the narrative within, but only display the protagonist in a dynamic, often physics-defying pose. *Daredevil* #1 depicts the red-horned superhero suspended in midair above the New York skyline, his face obscured in shadow but his eyes and horns glowing red; his eyes peer directly at the reader (ironically, given his blindness). In free fall, he strikes an upside-down acrobatic pose as the cable attaching the two ends of his billy club gracefully swirls around him in an intricate pattern. The red of the costume and billy club are the only traces of color in the image (aside from the company and title logos and artists' signatures); Daredevil thus stands out against the drab, almost sepia-toned background. A slight lens flare on the tip of the billy club evokes the medium of photography, emphasizing that this is a moment frozen in time: a snapshot rather than an image-event with duration. And even without motion lines or any other signifiers of movement, the image is incredibly dynamic due to the intricate pattern woven by the billy club's trajectory. The film version (see figure 4.6), naturally, adds movement to the composition: the building rushes past as Daredevil falls through the air toward the streets below; the cable thrashes through the air as the grappling hook rushes directly at the camera, echoing the direct address of Daredevil's gaze from the comic image. As in the previous example, the film's limited palette strips almost all color from the original drawing. The final lines of the film, spoken in voiceover over this image and those preceding it, make the connection to the "Guardian Devil" story explicit: "I prowl the rooftops and alleyways at night, watching from the darkness. Forever in darkness. A guardian devil."

Given the vast difference in sales between contemporary comics and blockbuster films, it's fair to say that the film versions of long-running comics characters are, for most viewers, the primary points of entry into these narrative worlds. Smith and Quesada's run on *Daredevil* was framed similarly, ending the numbering of the previous series (after 380 issues published over thirty-four years) and starting again at #1. In the bottom-left corner of the cover, however, below the artists' signatures, reads the number "381": this is the "true" issue number, counting from 1964. Thus *Daredevil* #1 brands itself as part of the old tradition as well as the beginning of a new one simultaneously. Pointing to *this* cover specifically is thus charged with significance beyond the aesthetic force of the image itself, since the film adaptation operates in the same way as the relaunched series, telling a story that combines new and familiar elements; it's framed as an entry point for new viewers, but longtime fans of the character will have their knowledge of the comic books rewarded as well, through mimetic compositions like this one. Like the comic, the film is both a continuation of what has come before as well as a reboot, a "new #1."

ABOVE
FIGURE 4.9. Still from
Batman Begins

RIGHT
FIGURE 4.10. Cover
of *Batman* #608

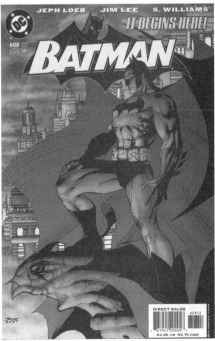

In the case of both the opening and closing shots, based as they are on comic book covers that exist outside of narrative, the memory images that they bring forth produce associations that are primarily aesthetic. The viewer gets a Proustian charge of reminiscence, but divorced as these images are from any narrative context, the experience may not go much deeper than that. This is not the case with the third and final mimetic composition that I want to analyze, which occurs at the climax of Elektra's fatal battle with Bullseye. The image in question depicts Bullseye impaling Elektra with her own weapon, and was originally featured in *Daredevil* #181, an issue whose cover boasted "Bullseye vs. Elektra: One Wins, One Dies." In the comic, this image appears in a borderless panel against a white background (with a pink stripe that dissolves to white as it approaches the characters): in this way, it is abstracted from both time and space as conventionally depicted in comics. The lack of dialogue or sound effects on the entire page lends it a slow, almost timeless quality. The dimensions of the image on the page also lend it additional significance, especially when contrasted against the series of thin, horizontal panels on the other side of the page: like the splash pages in *Watchmen* #12, it stands out by virtue of its deviation from the norm. In other words, the image's stylistic features encourage the reader to slow down and contemplate the significance of this narrative event. It's this context that the reader imposes on the film version, a shot that appears onscreen for less than two seconds. While the previous two examples existed somewhat outside of the narrative, both in their comics and film versions, this mimetic composition represents a crucial turning point in the plot whose narrative significance is further heightened intertextually. The film's intensified continuity editing patterns demand that the film not rest on any one shot for longer than a few seconds; and though the equidistant snapshots continue to fly through the projector, this image stands out amid the flow and lingers in the viewer's memory, if not perception. This is because its particular indexical quality calls upon the viewer to participate or, more specifically, to "look at" the original comics image at which the mimetic composition points, and to read them simultaneously. As Doane writes, "The index, more insistently than any other type of sign, is haunted by its object":[44] it may be read in isolation by the segment of the audience that doesn't recognize the allusion, but this misses part of what makes comic book films like these such densely intertextual and intermedial objects.

All of the remediating strategies discussed in this book represent an active negotiation between comics and film in one way or another. The specificity

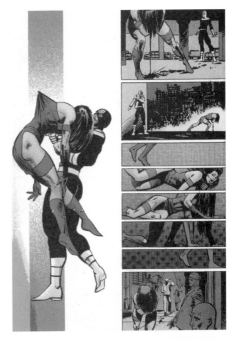

of compositional mimesis as a visual practice—*this* shot recalls *this* panel from *this* comic—puts this into stark relief, clearly demonstrating how the comic book film is read as an intermedial object, composed not just of multiple texts but of multiple media. *Daredevil* is an interesting case study because, for the most part, it eschews the more stylistically self-conscious strategies of remediation (e.g., split screen, as discussed in the previous chapter) and relies primarily on textual references that would slip by unnoticed for anyone not already in the know. Compared to a film like *Sin City*, whose extreme stylistic choices are only rationalized with the understanding that it's based on a comic book, *Daredevil's* allusionism is not stylized in such a way that calls attention to its intertextuality; rather, it simply adds another layer of meaning that enhances the experience of the film for those viewers who are as engaged with the comic book history of the character as they are with the film itself.

Motion Lines and Motion Pictures

Compositional mimesis involves remediating specific comics images and bringing them to life, in a manner of speaking, by restaging them with live actors and adding movement. But there's a difference between remediating static images and remediating the condition of stasis itself or, perhaps more accurately, the means through which comics imply movement with only static images. Expressive intermediality, which involves using film style to evoke the aesthetics of certain stylistic conventions associated with the comics medium (not its formal system, which is covered by formal intermediality), does precisely this. This category tends to trouble the ontological difference between drawing and photography by imposing conventions specific to drawn media like comics onto cinema. Expressive intermediality can encompass a fairly broad range of effects, including impossible lighting or a painterly use of color; the abstraction of objects from their surroundings (i.e., the elimination of backgrounds); the caricaturing of reality through larger-than-life props, sets, and makeup; and the imposition of effects particular to or predominantly associated with comic book representations onto an otherwise live-action (or seemingly live-action) shot. The effects thus produced purposefully draw the viewer's attention to film style and its artificiality in precisely the way that classical continuity, and even intensified continuity, generally seeks to avoid.

In this context, the relevant convention being remediated is motion lines, which are used in comics to give the reader a sense of movement and trajectory within a single static image, as we saw at the outset of this chapter with regard to *Showcase* #4. Unlike compositional mimesis, the results here should be very evident to any viewer of the film, not just those familiar with the comics, for two reasons: first, no prior knowledge of another text or canon is required, since these aren't allusions to a specific text; second, the effect is not a natural feature of cinematography or a common feature of live-action cinema and therefore stands out as an obtrusive stylistic effect.

Scott McCloud points out that motion *blur* is produced in films whenever the object filmed moves faster than the camera shutter, but motion *lines* are conceptually and visually distinct from this phenomenon.[45] They are clearer, cleaner, more precise, and serve a very different purpose compared to blur. Whereas motion lines in comics are always a deliberately used narrative and stylistic choice, motion blur is an inherent and unavoidable quality of cinema. In fact, it's often seen as a *defect* of the medium, especially by technically minded filmmakers like James Cameron and Peter Jackson, who have spearheaded an attempted transition from 24 to 48 frames per second that would effectively eliminate motion blur from cinema.[46]

Neil Cohn asserts that motion lines are one of many conventions of comics' visual language that are understood because of their widespread usage, not because they resemble their meaning:[47] in other words, this is a symbolic effect, not an iconic one. "Conventional representations like motion lines," Cohn writes, "are all understood better with age and more experience reading comics."[48] While this is certainly true of dialogue balloons, which do not in any way *resemble* the nonvisual phenomenon of spoken speech, motion lines are a more complex case. Take what has been mistakenly interpreted as a remediation of motion lines in *The Matrix*, about which Costas Constandinides writes, "Motion lines are actually reproduced for . . . the bullet time effect in *The Matrix* in a style that can only quote motion lines in comic books,"[49] referring to a scene in which bullets fired at Neo leave a visible trace in their wake. Rather than lines, however, the trails left by the bullets in this scene look more like visible sound or heat waves; as a result, they appear to the viewer as natural (if usually invisible to the naked eye) translucent ripples in the air rather than an artificial addition to the scene; their visibility seems to be a product of the slow-motion effect rather than an imposition of a comics convention onto the film's stylistic system. Expressive intermediality, by contrast, represents a break with photographic reality in favor of representing a world as it would appear in a comic book panel, through that medium's particular idioms and conventions. *The Matrix* naturalizes motion lines within its storyworld and makes them appear organic to the image, and therefore does not meet this criterion. However, another film written by Lilly and Lana Wachowski (who also codirected *The Matrix*) does remediate motion lines: *V for Vendetta*. Motion lines only appear in one scene of the film in which V dispatches a squad of special operatives and a government official in slow motion. As we'll see in the next section of this chapter, slow motion is also key to the remediation of stasis in the comic book film, but what's more significant about this scene is the use of motion lines following from the tips of V's knives. In contrast to *The Matrix*, these motion lines are patently artificial and cannot be interpreted as an effect of the slow motion or a natural (if usually invisible) feature of the environment. Rather, this is a deliberate stylistic intrusion that remediates the motion lines of comics.

According to McCloud, Ndalianis, and others, motion lines are largely responsible for the dynamism of comics art.[50] Additionally, motion lines represent a possible counterargument to Gardner's assertion that comics are the least efficient narrative medium.[51] Motion lines actually provide an extremely efficient means of representing a span of time in a single privileged instant, showing the final result of an action and the trajectory leading to it simultaneously. To date, very few live-action films have remediated comics' motion lines, especially compared to compositional mimesis, which runs rampant throughout comic book filmmaking. This is most likely because motion lines are redundant in a moving image medium; since movement in film is explicit rather than implicit, seen rather than inferred, the only cinematographic purpose of motion lines would be purely aesthetic and ornamental, as opposed to the comic, where they provide information that allows the viewer to make sense of the narrative action. This is certainly the case in the scene from *V for Vendetta* discussed above. Thus, it seems that motion lines in cinema have a similar overall effect as some of the split-screen compositions in *Hulk*: the result is both more stylistically self-conscious—less immediate, more obviously mediated—and superfluous to the film's narration. Just as *Hulk* employs split screen to redundantly show the same action from two different angles, *V for Vendetta*'s motion lines suggest movement where movement is already plainly perceivable to the viewer. It's style used not at the *expense* of substance but in addition to it.

Another reason, perhaps, for the rarity of motion lines even in comic book films is the issue of tense. It's widely understood that film necessarily takes place in the present tense; even in flashbacks, whatever shot is onscreen is occurring "now" in terms of the viewer's consciousness and perception. Comics, because of the simultaneity of panels on a page and the freedom of the viewer's gaze, are somewhat more complicated than that, but for the purposes of this discussion we only need to consider the tense of the individual panel. When motion lines are used in a comics panel, they are effectively visualizing the immediate past in an abstract way—a past, it's important to note, that the reader doesn't otherwise see. While the tense of certain other image elements is fundamentally tied to the reading

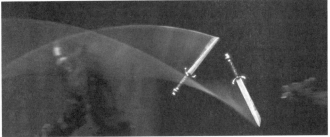

FIGURE 4.13. Still from *The Matrix* and FIGURE 4.14. Still from *V for Vendetta*

process—in a panel containing two dialogue balloons, for instance, the first balloon will be relegated to the past as soon as the reader moves on to the second balloon—motion lines tend to remain definitively in the narrational past. Another example of cinematic motion lines appears in the climactic moments of *Superman* and demonstrates this in a more complicated way than *Vendetta*. In order to reverse a natural disaster that resulted in Lois Lane's death, Superman reverses the rotation of Earth, thereby turning back time. In representing this feat, the camera assumes an extreme long shot of Earth itself; the microscopic figure of Superman is invisible from this distance, but we can track his movement through a white motion line that wraps around the planet. A frame capture from this shot—such as figure 4.15—reads very much like a comic book panel, with the motion line indicating Superman's previous trajectory up to his current coordinates. The motion line is used strategically here to make an otherwise indiscernible action—Superman flying around the world—legible to the viewer. Without the motion line, it would merely appear as though Earth's rotation slowed, stopped, and then proceeded in the other direction of its own accord. In this case, then, the convention functions very similarly to its use in comics, making visible what would otherwise not be visible, using a symbolic

FIGURE 4.15. Still from *Superman*

visual device to communicate an otherwise unrepresentable action. Traces of the past, moreover, remain visible in the cinematic present, as they would be in a comic panel. But movement is actually key to this shot as well. In a static frame such as figure 4.15, Superman's trajectory is legible but Earth's movement is not. We need the cinematic movement to understand the relationship between Superman's superspeed flight around the planet and the planet's altered rotation. So whereas the motion lines were entirely supplemental to the represented movement in *V for Vendetta*, here they are additive: a symbiosis of the different mediums' representational codes.

A final example further complicates the situation. In *Scott Pilgrim vs. the World*, motion lines (and other instances of expressive intermediality) are used throughout the film in an extremely self-conscious and overtly stylized fashion. Since *Scott Pilgrim* is the subject of a lengthy analysis in the next chapter, I will limit my comments here to its use of motion lines specifically. Largely, their use aligns with that seen in *V for Vendetta*: for instance, in fight scenes, punches, kicks, and jumps most often leave a trail of—to paraphrase Wolk's words quoted at the beginning of this chapter—parallel lines of (CG) ink. While visually distinct from the wispy lines in *Vendetta*, they function similarly as nondiegetic (and narratively redundant) traces of movement. But there is also a unique application of this aesthetic device, seen in one scene when Scott and his friends are socializing at the Rockit prior to his band's gig. Scott's seventeen-year-old girlfriend, Knives Chau, has just arrived, and promptly throws herself at him. As she kisses him, the film ramps into slow motion and CG hearts flutter about their lips. This creates an awkward moment for the entire group, but especially for Scott, who is trying—more than a little desperately—to impress his true crush,

Ramona Flowers, who bears witness to the entire spectacle. What happens next is a panel-for-panel remediation of a brief half-page sequence from the graphic novel *Scott Pilgrim's Precious Little Life* where the various characters glare at each other in turn. In the comic, the asymmetrical panel shapes and motion lines give the sequence a sense of visual dynamism, but the latter, unusually, aren't used to indicate movement per se; instead, they only reinforce the emotions and eyelines between the characters, none of whom are actually mobile in the scene.

FIGURE 4.16. Page from *Scott Pilgrim's Precious Little Life*

One of *Scott Pilgrim* director Edgar Wright's stylistic signatures through-out his oeuvre is the use of the whip pan and other kinetic in-camera shot transitions: in this short sequence, he uses quick zooms and focus racking to remediate this four-panel sequence in cinematic terms. In doing so, he makes use of motion lines, which now accentuate the movement, not of any-thing within the mise-en-scène, but rather of the camera lens itself during these quick zooms. The camera starts on Knives, who turns her head to look at Ramona; the camera quickly zooms out, settles on a two-shot, and racks focus to Ramona. This pattern repeats several times—Ramona to Stacy, Stacy to Scott, Scott to Wallace, Wallace to Jimmy—in quick, rhythmic succession. The latent movement in the comic becomes literalized in this sequence; however, instead of V's knives or Superman's flight, the motion lines are used to emphasize the movement of Wright's kinetic camera and the perspectives it creates: in other words, the cinematic apparatus itself is being put on display. This example further emphasizes how motion lines are symbolic and nondiegetic, tied to representational convention rather than diegetic movement. Indeed, my argument throughout this book has been that the cinematic remediation of comics tends to lay bare the inherent arti-fice of cinema, putting style on ostentatious display in a way that forces the viewer to take notice. This often involves breaking the rules of classical style, but this sequence manages to maintain visual continuity while also being stylistically conspicuous. Indeed, the sequence presents extremely coherent spatial geography: each zoom and cut happens on a precise eyeline match, and characters often reappear within each other's shots, which allows the viewer to grasp the spatial relations between them with precision. And yet the fast zooms remind us that we're watching a world mediated by film, while the motion lines remind us that we're watching a film whose style is itself mediated by comics. The laws of continuity editing and the ostenta-tious remediation of comics through film style are not, in this case, mutually exclusive. Nevertheless, it remains salient that comic book conventions are being privileged over the "invisible," self-effacing style afforded by continu-ity editing, that the act (and fact) of mediation is being emphasized over the illusion of unmediated access to the diegetic world.

FIGURES 4.17, 4.18, AND 4.19. Stills from *Scott Pilgrim vs. the World*

Panel Time: Visualizing the Reading Experience through Slow Motion

The final manifestation of temporal remediation in the comic book film is also the most complex and yet, increasingly, among the most widely seen in comic book films and beyond. Its complexity lies in the fact that it doesn't remediate the *aesthetics* of the medium but rather the *reading process* that is unique to comics. How does the reader interpret and synthesize a narrative from the series of discrete static images offered by a comic book? The answer is closure—"the mental process whereby readers of comics bridge the temporal and spatial incompleteness of the diegesis that occurs in the gutters between panels, thereby participating in the creation of narrative"[52]—which is the most fundamental process of reading comics, performing tasks equivalent to cinematic movement (between frames) and editing (between shots): "In a very real sense," McCloud writes, "comics *is* closure."[53] And just as gutters play a salient role in the construction of comics, closure plays a salient role in the experience of reading them. In cinema, the rapid succession of still images allows viewers to perceive uninterrupted movement on the screen: due to the lack of perceivable visual downtime between each frame, the brain automatically performs a process analogous to closure when watching a film, connecting what are actually discrete images into what is ultimately perceived as fluid motion. McCloud argues that comics readers must consciously work to produce the same effect of seamlessness whenever they read comics, actively filling in the gaps between panels and thereby turning the gutter into a site of productivity and collaboration.[54]

Though this theory has assumed prominence in comics scholarship, I think McCloud overemphasizes the reader's participatory role between panels; indeed, the vast majority of comics are expressly designed so that readers *don't* need to perform the kind of mental work he describes. In most mainstream comics, closure as a conscious readerly process only becomes necessary when presented with visual or narrative ambiguities that create interpretive difficulties. In Thierry Groensteen's words, "The continuity attributed to the fictional world . . . allows [readers] to *effortlessly* fill in the gaps of the narration."[55] McCloud's example of closure is a two-panel sequence in which the first panel shows an angry man swinging an axe at another man, screaming "NOW YOU DIE!"; the second panel is a long shot of a skyline with the exclamation "EEYAA!!" superimposed above the buildings.[56] McCloud claims that every reader must *consciously* imagine the specifics of the murder.[57] Following Groensteen, I would counter that knowing a murder took place (we already know that an angry man was swinging an axe) is sufficient to understand the scene and that most readers will be willing to proceed with the narrative while accepting this minimal amount of narrative ambiguity: how quickly the axe was swung, where it made contact, and other grisly details aren't necessary to reach a functional degree of narrative comprehension. If the victim is shown alive and well later in the narrative, only then does the representational gap become significant (because it was deliberately misleading the reader), but otherwise we are given enough information to proceed without confusion. Nevertheless, the concept of closure as conceptualized by McCloud has taken firm hold in comics studies, perhaps because it allows us to understand the medium in a way that brings it closer to cinema, a medium with a greater body of scholarship and theory than comics, not to mention critical prestige and cultural currency. The theory of closure smooths over the gaps inherent in comics, imbuing it with a sense of aesthetic unity, while also granting the reader a significant degree of agency: both are very appealing ideas for those looking to justify comics' aesthetic value.[58] Even if closure is not a necessary *fact* of reading comics, it has certainly influenced the way we *conceptualize* the act of reading them in the wake of McCloud's *Understanding Comics*, which has become comics studies' equivalent of Bordwell and Thompson's *Film Art*.

Other, less controversial aspects of the comics reading experience are also relevant to the present discussion. For instance, it is unambiguously the case that comics consist of sequentially organized static images.[59] They may be dynamic static images, per Ndalianis, but they are static nonetheless. Luca Somigli, translating scholarship on Italian *fumetti*, writes:

> As Daniele Barbieri explains in his excellent structural study of the comics medium, the panel itself is not simply an image frozen in time, but it can be used to represent a duration through a number of different techniques (use of motion lines, repetition of the image as with an overexposed photograph, particular arrangements of the balloons, and sound effects, etc.): "Therefore, we have one image—traditionally corresponding to one instant—within which there is a duration. With the comics, the panel no longer *represents* an *instant*, but a *duration*: just like cinema."[60]

The difference between cinema and comics, then, is not in *what* they each represent (a duration of time) but in *how* they represent it: via the static privileged instants (or image-events) of comics or via the flow of cinema's any-instant-whatevers. Although movement is absolute—an object is either in motion or at rest—there are degrees of movement, and slow-motion cinematography inarguably works to bring photographed movement *closer* to stasis than it otherwise would be if shot and projected in the "real time" of 24 frames per second. In other words, film's representational flexibility vis-à-vis time allows viewing duration and diegetic duration to be distinct from each other, just as they are in comics. Any cinematic intervention that divorces viewing duration from diegetic duration may thus potentially qualify as figural intermediality, which refers to the cinematic remediation of the reading experience of comics: in other words, closure.

Though "real time" is not often adhered to by films for their entire running time—a film that takes two hours to view usually represents much longer than two hours of diegetic time—it is usually the default mode of representation within each shot because it most closely mirrors our natural perception of the world.[61] Doane's explanation of cinematic "real time" is worth quoting in full:

> In the technical language of filmmaking, the term *real time* refers to the duration of a single shot (assuming the shot is neither fast nor slow motion). If the physical film is not cut and its projection speed equals its shooting speed (usually somewhere between sixteen and twenty-four frames per second), the movement on the screen will unfold in a time that is isomorphic with profilmic time, or what is generally thought to be our everyday lived experience of time—hence the term *real*. The time of the apparatus matches, is married to, the time of the action or the scene.[62]

Naturally, there is some controversy over whether a mechanically standardized "real time" could ever jibe with individuals' subjective experiences of time; for instance, Bergson argues that "each individual inhabits their own unique temporal flow," making time "highly subjective" rather than rigidly objective.[63] The term "real time" should therefore be understood not as an objective account of time but rather as a cinematic construct whereby the shooting speed (measured in frames per second) matches the projection speed, resulting in an equivalence between diegetic time and viewing duration. By contrast, there is no possibility for "real time" in comics, because there will never be a perfect or guaranteed correlation between the diegetic duration of the narrative and the reading time of its narration. Indeed, the reader's ability to advance through the narrative at his or her own pace suggests a closer relationship to psychological time, which may be closer to Bergson's understanding of lived time than to Doane's cinematic real time (which, in the case of static long takes, often feels psychologically shorter or longer than its "real" duration, especially when intensified continuity editing conditions viewers to expect cuts at least every few seconds). The cinematic remediation of comic books may therefore manifest in a disavowal of real time, in an increased sense of temporal flux that results in a phenomenological ebb and flow.

In the wake of *The Matrix*, which popularized a unique articulation of slow-motion cinematography that became known as "bullet time" (using, it should be noted, a variation on Muybridge's multicamera setup), extreme slow-motion photography became a popular and common visual effect in Hollywood blockbusters, including many comic book films. What I refer to as the "panel moment"—a shot in a comic book film in which the frame rate alternates between real time and slow motion, replicating the elastic temporality of the comic book and the process of closure between privileged instants—is distinct from, though often confused with, bullet time. The confusion is understandable, given their shared reliance on slow motion, which Bob Rehak has evocatively described as the "romanticization of the pause."[64] The most significant distinction between these two articulations of slow motion is that while bullet time serves both narrative *and* stylistic functions, panel moments serve no ostensible narrative function; they only exist as a function of remediating the comic book medium and, more specifically, the reading process. By contrast, bullet time is used in *The Matrix* because characters like Neo, Trinity, and Morpheus have the ability to bend and slow their own subjective experience of diegetic time. In other words, time is being altered in both the world of the film and in the screen representation of that world; both the audience *and* the characters experience the narrative events depicted in bullet time. Similarly, in *Spider-Man*, Peter Parker's "spider-sense" is represented in a style similar to bullet time, demonstrating his superior reflexes and response time compared to normal people. When his spider-sense is activated by nearby danger, Peter experiences the world in bullet time, allowing him to outmaneuver his aggressors. In both *X-Men: Days of Future Past* (2014) and *X-Men: Apocalypse* (2016), playful sequences involving mutant speedster Quicksilver make use of intermittent slow motion to depict the character's subjective perception of the world while also making his movements visible and legible to film audiences. As in *The Matrix*, the use of slow motion is motivated in these cases by the character's perception and experience of the world rather than—or in addition to—the aesthetic effect that it produces. In a sense, these scenes take place in real time *and* slow motion, because the "real time" experienced by the characters is different from ours. In panel moments, however, the characters depicted do not experience the world more slowly, just as comic book characters do not experience their world as a series of static instants; in both cases, it is only the reader or viewer whose temporal experience is altered. When certain moments are presented more slowly than others, it is solely to heighten the aesthetic impact of the composition and to allow the viewer more time to contemplate the image: in other words, to privilege certain instants among the any-instant-whatevers that compose the film. While bullet time makes manifest the subjective experience of the characters, panel moments visualize the experience of the comics reader. Recalling the discussion of motion lines above, panel moments are therefore an entirely nondiegetic effect.

While panel moments have appeared in various comic book films—only a few of which are discussed here—the example par excellence comes from *300* and is known as the "Crazy Horse" shot, so called for the name given to the multicamera rig used during its filming. The shot, which lasts for a full seventy-two seconds, is possibly the most memorable one in the film that is not also a mimetic composition referencing the original graphic novel. In the shot, which can almost be considered a self-contained battle sequence, King Leonidas slashes his way through several enemy soldiers before hurling his spear through the air; the camera follows the spear as it flies and finally hits its target, impaling a soldier and sending him to the ground; he slashes through several more enemies, and the shot completes as he buries his sword in a fallen enemy soldier. Throughout the shot, the speed of playback changes about twenty times in total, alternately ramping up into slow motion to emphasize an arresting panel moment before ramping down to hasten the transition to the next such moment: the variations in playback speed mirror the process of closure as defined by McCloud, pausing over the "panels" and rushing through the connective tissue contained in the "gutter" that separates them. The effect of this shot in particular was achieved by shooting with three cameras at once—each equipped with a lens of a unique focal length but all shooting from the same angle[65]—all recording at 150 frames per second,[66] much faster than the typical frame rate of 24 frames per second. In postproduction, these separate shots were edited together to create the illusion of one seamless take, with twenty-seven cuts masked by digital morph and zoom effects.[67] The presence of these hidden edits rein-forces the illusory nature of temporal flow in *300*, where what appears fluid is actually made up of separately filmed elements that are stitched together in postproduction using digital editing technologies. Stephen Prince describes the scene thusly: "The action appears to be covered in a single camera move, and this appearance conceals the actual basis of the sequence that lies in montage. The wholeness of space here is a digital palimpsest, but one that advertises its constructed origins through the insistent artifice of the speed ramps."[68] The shot is also intermedial insofar as it remediates how comics are read—as a series of separate images that are connected together only by the reader's intervention—via a series of panel moments, which provide a seamless rendering of duration that also isolates privileged instants.

FIGURES 4.20, 4.21, AND 4.22. Stills from *300*

Prince also writes that "the abrupt zooms and speed ramps give the shot a hyper-kinetic quality, a herky-jerky, spasmodic energy, a degree of artifice so pronounced that the viewer is forced to take notice."[69] Indeed, such moments of extreme stylization demand that the viewer pay attention not just to the narrative but also to the film's self-consciously intermedial style of presentation. Films like *300*, *Scott Pilgrim vs. the World*, and *Sin City* put comic book film style on the same level of importance as narration, even as style and narration often work separately rather than together: the style works to create *intermedial* meaning rather than, or in addition to, narrative meaning. While other scholars have picked up on the connection between slow motion and comic book form, the discussion has largely confused the differences between panel moments and bullet time outlined above. In a chapter about comics aesthetics in film adaptations, Burke writes that "bullet time does not de-narrativize the film as some digital effects might, but allows the spectator to explore the narrative spatially (much as they would in a comic), viewing several areas of interest with a degree of participation rarely afforded by cinema's relentless images."[70] His analysis is entirely apt with reference to bullet time, but the panel moments found in films like *300* don't actually perform such spatializing work. Constandinides also writes about *The Matrix*, *300*, and *Wanted*—a film based on a graphic novel by Mark Millar and J. G. Jones—as though they all employ slow motion in the same way, referring to what I have called panel moments as "in-between moments" or as "blood-spraying time" (and, moreover, not making any distinctions between this effect, bullet time, and traditional slow-motion cinematography, despite considerable aesthetic, narrative, and technological differences between each). He notes that "the different temporal rhythms of motion and digital compositing replace *the gutter* between comic book panels," which is accurate for much of *300* and some of *Wanted*, but none of *The Matrix*.[71]

Wanted does indeed feature several panel moments, but they are interspersed among a variety of other slow-motion-based stylistic interventions that collectively give the action scenes a "jagged, staccato rhythm," to use McCloud's phrasing.[72] One of the first instances of slow motion occurs just a few minutes into the film as an assassin runs down a hallway, bursts through a window, and flies between buildings, guns blazing and covered with shattered glass. Unlike *300*, the slow motion here and elsewhere in the film is, in fact, diegetically motivated: this assassin, along with many of the film's central characters, has the ability to respond to stimuli incredibly quickly (the pseudo-scientific reason given by the film is that their hearts beat upward of four hundred times per minute, producing excessive amounts of adrenaline). At this point in the narrative, this hasn't been explained to the viewer, but there is a shot that suggests that the slow motion is linked to the assassin's subjectivity. In this shot, which directly precedes the transition to slow motion, we see the world from the assassin's point of view: the first-person perspective, shot reverse shot editing pattern (the shot is bookended by close-ups of the assassin's eyes), and the throbbing of the frame in time with the heartbeats on the soundtrack all align the camera's perspective with that of the character. After this point, the slow motion reflects the character's subjective experience of time, as in *The Matrix*. Within this shot sequence, however, there are several instances in which the camera ramps back to regular speed, giving a dynamic, staccato rhythm to the scene: in other words, panel moments. The reader may think I have contradicted myself here, since panel moments by definition are not associated with a character's subjectivity; however, that remains the case in this example, since the *regular speed* cinematography is a purely aesthetic effect untethered to the assassin's slowed experience of time. Therefore the panel moments in this sequence are merely the inverse of those seen in *300*, in which the regular speed footage is associated with Leonidas's perspective while the slow motion represents a purely stylistic intervention.[73]

While not diegetically motivated, panel moments may also serve a narrative purpose: to increase the legibility of rapid or ephemeral moments. As we saw at the outset of this chapter, comics are extremely well suited to representing fast movements—like the Flash running—that cinema would have difficulty showing clearly in real time. By contrast, comics offer the opportunity for *every represented moment* to be pored over and scrutinized: diegetic duration holds no sway over the reader, and cannot prevent him or her from focusing on the most miniscule of details. The panel moment can't offer this, but it's a step in that direction, away from real time and toward panel time. *Wanted* features a cheeky demonstration of this in a shot wherein the protagonist, Wesley, smashes a keyboard across his coworker's face. He strikes the blow at full speed, letting loose many of the keys; the missing letters then hang in midair, virtually static in a panel moment, allowing us to make out the phrase "FUCK YOU" (the second "u" is a tooth), before real time resumes and the keys fall quickly to the ground. This is precisely the kind of visual play that only seems possible in the static world of comics but that the panel moment makes legible to film viewers; if played in real time, the keys would be a blur and the joke would be lost. Panel moments enable

FIGURE 4.23. Still from *Wanted*

these kinds of privileged instants to be appreciated onscreen longer than their diegetic duration: not indefinitely, nor even for as long as the reader cares to look before moving on, but nevertheless untethered both from real time and the psychological time of the characters.

This technique works similarly well for complicated action choreography, allowing the skirmishes between superheroes and villains to be witnessed with specificity rather than as an indistinguishable flurry of attacks and counterattacks. The latter is what many contemporary action films seem to provide, ignoring classical continuity construction and editing patterns in favor of audiovisual chaos. The opening sequence of *Avengers: Age of Ultron*, with its constantly mobile camera—there's no stable 180° line governing our perspective here—and frenetic action, is a perfect example of what Matthias Stork has dubbed "chaos cinema."[74] Though presented in one seemingly unbroken take—the mind reels at the amount of CG montage going on within this single "shot"—rather than a succession of quick cuts, it's nevertheless much more a kinetic experience than a coherent presentation of characters moving through space; as a hyperbolic revision of the tracking shot following the assembled Avengers battling through hordes of aliens in the third act of *The Avengers*, this opening set piece certainly ups the ante on superheroic spectacle. Before finally cutting, the shot reaches its climax in a panel moment that displays the entire team in profile, lunging toward offscreen right. The shot is obviously carefully designed, its CG elements composed and layered in depth across multiple planes of action to showcase each individual character in the most dynamic way possible. In short, it's like a comic book panel at the end of an otherwise very cinematic action sequence, a brief respite of near stasis following the relentless momentum of the camera during the preceding action beats. Similar to a single splash page punctuating the end of a comic book, the panel moment hits all the harder due to its placement at the climax of this chaotic long take, with which it contrasts sharply. The action scenes in *The Amazing Spider-Man 2* also employ panel moments in this way to reproduce the elastic temporality associated with comics reading and to privilege important instants in the flow of images. However, instead of using a single panel moment to emphasize the end of a spectacular sequence, *The Amazing Spider-Man 2* (and, to a lesser extent, its predecessor *The Amazing Spider-Man* [2012]) incorporates panel time throughout as a way to make its complex action choreography legible and to create comics-like variation in its editing rhythms.[75] Recalling the compositional mimesis of *Daredevil* discussed earlier in this chapter, *The Amazing Spider-Man*'s final shot combines an allusion to the cover image of *The Amazing Spider-Man* #301 (June 1988) with the added slow-motion emphasis of panel time.

It's no coincidence that many of the most visually striking applications of slow-motion cinematography have appeared in comic book films, though panel moments certainly don't exhaust the ways in which comic book film style demonstrates an interest in manipulating the representation of time. Films like *X-Men: Days of Future Past* and *Avengers: Age of Ultron* both use slow motion to make Quicksilver's superspeed legible (and the latter also uses *V for Vendetta*-esque motion lines to that effect, usually in lieu of slow motion rather than in addition to it). The original Spider-Man trilogy uses bullet time to represent the superhero's heightened sense of immediate danger.

FIGURE 4.24. Still from *Avengers: Age of Ultron*

LEFT
FIGURE 4.25. Cover of
*The Amazing Spider-
Man* #301

BOTTOM
FIGURE 4.26. Still
from *The Amazing
Spider-Man*

Dredd (2012) uses extreme slow-motion cinematography—shot at up to 3,000 frames per second![76]—to visually represent the warped subjectivities of drug users under the influence of a time-bending psychedelic. If cinema's gutter exists in the moments between frames—the "lost time" of Muybridge's chronophotography—such advances in slow motion minimize that gutter past the point of negligibility. In addition to its rampant use of slow-motion effects, *Wanted* also features two scenes in which time comes to a halt and then reverses. A bullet freezes in time after producing an exit wound; time then continues in reverse, showing us the bullet's complex trajectory—through, for instance, the hole in a donut—culminating with its reentry back into the gun from which it was fired. The initial freeze frame undoubtedly functions as a panel moment, stopping time out of sheer aesthetic interest, as do some of the slower and more intricate shots within the sequence (e.g., the donut in figure 4.28). But this reversal of time's arrow represents an interest in time's malleability that is broader than the panel moment or slow motion. (We also see this in Superman's reversal of Earth's rotation at the climax of *Superman*.) Cinema has been "perceived as *the* exemplar of temporal irreversibility,"[77] but Wesley's bullet and Superman are similarly able to defy the laws of time, just as comic book readers are free to flip through pages as they choose, traveling to the past or future at will, and surveying a span of time simultaneously as it's arrayed across the page. Digital cinema—and especially its attendant home video technologies—further dissolve the link between cinema and temporal linearity.

Given comic book film style's inherent interest in issues related to movement, comic book films employ a variety of stylistic means to appropriate, play with, and negotiate the dynamic stasis and elastic temporality associated with the comic book medium. Compositional mimesis provokes a memory image of a comic book panel whose stasis contrasts with the moving image remediation being viewed; the use of motion lines in live action appropriates a symbolic convention from comics; and the panel moment, as well as other divergences from real time cinematography, replicate the unregulated temporal fluidity of comics as well as the staccato rhythm of the reading experience. Some films employ these techniques subtly, others obviously. Many filmmakers may not even be aware of the connections being forged between these two media when they stylize their films in these ways. (For all I know, *Wanted*'s panel moments may very well be failed attempts at replicating *The Matrix*'s bullet time, their evocation of closure being an inadvertent but productive by-product of this failure.) Indeed, the kinds of

FIGURES 4.27, 4.28, AND 4.29. Stills from *Wanted*

stylistic interventions that I've discussed in this chapter may be common enough in contemporary Hollywood cinema that many viewers now let them pass by unnoticed; speed ramping, for instance, is increasingly used in all manner of blockbusters, as well as video games and live sports' "instant replay," wherein it serves to heighten the perceived impact and make fast, intricate movements more legible to viewers. Stylistic gestures such as the panel moment thus have the potential to be not just intermedial but *polymedial*, evoking a variety of media simultaneously. The next chapter explores two comic book films in depth that embody the environment of polymedia, remediating comics as one part of a larger media ecology.

CHAPTER 5

THE POLYMEDIAL COMIC BOOK FILM

The preceding three chapters have unpacked the main ways in which cinema's ongoing fascination with the form, conventions, and content of comic books have manifested in innovative or novel approaches to film style. But the phenomenon of remediation is hardly limited to this one intermedial trajectory; like film, comics exist within a broader media ecology and are just as likely to be interested in representing other media using their own unique formal mechanisms. This is a rich enough vein that it could be the subject of its own monograph concerning the role remediation has played in the historical poetics of comics; for the purposes of the present investigation, however, this phenomenon has the potential to complicate film adaptations of comics that are interested in remediation, resulting in films whose stylistic systems remediate a wide variety of media in addition to comics. This is certainly an apt description of two of the densest and most complex examples of comic book film style to date: Edgar Wright's *Scott Pilgrim vs. the World* and Zack Snyder's *Watchmen*. While both of these films remediate comics in ways that recall and extend the conversations that began earlier in this book, this is not all they do. In adapting comics texts that are themselves rife with remediation—with targets ranging from video games, anime, television, and various forms of prose, to name just a few—*Scott Pilgrim* and *Watchmen* perform what I call second-order remediation, essentially becoming self-contained media "ecosystems" unto themselves.[1] Second-order remediation is omnivorous, wide-ranging, and polymorphous; these films don't just represent one additional medium using the distinct representational processes of another, but rather filter an array of different media through a cinematic sieve. While previous chapters attended to the representation of comics through film specifically, *Scott Pilgrim* and *Watchmen* don't limit themselves in this way, instead adopting an "everything-but-the-kitchen-sink" approach. These are not merely cinematic remediations of comics, but cinematic remediations of comics that are themselves chockablock with remediations of their own. It is here that the focused intermediality discussed in previous chapters gives way to a more all-encompassing *polymediality*.

As coined by the cultural anthropologists Mirca Madianou and Daniel Miller, polymedia refers to an environment within convergence culture wherein media—referring collectively to technologies, platforms, and applications—are defined primarily based on the "communicative opportunities" they represent rather than by their inherent or distinctive qualities compared to other media. These different media collectively form "an 'integrated structure' within which each individual medium is defined in relational terms in the context of all other media" rather than as discrete and autonomous forms. In this context, "the emphasis shifts from a focus on the qualities of each particular medium as a discrete technology, to an understanding of new media as an environment of affordances."[2] While Madianou and Miller are primarily interested in the ways that polymedia has transformed how transnational families navigate their interpersonal communications across national borders, the concept of polymedia can also be adapted to illuminate the approach to film style taken in films like *Scott Pilgrim* and *Watchmen*. Similarly to how social actors select and switch between the media they have at hand to satisfy the various social, emotional, and moral requirements of different communicative acts—"what cannot be achieved by email, can be accomplished by webcam, or instant messaging or a phone call"[3]—so too can films remediate various media in order to draw upon the specific narrative and aesthetic effects and affects uniquely associated with them. In so doing, they don't just become hypermediated; they also reflect a world that is itself hypermediated. So while comic book film style and remediation in general are not new or digitally specific phenomena by any means, polymedia seems only to emerge in the screen-saturated contemporary world. As Steven Shaviro puts it in *Post-Cinematic Affect*, we now live in spaces where "nothing is direct or 'unmediated,' and nothing exists outside of the mediasphere."[4] For Madianou and Miller, "Polymedia is ultimately about a new set of social relations of technology, rather than merely a technological development of increased convergence."[5] In terms of film aesthetics, though, polymedia can also refer to the ways in which film texts incorporate a heterogeneous variety of media forms into their stylistic systems, denying the primacy of the "cinematic" over other modes of mediated expression. Instead, polymedia recognizes cinema's place as one medium within an increasingly screen- and image-saturated world.

Again, while this state of affairs is not totally determined by technological factors, polymedia is obviously enabled by media convergence, and specifically the digitization of media and social/cultural experience more generally. Polymedia is a consequence of media convergence and widespread remediation,[6] the combination of which has exploded the number of media and facilitated their availability on a massive scale. To some extent, many of these media are interchangeable in terms of their use value, and even more so in terms of their shared (digital) technological basis. In such a massively mediated environment, the demarcation of individual media—their unique identities as discrete technologies, platforms, or applications—becomes increasingly blurred. While cinema is certainly beyond the scope of Madianou and Miller's study, it has hardly been immune to this symptom of media convergence. As André Gaudreault and Philippe Marion write in *The End of Cinema? A Medium in Crisis in the Digital Age*,

> We are ... at grips with a system that is coming to the forefront by way of the fragmenting of other media (which are sometimes described as *hypermedia*). This system is replacing an older one in which media enjoyed relative autonomy. To put it more extremely, we might even say that the media at greatest risk of acute crisis in today's media chorus, those media that risk becoming isolated, are those that do not hybridize.[7]

For cinema, this phenomenon started emerging most forcefully in the 1990s when moving image media began the transition to digital in earnest. As Bolter and Grusin recognize, "Hollywood films, such as *Natural Born Killers* [1994] and *Strange Days* [1995], mix media and styles unabashedly." They link this directly to the contemporaneous "[televised] news programs [that] feature multiple video streams, split-screen displays, composites of graphics and text—a welter of media that is somehow meant to make the news more perspicuous."[8] The aesthetic revolution that television news was experiencing at this time can be traced back to MTV in the 1980s, when discrete instances of images and text were being "fragmented, rendered discontinuous, divisible, and liable to recombination . . . like never before."⁹ We might also connect this aesthetic with the logic of the desktop computer and its multiple "windows," which was emerging around the same time.

Predating all of these, however, is another multiply "windowed" text-image hybrid: comics. It may merely be coincidence, but as media converge they increasingly draw on the representational techniques and aesthetic features that have always defined comics as a medium. Jared Gardner has made a similar observation regarding the overlap between the logic of new media and that which has been inherent to comics from the medium's earliest incarnations:

> If the digital age is marked by a shift toward the open-ended combinations of the database over traditional narrative, as Lev Manovich and others have argued, comics has necessarily foregrounded the activities of selection, combination, and navigation from its origins. Indeed, . . . it is the structural affinities of the comics form with the "database aesthetic" that has contributed to the increasing visibility and relevance of the comics form in the twenty-first century.¹⁰

It's strange that Bolter and Grusin seem to question the ability of these techniques to render the news in a lucid manner, since they demand active rather than passive viewing, require a variety of modes of engagement (reading, viewing, hearing), and encourage viewers to make connections between the different flows of information on simultaneous offer. The skills that comics readers have always had become increasingly useful, if not crucial, in this environment: "As film completes its ongoing translation into digital media," Gardner continues, "comics are suddenly increasingly relevant once again to the work of making movies."¹¹

Though comics can hardly be described as new media, their particular formal properties have made them useful frames for the kind of media hybridization that defines convergence culture in general and polymediality in particular. As *Scott Pilgrim* and *Watchmen* demonstrate in their original form as sequential art, the representational flexibility of comics—with its dynamic combination of stylized drawn images, graphic text, multiple juxtaposed windows on the diegesis, and the necessity of an active reader to connect all of these features together—allows the medium to easily represent a variety of other media, and in ways that are increasingly echoed in a variety of other mediated contexts. Comic book film style—with its previously demonstrated interests in combining text and image, in fracturing and multiplying screen space into multiple simultaneous views, and in representing time in an abstracted manner—can be extended to polymedial status fairly naturally. Using *Scott Pilgrim* and "The Ultimate Cut" of *Watchmen* as case studies, this chapter explicates the ways in which comic book film style may give way to a more polymedial approach, integrating film and comics within a larger integrated structure of media. These two films, however, achieve this in different ways. While *Scott Pilgrim* embodies a "post-cinematic" approach that seamlessly incorporates a variety of media into its representational style, switching between and often combining them into densely polymedial flourishes, *Watchmen: The Ultimate Cut* presents a variation on transmedia storytelling, positioning the comic book film as one component within a larger structure of texts and media. We'll begin by looking at *Scott Pilgrim*.

Scott Pilgrim vs. the Hypermediated World

As Shaviro defines it, the "post-cinematic" era is one in which "digital technologies, together with neoliberal economic relations, have given birth to radically new ways of manufacturing and articulating lived experience."[12] Under a post-cinematic regime, "all phenomena pass through a stage of being processed in the form of digital code," and as a result we can no longer "meaningfully distinguish between 'reality' and its multiple simulations; they are all woven together in one and the same fabric."[13] This perfectly describes how the characters in Wright's film adaptation of Bryan Lee O'Malley's graphic novel series live their lives and experience their surroundings, as well as the subject position that the film constructs for its viewers via subjective third-person narration. The plot of *Scott Pilgrim*, in both its printed and cinematic manifestations, filters a generic romantic comedy premise (boy meets girl . . .) through the conventions of other media, and platform/fighting video games (. . . boy must be victorious in an increasingly difficult series of "boss battles" to get/rescue girl) in particular. Twenty-three-year-old Torontonian Scott Pilgrim, enamored of recent American émigré Ramona Flowers but dating seventeen-year-old Knives Chau, must combat Ramona's seven evil exes in order to win her heart. Significantly, Scott and his friends are obsessed with the video games of their youth, the aesthetics and narrative logic of which factor into O'Malley and

Wright's representations in various ways. While the narrative can easily be read as an allegory about the difficulties of accepting a potential romantic partner's past baggage (and them accepting yours), neither the comics nor the film presents the hypermediation of the diegesis as anything other than the literal truth of this storyworld; when the narrative adopts a video game logic, it is not tied to Scott's subjectivity or that of an unreliable narrator. On these grounds, the film has been understood as a contemporary exercise in magical realism,[14] as has the comic,[15] but both are better described as reflections and manifestations of a post-cinematic media ecology in which "video screens and speakers, moving images and synthesized sounds, are dispersed pretty much everywhere"[16] and therefore have a profound impact on how we see and interact with the world.

In O'Malley's original series of six graphic novels, the comic book medium functions as the filter through which video games and other media are represented: for instance, diegetic music is communicated through the established sonic conventions of comics (including chord charts to play the songs yourself),[17] and many of O'Malley's stylistic choices reflect the influence of manga (Japanese comics)[18] and anime (Japanese animation). Comics is thereby the vehicle through which the media-saturated lives of Scott and his friends are communicated to readers in O'Malley's work. In shifting the vehicle of representation to film, Wright's *Scott Pilgrim* adds comics to the list of media being remediated. Indeed, the film arguably remediates comics—a medium that, unlike video games or music, has no role or bearing on the characters' lives or experiences—to a greater extent than any other medium. Unlike the comics' remediation of video games, the film's remediation of comics is *not* diegetically motivated but can rather be understood only as an acknowledgment of the narrative's original incarnation, as in other comic book adaptations wherein comic book film style manifests nondiegetically. In *Building Imaginary Worlds*, Mark J. P. Wolf suggests that "how an audience first enters into an imaginary world, and the sequence in which the various works making it up are experienced, can greatly shape the audience's experience of that world."[19] *Scott Pilgrim*'s remediation of comics, then, performs multiple functions simultaneously: it contextualizes the film as a comic book adaptation and as a "comic book come to life," and increases the visual density of the hypermediated post-cinematic world in which the narrative takes place.

Video games are particularly crucial to the narrative, not only in terms of how the representations are stylized and abstracted from a verisimilitudinous reality, but also with regard to the basic logic upon which the storyworld operates. As Padmini Ray Murray describes the comics series,

It meshes a naturalistic narrative and visual style with surreal episodes staged in a video game universe, which gives the comic an almost magic realist feel. *Scott Pilgrim* is a text that embodies transmediality, its very premise assuming at least a notional understanding of video games. In order to be with Ramona, Scott Pilgrim has to defeat her seven evil exes in elaborately staged battles that draw liberally on a vocabulary familiar to gamers—an economy where skills, resources and tenacity are embodied in material objects such as swords, gold coins and levels, and without this awareness, understanding of the comic is notionally incomplete.[20]

What Murray doesn't address here, however, is that there is no sharp division between the "video game universe" and the "naturalistic" universe; in both the comic and the film, the characters move fluidly between them to the point that they cannot really be meaningfully distinguished from each other. Even the most quotidian task is infused with video game aesthetics: for instance, when Scott goes to the bathroom, a power bar with the word "PEE" appears behind him, which drains as his bladder does. Video game conventions are alternately incorporated as digitized elements within the diegesis, such as an extra life icon that appears as a reward after a successful fight, or as their real-world equivalents, such as the flurry of Canadian coinage that replaces the bodies of enemies after they're defeated in battle. Video game conventions such as these are transplanted into the film's contemporary Toronto setting throughout, without comment, as though there was no ontological distinction between playing *Super Mario Bros.* (1985) on a Nintendo and playing bass at band practice.

In his analysis of Richard Kelly's *Southland Tales* (2006), Shaviro identifies the omnipresence of media as an alienating and dislocating experience. He argues that "*Southland Tales* surveys and maps—and mirrors back to us in fictive form—the excessive, overgrown post-cinematic mediasphere. The film bathes us in an incessant flow of images and sounds; it foregrounds the multimedia feed that we take so much for granted, and ponders what it feels like to live our lives within it."[21] *Southland Tales'* "traditionally 'cinematic' sequences are intermixed with a sensory-overload barrage of lo-fi video footage, Internet and cable-TV news feeds, commercials, and simulated CGI environments"[22] that become as oppressive as the surveillance state that the film critiques. Like Kelly's film, *Scott Pilgrim* reproduces the experience of living in such a post-cinematic mediasphere: "sensory overload" is an apt description of the experience of watching Wright's film, as many reviewers have pointed out.[23] But where *Southland Tales* is apocalyptic, *Scott*

FIGURES 5.1 AND 5.2.
Stills from *Scott Pilgrim vs. the World*

Pilgrim is optimistic, playful, and even nostalgic about our interactions with media. For these characters, digital media provides a framework through which to view, understand, and participate in the world. For the viewer, the cinema screen becomes the means through which these various technologies are condensed and contained, their aesthetic markers put on display and to narrative use: the "sensory overload" Shaviro refers to may overwhelm the viewer, but it never overwhelms (digital) cinema's representational capacities. Despite its polymedial aesthetics, intermedial origins, and largely digital production, *Scott Pilgrim* remains a film with a mode of address not dissimilar to more conventional films.

Narratively speaking, *Scott Pilgrim* is ultimately a bildungsroman, and it's largely the framing of the story as a video game that enables Scott to grow as a human being and achieve a measure of self-actualization by the film's conclusion. Video games, premised as they are on the sequential completion of tasks organized into discrete levels, impose a goal-oriented structure onto Scott's heretofore shiftless life. At the beginning of the narrative, Scott is drifting; still broken-hearted one year after his breakup with Envy Adams, his nascent relationship with a high school student six years his junior represents a regression into immaturity for the unemployed university graduate. After he meets Ramona, an American expatriate who has actively run away from her past by moving to Toronto, she becomes the goal to which he aspires. As defined by Jesper Juul, the experience of playing video games is designed around such a set goal, which, even in virtual space, is associated with tangible consequences, feelings, and actions for the player. He divides goals into the following three components:

1. Valorization of the possible outcomes: Some outcomes are described as positive, some as negative.
2. Player effort: The player has to *do* something.
3. Attachment of the player to an aspect of the outcome: The player agrees to be happy if he or she wins the game, unhappy if he or she loses.[24]

Most obviously, the second component allows the film's narrative to proceed; the static, apathetic version of Scott that exists prior to the events depicted in the film is not an active protagonist, but *Scott-as-player* is. The positive valorization of Ramona and their relationship encourages Scott to pursue his goal, despite the increasing difficulty of the challenges in his path. In the midst of this pursuit, Scott becomes invested in completing the "game" irrespective of the goal: his happiness rests on successfully completing the "game" because his dignity is at stake. It's only after he tries, fails, and tries again—even though the chance to date Ramona is seemingly lost—that he is able to earn "the power of self-respect," which is visualized in the film as an "achievement" or "trophy" (an optional side goal that players may choose to pursue while playing a video game). The structure of the narrative is thus thoroughly indebted to the medium of video games; at the same time, however, it represents a diegetic intertextual link to O'Malley's comics, since the film borrows that structure from its source material. This layered appropriation is typical of the film's aesthetic strategy as well: as we'll see later, the film remediates comics at the same time, and using the same techniques, as it does video games.

According to Juul, video games are "half-real" insofar as the inhabited virtual world is imaginary while the rules according to which the player engages with that world are real.[25] *Scott Pilgrim*'s world also seems half-real, straddling the line between video game fantasy and mumblecore-esque

FIGURE 5.3. Still from *Scott Pilgrim vs. the World*

banality, but this appearance warrants a more complicated interpretation. We've already established that the film doesn't oscillate between these two modes but rather combines them (and many more) into a single ontology. The characters in *Scott Pilgrim* don't seem to distinguish between video games, manga, Japanese animation, and their "real" lives; the film doesn't make such distinctions in representing them; and the digital mode of production and distribution doesn't make such distinctions in creating and exhibiting them. In a post-cinematic world, even the real half of Juul's "half-real" is necessarily mediated.

Jeff Thoss argues that both the film and comic book versions of *Scott Pilgrim* "deny their actual mediality to engage in a competition of simulating yet another medium—the video game."[26] The first thirty seconds of the film version alone demonstrate a much more complicated state of affairs than this, in which film style is deployed to create a polymedial representation consisting of both comics and video games remediated cinematically. As we saw in previous chapters, comic book films often begin with credits sequences that announce the intermedial nature of the representations to follow, indicating that the film is to be understood as a live-action comic book, or a comic book "come to life." In a variation on this, *Scott Pilgrim* begins with a digitally degraded version of the Universal logo that suggests that the film to follow is a video game "come to life" or, at the very least, a heavily digitized and mediated representation of the world. (The fact that the film is produced by Universal, whose logo is a globe, literalizes nicely the idea that the world has been digitized.) The degree of pixelization and the eight-bit chiptune[27] timbre of the studio's refashioned fanfare collectively evoke a very particular era in gaming history, marked by low-resolution "sprites" as avatars, two-dimensional imagery, and primitive synthesized soundtracks. The film quickly segues from this eight-bit aesthetic to full live action, albeit one heavily invested in other media, and comics in particular. The opening narration—which is visible onscreen *and* audible as a voice-over on the soundtrack—first announces the film's comic book affiliation through the use of onscreen text written in the same typeface as the comics. The camera then tilts down to reveal a snowy Toronto street; a musical flourish from *The Legend of Zelda* (1986) game series plays on the soundtrack as the camera settles on its first mimetic composition. This shot mirrors the first page of *Scott Pilgrim's Precious Little Life*, with the dialogue balloon realized on the film's audio track. Less than thirty seconds into the film, then, it seems that both comic books and video games will be remediated to significant degrees throughout: more specifically, however, the video game medium has been associated with movement (such as the camera movement in this first shot) and the narrative logic governing the diegetic world, whereas the comic book medium has been associated with narrative exposition, compositional choices, and other nondiegetic interventions. In keeping with the concept of the post-cinematic, however, the divisions between these various languages are not strongly enforced. For instance, the film's sporadic use of voiceover narration reads onscreen comics-style captions aloud, associating the technique with comics, and also comments on victories, defeats, goals achieved, and countdowns, thereby also associating the technique with video games. Both medium-specific tasks are performed by a single voice, though the video game–inspired utterances are sonically degraded, as if produced by a vintage arcade machine. Thus even the narrator's voice resists being associated with a single medium and instead embodies the film's polymedial fusion.

Far from denouncing the cinematic, as Thoss claims, *Scott Pilgrim* is actually heavily invested in the materiality of film. The opening credits sequence, which follows the first scene, explicitly references avant-garde cinema in its use of painted and scratched film. The imagery is strongly reminiscent of drawn-on-film animation or scratch films like Len Lye's *A Colour Box* (1935) or Norman McLaren's *Boogie-Doodle* (1948), featuring bold color clashes,

FIGURES 5.4 AND 5.5.
Stills from *Scott Pilgrim
vs. the World*

FIGURE 5.6. Page from
*Scott Pilgrim's Precious
Little Life*

symbolic representations of characters (e.g., a pair of *sai* for Knives Chau, a guitar for Stephen Stills), and abstract lines and movement—all syncopated to the grungy musical soundtrack. The sequence serves many functions in the film: to give viewers the opportunity to acclimatize themselves to the film's particular rhythms and visual energy;[28] to subtly establish traits or images associated with each character; and to provide a visual representation of Knives's internal reaction to Sex Bob-omb, Scott's band.[29] The sequence may also be interpreted as an example of expressive intermediality, insofar as it forgoes the use of a camera to produce images and instead introduces comics' drawn aesthetic into the proceedings, albeit substituting paper with celluloid.[30]

The post-cinematic draws on the avant-garde insofar as both push against the perceived limitations and boundaries of media. As Lev Manovich describes it,

> When the avant-garde filmmakers collaged multiple images within a single frame, or painted and scratched film, or revolted against the indexical identity of cinema in other ways, they were working against "normal" filmmaking procedures and the intended uses of film technology. (Film stock was not designed to be painted on.) Thus they operated on the periphery of commercial cinema not only aesthetically but also technically.[31]

In this light, the opening credits of *Scott Pilgrim* read very clearly as a mission statement, as a declaration that the interests of the avant-garde—operating on the periphery of the mainstream, going against "intended" or "normal" uses of technology—no longer hold in the digital era of filmmaking. Experiments in polymediality that were once considered avant-garde have become increasingly common today. To quote Manovich again: "The avant-garde move to combine animation, printed texts, and live-action footage is repeated in the convergence of animation, title generation, paint, compositing, and editing systems into all-in-one packages. . . . All in all, what used to be exceptions for traditional cinema have become the normal, intended techniques of digital filmmaking, embedded in technology design itself."[32] It is largely through experiences in intermediality like comic book film style and polymedial films like *Scott Pilgrim* that these changes have taken place. The opening credits' evocation of avant-garde cinema and its emphasis on the materiality of cinema also emphasize *Scott Pilgrim*'s status *as a film* as well as a representative and embodiment of post-cinematic logic.

As the film continues, the use of comics aesthetics becomes more conventional, functioning mostly in the ways that I've described in previous chapters—which is to say, rather than serve the medium-specific purpose that they would in a comic book, these stylistic interventions often duplicate information that is also provided through traditionally cinematic means. For instance, many sound effects that appear on the audio track are also doubled on the image track, appearing graphically as they would in a comic book. *Scott Pilgrim* is notable, however, for its embrace of the various means through which comics visually represent sound. In chapter 2, we saw examples of expressive intermediality via visual onomatopoeia in *Batman: The Movie* and *Super*; in both cases, this was the sole instance of comics' sonic strategies being cinematically rendered. *Scott Pilgrim* features multiple instances of graphic onomatopoeia, including visualizations of Stephen's musical vocalizations ("YEAH!"), a string of "RRRRRRRRs" representing an end-of-school-day bell, "DDDDDDDDDs" representing a steady stream of plucked notes on the electric bass, the "DING-DONG" of a doorbell, and repeated "THONKs" as Scott bangs his head against an electrical pole. In all of these cases, the visualized sounds are not static parts of the moving image, as they were in *Batman: The Movie*. Instead they seem to issue forth from their diegetic source; their animation within the frame represents the

FIGURE 5.7. Still from *Scott Pilgrim vs. the World*

FIGURE 5.8. Two-page spread from *Scott Pilgrim's Precious Little Life*

FIGURE 5.9. Still from *Scott Pilgrim vs. the World*

main difference between the comics and film versions of this convention. And though they don't exist within the diegesis—the sounds exist in the storyworld as sounds but not as both sounds *and* visible objects—they are nevertheless integrated into the three-dimensional space and are often partially obscured by diegetic mise-en-scène elements. In comics, by contrast, representations of sound usually (though not necessarily) appear on top of or above the diegetic world, as a separate layer, in order to remain legible and distinct from the rest of the image.

In one exception to the nondiegetic rule, when Knives professes her love for Scott in the aisles at Sonic Boom—an actual Toronto record store but also a reference to a finishing move in the *Street Fighter* video game series—the word "LOVE" appears in cloud-like pink letters, floating from her mouth toward Scott. At first, it seems that this will follow the same laws as other sonic visualizations, but when the Ramona-smitten Scott waves his hand, the letters evaporate into a pink mist. This is a rare moment of self-reflexivity with regard to comics; while the film is fairly self-reflexive about its relationship to video games throughout—characters are seen playing and talking about games as much as we see them living one—the film's stylistic relationship with comics doesn't otherwise manifest within the diegesis. With a wave of his hand, Scott implicitly recognizes that he's in a comic book as much as he's in a video game.

The film also remediates other ways in which comics represent aural phenomena that weren't explored in chapter 2. Aside from dialogue and onomatopoeia, sound most commonly manifests as "impact stars," jagged lines or shapes that resonate from or surround the source of a sound, which is also usually a point of violent impact. In comics, these shapes may be used in combination with onomatopoeia (e.g., an impact star surrounding an onomatopoeic word, as in figure 2.5) or on their own. As examples of the latter, lightning bolt–shaped images appear when Kim Pine strikes her kick drum (a mimetic composition based on the bottom-left panel in figure 5.10) or when Scott plays his bass in the opening scene. In comics, these effects stand in for sound, but in the film they become a supplement to it, emphasizing the cacophonic grunge of Sex Bob-omb. In the comic, these shapes are the only visual clues that help the reader imagine Sex Bob-omb's sound; the overall impression given by a page like figure 5.8 is that the band is fast, loose, and loud. As Camilo Diaz Pino observes, the use of chord charts suggests that the songs require only "a basic competence" to play, framing "musical creation and performance above all as participatory, inclusive, communal and fun."[33] The film version, by virtue of its soundtrack, is unquestionably more specific. Combined with close-ups (many of the compositions mirror specific panels) and the quick, rhythmic cutting, these visual supplements give the film version all the dynamism of the comic book while rendering in precise detail what the comics leave to the reader's imagination. The sonic shapes don't convey unique narrative information—instead they provide a visual corollary to the soundtrack—but they do contribute to the polymedial density of the film image. In being remediated by the cinema, moreover, the meaning of these aural techniques changes from a figural representation of sound—a storytelling tool—to an iconic representation of the comics medium that serves an indexical function. In the same way that compositional mimesis brings a particular panel to the viewer's consciousness through visual resemblance, expressive intermediality brings the *medium* of comics to mind. If they don't communicate narrative information, such techniques nevertheless emphasize the hybridity and intermediality inherent in comic book film style. In this case, the remediation of comics conventions through film style completely undermines and transforms its original, medium-specific purpose.

Another common comics convention that we see throughout *Scott Pilgrim* is the use of onscreen text as captions. As suggested in the analysis of the opening shots, extra-diegetic onscreen text is primarily used as an expository

FIGURE 5.10. Still from *Scott Pilgrim vs. the World*

tool, a visual equivalent to voiceover narration (which is an apt description for how captions are most often deployed in mainstream comics). In many cases, the use of onscreen text is completely analogous to its use in comics: both provide efficient means of conveying narrative information in a purely visual (and nondiegetic) way. The vast majority of films that employ onscreen text do so sparingly, often to establish the narrative's historical and geographical setting. A film like *Hulk* uses text in precisely this way, but alludes to comics simultaneously by using a comics-esque typeface; in keeping with their remediation of word-image hybridity, *American Splendor* and *Kick-Ass 2* do the same thing, but increase the visual similarity to captions by encasing the text in a rectangular box. Like comics themselves, however, *Scott Pilgrim* is again notable for using extra-diegetic text in a wider variety of ways than the previous examples. This is apparent from the opening shot (see figure 5.4), but then as characters are introduced, small black boxes with narrative information (name, age, and an additional trait) appear in the frame. This strategy is taken directly from the comics, as is the use of chapter titles, which appear sporadically throughout the film. These don't necessarily mark key turning points in the narrative: for instance, one of the captions simply reads "SO YEAH," superimposing the characters' idiomatic and disaffected speech onto a scene transition, as though the film itself was ambivalent about the narrative's direction. Often they are references to the comics, and thereby function as diegetic intertextuality as well as expressive intermediality; for instance, the caption "THE INFINITE SADNESS" marks a low point for Scott in the narrative while also citing *Scott Pilgrim and the Infinite Sadness*, the third in the graphic novel series.[34]

FIGURES 5.11 AND 5.12. Stills from *Scott Pilgrim vs. the World*

As should be clear by now, the film is extremely flexible and generous in its deployment of comics' various expressive strategies. Onscreen text is not used in isolation from other remediated elements but is combined with them. For instance, in figure 5.12, onscreen text is combined with comics art in a crossover between the explicit and expressive categories of intermediality. The right side of the frame darkens (one of many instances in which the on-set lighting is manipulated to emphasize parts of the image), and diegetic time seemingly freezes for a moment of expository narration; as the voice-over informs us of the backstory behind Scott's haircut-related paranoia, a crude comic book image of the title character appears in the darkened screen area, diagramming the date of his last professional haircut. Remediating the instant replay of televised sports, the aforementioned narrator draws our attention to salient parts of the image with arrows and lines of emphasis that appear as if drawn in real time. In this case, the narrator and the text convey more or less the same information, but the dynamism of the shot is unquestionably aided by the addition of Scott's cartoon double.

The film's use of onscreen text is perhaps at its most radical, however, when it contributes information not provided through other cinematic means. The best example of this occurs in the scene immediately following Scott's disastrous first conversation with Ramona, which comprises a short series of five shots, each of which features onscreen text. Specifically, each shot features between one and three words, and the entire series collectively forms the complete sentence "And then / he stalked her / until / she left / the party" (the slashes indicate how the text is divided between the shots). Given in this piecemeal manner, the editing imposes a distinctly staccato rhythm on the viewer's reading of the text, much like that which Scott McCloud associates with comics itself.[35] Interestingly, the comic book version of this scene features the complete sentence at the top of the page, and thereafter the images are presented without additional textual narration.[36] Wright's use of text and its placement within the shots forces the viewer to roam around the film frame in the same way that the comic book reader navigates a hyperframe: not necessarily from left to right, but rather following a different and unpredictable path on each individual page based on the particular arrangement of images and text and the whims of the reader.

Scenes edited in such an atypical manner may arguably be considered figural remediations of panel time, albeit in a radically different form from its articulation via selective slow motion in films like *300* and *Wanted*. In comics, duration is expressed via a series of discrete moments of varying lengths (individual panels) separated by temporally indeterminate ellipses in the representation (gutters), sutured into a coherent narrative through the intervention of the reader (closure). In films like *300* and *Wanted*, we saw closure visualized through the intermittent use of slow motion, which remediates the imaginative aspect of the comics reading experience in which the reader intervenes and internally produces the "missing" moments between panels. The scene just described in *Scott Pilgrim*, however, is doing something very different insofar as it retains the existence of "gutters" between panels; instead of smoothing over the gaps between panels (or panel moments) with any sort of additive connective tissue, this short sequence presents shot-to-shot relations that are marked by self-conscious narrative ellipses, like those between each comics panel. In other words, what is absent in comics—classical cinema's (illusory) sense of temporal fluidity and wholeness—remains strikingly absent in this scene's filmic remediation. Not only does the viewer *literally* read these frames, following the text around the screen space and assembling the discrete utterances into a coherent phrase, he or she must

FIGURES 5.13, 5.14, 5.15, 5.16, AND 5.17.
Stills from *Scott Pilgrim vs. the World*

FIGURE 5.18. Page from *Scott Pilgrim's Precious Little Life*

also combine the content of the text and the accompanying images in order to fully understand the scene's narration: the combination of these two activities is also the combination of the processes of comics reading and movie watching. Unlike many of the remediation strategies examined in this book, this scene incorporates comic book form in a way that resembles comics—remediating both its word-image hybridity and gap-based narration—while also avoiding narrative redundancy.

At other points in the film, the editing elides over indeterminate chunks of diegetic time, again evoking panel time but for a different purpose. Take, for instance, the transition out of an earlier scene in which Scott first sees

Ramona at the Toronto Reference Library. After Knives asks the conspicuously stupefied Scott if he knows her, he continues to stare, dumbfounded by the appearance of the girl previously seen only in his dreams. The camera holds on a close-up of his face for what seems like a moment too long, and then his Sex Bob-omb bandmate Stephen intrudes into the frame, commanding Scott's attention. We suddenly cut to a medium-long shot of the band in the middle of practice. The editing falsely implies that the two moments are immediately subsequent in diegetic time by matching the shots together in a seamless way; the shots *seem to* flow together and thereby present a consistent span of time and space, but they do not (note, for instance, that Scott's wardrobe has changed between the two shots). The result is deliberately jarring, representing Scott's distracted subjectivity as he drifts through his day after seeing Ramona, but it also reproduces the indeterminacy of the temporal ellipses between comics panels. The film elides the time between these two instants, just as comics elide time in the gaps between panels; it incorporates this gappiness into its editing, putting comics' inherent lack of temporal fluidity to work in a cinematic context. Whereas panel moments visualize the process associated with the theory of reading comics (closure), *Scott Pilgrim*'s gappy editing evokes comics as they appear on the page, as a series of somewhat disconnected narrative events whose connective tissue is lost to ellipses.

Scott Pilgrim also plays with the shape of the shots themselves in a way that recalls *The Dark Knight*'s use of shifting aspect ratios in its IMAX presentation. In chapter 3, I argued that the use of shifting aspect ratios in Nolan's film subtly evoked the mercurial panel shapes seen in many comics (at least those without "waffle-iron" style pages, in which all panels share the same dimensions: e.g., see figure 3.3). In *Scott Pilgrim*'s case, this same strategy is deployed to remediate not just comics but also video games. As such, the film's shifting aspect ratios become polymedial.[37] In many games that feature full-motion video "cut scenes"—fully animated sequences in which gameplay is temporarily suspended and the narrative is advanced—the transition from a participatory to a spectatorial mode of engagement with the game is marked by an aesthetic shift from a "full screen" display to a "letterboxed" view. According to Harper Cossar, this is a visual strategy intended to distinguish active gameplay from passive video scenes while also capturing some of the cultural capital associated with cinematic works on behalf of games. I quote:

Sports games utilize the letterboxed view when something extraordinary—a shot or play—is worthy of spectatorship. The 4:3 monitor view collapses to a letterbox view. When this occurs, a remarkable transformation takes place that is virtually untapped with regard to media studies; the participant playing the game is cued by an aesthetic shift in aspect ratio and simply *becomes a spectator*.[38]

This is precisely how *Scott Pilgrim* styles its fantasy sequences; while dreaming, Scott becomes a passive spectator, often gaining knowledge that he will use in future "gameplay" (i.e., his life). Thus when the film reappropriates letterboxing from video games, it carries with it the associations it gained through its use in that medium. The letterboxed view of Scott's dreams, however, is not fixed; the frame is mobile, imparting a subtle oneiric quality to the images, moving in closer and gradually subsuming the negative space at the top and bottom of the screen. When the letterbox is entirely eliminated, Scott wakes up: the cut scene is over and "gameplay" resumes. Letterboxing

FIGURE 5.19 AND 5.20.
Stills from *Scott Pilgrim vs. the World*

is similarly used immediately prior to each major fight scene—cut scenes are commonly used in video games to set up battles or challenges—in which it again evokes both comics (by manipulating the shape of the frame, treating it as a malleable panel) and video games (appropriating the letterbox's narrative connotation in that medium) using the same technique.

This is one stylistic strategy whose trajectory across media is worth unpacking. While I think that Cossar's argument has a great deal of merit, he misidentifies the lineage of letterboxing, referring to it as a "filmmaking strategy" rather than a distribution format. Though panoramic images existed prior to widescreen cinema, the formalization of widescreen aspect ratios is a cinematic innovation. Letterboxing was introduced for home video formats (like RCA VideoDisc, Laserdisc, VHS, DVD, and Blu-ray) in order to maintain the original theatrical aspect ratio of widescreen films on 4:3 television sets. Strictly speaking, letterboxing doesn't refer to widescreen aspect ratios but to the particular kind of image created when widescreen images are presented on more square-shaped screens, particularly in nontheatrical (i.e., home video) contexts. When video games and the other digital video-based media discussed by Cossar first remediated the look of letterboxed video, it was a means of appropriating the cultural capital associated specifically with letterboxed *home video*—the preferred format of highbrow cinephiles and the only way to see film images as originally composed for the cinema screen at home—rather than theatrical widescreen film. *Scott Pilgrim*'s use of dynamic letterboxing relates specifically to video games' use of the technique to formally demarcate passive narrative sequences from active gameplay. Letterboxing begins as a remediation of widescreen for home video formats, which then becomes remediated by video games as an aesthetic and narrative device; these associations carry forth when it is again remediated in *Scott Pilgrim.*

Related to the use of shifting aspect ratios and letterboxing is split screen, which is another strategy previously discussed in chapter 3. Much of the split screen in *Scott Pilgrim* is conventional and not sufficiently distinct from its use in films like *Hulk* to warrant extended consideration; as in *Hulk*, the technique is often used to present simultaneous shot reverse shots in a single frame. However, it is worth noting how other instances of split screen become polymedial, remediating a variety of media simultaneously, namely comics, anime, and video games. Unsurprisingly, split screen is arguably the aesthetic strategy most closely linked to the contemporary sense of hypermediation, since it breaks the illusion that the window (be it a cinematic

FIGURE 5.21. Still from *Scott Pilgrim vs. the World*

frame, a television screen, a tablet, a computer, etc.) presents an unmediated presentation of the world; the co-presence of multiple windows within the larger framework necessarily fragments the single-perspective view associated with natural (human) vision. Computer operating systems, the Internet, and contemporary cable news networks are all everyday examples of the kind of hypermediation parodied in *Southland Tales* and pastiched in *Scott Pilgrim*. These, however, are not the media that contribute to Scott's worldview.[39] Video games most often employ split screen as a means of accommodating simultaneous multiplayer gameplay; in this mode, the screen is divided into two to four player-specific frames. It is precisely this kind of split screen that is evoked in the film's final fight, in which Scott and Knives team up against Gideon, the seventh and final Evil Ex.

Anime's use of split screen—which also tends to be used during fight scenes—is arguably already an aesthetic choice remediated from digital games.[40] However, it is regularly employed in *Scott Pilgrim* to produce a visual style distinctly associated with anime (which is itself remediating manga). The limited animation style associated with anime, which "drastically decreases the number of drawings used for character movements, relying on other effects to impart a sense of movement,"[41] is often typified by a static character (in the requisite action pose) against an abstract background of colorful streaking light. The result contains no foreground movement whatsoever but nevertheless implies it because of the dynamic background.

It is precisely these kinds of images, often combined with split-screen imagery, that best represent the polymediality of *Scott Pilgrim*.

The fight scene between Scott and Evil Ex #2, Lucas Lee, presents several such moments. In figure 5.22, the frame is divided horizontally into two long rectangular subshots; the two characters are shown in profile, and do not move to any significant degree within the frame, while the background streaks with horizontal lines of colored light: this is a live-action version of the limited animation of anime. As was the case with the remediation of onomatopoeia, the original purpose of the device is made redundant in its new context—replaced by live-action cinematography—and retains only a superficial resemblance to its originary medium. A second example from later in the same sequence provides an even denser combination of media. The diagonal split screen in figure 5.23 remediates comics in two ways (the split screen evokes the co-presence of panels; the onomatopoeic "HHHs" as the skateboard grinds the rail remediate comics' word-image hybridity, not to mention diegetic intertextuality, since the characters and situations originated in the comics series), video games in three ways (the multiplayer-esque split screen; the speedometer in the upper-right corner; and the letterboxed frame, indicating a cut scene since Scott is merely a spectator, not an active participant), and anime in two ways (the split screen; the lack of figure movement combined with an active, streaking background evoking limited animation). It is through such simultaneity that we see most clearly how *Scott Pilgrim* combines various media into densely polymedial moments. This seems like it would be a particularly complex example from the film, but equally multifaceted cases are common throughout.

Ultimately, it's beyond the scope of a single chapter to exhaustively catalogue *Scott Pilgrim*'s polymedial richness. In addition to the crucial role played by video games in the structuring of the film's narrative and its aesthetics, the thorough remediation of comics throughout, and occasional references to anime, the film also boasts a Bollywood-inspired musical number; a domestic scene between Wallace and Scott that features canned laughter, musical cues, and the sitcomic rhythms of *Seinfeld* (1989–1998); hand-drawn animated sequences;[42] the superimposition of a textual emoticon (":o") onto a character's face; elaborate kung-fu fight choreography; and more besides. All of these media or genres either represent means through which the film's characters express themselves in the world or through which mediated experiences give them a means of understanding or giving shape to the world around them. The film thoroughly embodies a post-cinematic

FIGURES 5.22 AND
5.23. Stills from
*Scott Pilgrim vs.
the World*

position in which all relevant media are voraciously consumed and amalgamated, stripped of their ontological uniqueness and much of their original medium-specific function. In such a polymedial environment, what were once thought of as discrete media forms are no longer easily separable; in *Scott Pilgrim*, cinema, comics, video games, anime, television, and other media exist within an integrated structure, enabling not only intermedial relationships to form through remediation but also allowing for more densely polymedial expressions that connect and combine three or more media forms through the shared vehicle of film style. As demonstrated above, the six modes of interaction between media can be put to use beyond the particular case of comics' relationship to film; this schema can equally describe a variety of intermedial and even polymedial relationships.

Like many contemporary comic book adaptations, *Scott Pilgrim* is more than just a film; it is also a transmedia franchise. Beginning life as a series of graphic novels, the narrative was adapted into the polymedial film analyzed here. The film's release was accompanied by the typical barrage of tie-in media objects—most notably a soundtrack, an animated short, and a couple of downloadable video games—and increased interest and visibility for the source texts, resulting in colorized reprints and a mobile adap(p)tation (*Scott*

FIGURE 5.24. Still from *Scott Pilgrim vs. the World*

Pilgrim's Precious Little App)[43] of the original comics, as well as a glut of comic book–inspired merchandise. While *Pilgrim*'s migration across these various platforms has been discussed in transmedia terms,[44] the narratives that these texts tell are largely closed off from one another. For instance, Ubisoft's *Scott Pilgrim vs. the World: The Game* (2010) doesn't advance the overall narrative of the franchise, though it does reproduce images and sounds from the comics and film while giving players the opportunity to extend their relationship with the property in general. This is not the ideal of transmedia storytelling as advanced by Henry Jenkins and exemplified by *The Matrix* franchise, in which a metanarrative is spread across a variety of texts and media, all of which feature stand-alone stories that provide a unique contribution to the whole: the franchise *in toto* should tell a single coherent story across multiple texts and platforms.[45] As a film narrative, *Scott Pilgrim vs. the World* is self-contained, telling a complete story unto itself, albeit one that originated in another medium. Its polymedial mode of address may draw on and assume prior knowledge of other media and genres, but it doesn't direct its viewers to other texts in the franchise (e.g., the comics) in order to assemble a larger transmedia narrative; rather, the other texts in the franchise tell the same narrative in different ways.[46] In this respect, the next case study embodies an alternative approach to polymediality, whereby various media circulate around the central text as a self-contained transmedia network.

Watchmen and Its Paratexts

Like *Scott Pilgrim*, Zack Snyder's *Watchmen* is an adaptation of a particular series of comics that themselves remediate a broader media ecology. While also a product of an increasingly digital media environment, *Watchmen* represents a very different articulation of polymediality than *Scott Pilgrim* in that it spreads its narrative across several different platforms; as a result, it becomes difficult to determine where "the text" begins and ends. This heterogeneous transmedia style is most fully represented in a multimedia home video release that has been designated *Watchmen: The Ultimate Cut* (hereafter *TUC*), which contains an extended 215-minute cut of the film,[47] the theatrical cut of the film, an array of bonus features, the complete motion comic adaptation, and a hardcover reprinting of the original graphic novel. For all intents and purposes, *TUC* is the *Watchmen* franchise in a box: a single multimedia work that remediates comics as well as other media, placing all of them in an integrated but simultaneously "conflictual structure that remains energetic and open-ended"[48] by virtue of the flexibility of home video formats and the possibilities of transmedia storytelling.

The bevy of supplemental material released alongside *Watchmen* is not merely a consequence of contemporary Hollywood marketing; as was the case with *Scott Pilgrim*, the film's polymediality is presaged by a storytelling strategy employed in the original graphic novel. The twelve issues that made up Alan Moore and Dave Gibbons's revisionist superhero series were released monthly between September 1986 and October 1987,[49] though the comics have received broader distribution and acclaim in their collected form as a graphic novel. *Watchmen* is notable in that both the monthly issues and the collected edition use the back pages usually reserved for advertisements and reader mail to feature supplemental materials presented as addenda to the comics. More specifically, these addenda pause the story's complex, non-linear, comics-based narration to elaborate on various characters' backstories and the history of the diegetic world, thereby deepening the reader's engagement with and knowledge of the story. They do so not via "character profiles" or other such contrivances, which are fairly common in superhero comics, but rather through *prose*, and predominantly literary genres specifically: for instance, chapters from retired superhero Hollis Mason's autobiography *Under the Hood* and an essay from *The Journal of the American Ornithological Society* are "reprinted" in full. The inclusion of these imaginary intertexts, which are seen in or alluded to within the diegetic world of the comics, itself represents an intermedial gesture that takes advantage of a common medium (the printed page) to incorporate other media into what may otherwise be interpreted as a conventional (at least in its presentation) superhero comic. These metafictional pieces are part of the diegetic world, but their formal difference and placement at the end of each issue (or between chapters in the collected edition) place them on the periphery of the text; in other words, they are presented as *paratextual* material.

As defined by Gérard Genette, paratexts are "those liminal devices and conventions, both within the book (*peritext*) and outside it (*epitext*), that mediate the book to the reader," including "titles and subtitles, pseudonyms, forewords, dedications, epigraphs, prefaces, intertitles, notes, epilogues, and afterwords," among other things.[50] In their ambiguous relation to the text proper, paratexts act as interpretive "thresholds,"[51] functioning to frame and demarcate the borders of the text, and to facilitate or mark the reader's entry into it. For Genette, they also represent an "undefined zone," being neither part of the text proper nor totally disconnected from it.[52] For Jonathan Gray, who has redefined the discourse on paratexts within the contemporary transmedia context, "a film or program is but one part of the text, the text always being a contingent entity, either in the process of forming and transforming or vulnerable to further formation or transformation" as a result of, among other things, paratextual material.[53] In short, Gray views the paratextual as always already textual, constituting and contributing to the formation of storyworlds just as much as a film. This adequately describes the positioning of *Watchmen*'s aforementioned pseudo-paratexts, which are certainly part of the text insofar as they enrich the reader's engagement with the storyworld, but whose status nevertheless seems to be supplemental rather than central to the primary narrative.[54] As a book, *Watchmen* contains more conventional paratexts as well: its cover(s), its title, and so on. The hardcover printing of the graphic novel contained in *TUC* features two afterwords, as well as reprints of Gibbons's artwork at various stages of completion. Genette would define these latter examples as nondiegetic peritexts, and we would not typically expect such material to be adapted in a film version; after all, they aren't part of the narrative even if they may contribute to a reader's understanding of the work.[55] In the analysis to follow, I primarily consider diegetic paratexts, which contribute to the construction—not merely the interpretation—of the fictional world. By virtue of the narrative's diffusion across these paratexts, they assume a more vital role in their franchise than, say, the *Scott Pilgrim* video game does. I argue that the cinematic *Watchmen* franchise as a whole, as represented by the *TUC* set, presents an alternative articulation of polymediality in which the various arms of the represented media ecology are not subsumed into the film but are rather distributed across a variety of paratexts—in other words, a strategy more in line with Jenkins's conception of transmedia storytelling.

Any cut of Snyder's *Watchmen* is already an intertextual and intermedial film, irrespective of its various paratexts, due to its adaptation and remediation of comics. To a greater extent than most comic book films, and practically unprecedented in the superhero film genre, *Watchmen* hews very closely to the characters and narrative of the graphic novel: in terms of diegetic intertextuality, an adaptation theorist would surely determine—perhaps after screening the film while following along in the (graphic) novel, as George Bluestone suggests[56]—that it is "faithful" to the original work in many respects. Indeed, Bob Rehak has described the film version as "a very ambitious experiment in hyper faithful cinematic adaptation,"[57] while Drew Morton has categorized it as emblematic of a "high fidelity" cycle of comic book adaptations.[58] A variety of critics received the film in similar terms, such that the notion of fidelity became central to the discourse surrounding the adaptation.[59] Rehak's claim is particularly peculiar, since the article in which his statement appears is largely devoted to explicating the narrative *divergences* made in the film adaptation as a result, he argues, of September 11, 2001. How might a film be considered not merely faithful but *hyper faithful* given these considerable differences? Such claims seem to be based largely on the film's use of the original comics "as script, storyboard, and design bible"[60] and can allow for differences in meaning or narrative so long as superficial visual resemblance is, for the most part, maintained. Cosmetic similarities between the film's mise-en-scène and the comics', as well as an incessant use of mimetic compositions, apparently more than compensate for the narrative alterations and condensation in the film version.[61]

The film's primary strategy for remediating comics—the adaptation strategies just mentioned are intertextual rather than intermedial—is the use of panel moments. As in other comic book films, the staccato rhythm thus produced emphasizes particular compositions, nearly arresting these moments amid the temporal flow and raising them to the privileged status of the comic book panel. For instance, the film begins with a scene suggested by a few panels seen in flashback in the first chapter (and again toward the end) of the graphic novel, in which the Comedian is attacked and ultimately thrown out of his high-rise apartment window; his murder becomes the catalyst for the rest of the "whodunit"-style narrative. The scene includes several panel moments, giving it a staccato, start-stop rhythm. The first true panel moment of the film occurs during this fight, when the Comedian's attacker punches him in the face. As the gloved fist makes contact, the shot ramps up into extreme slow motion, allowing this critical moment to register on the viewer with increased impact, before ramping back down to real time. In addition to remediating the reading experience of comics, the technique emphasizes both the force of the blow and the aesthetic effect of the shot. Another example occurs near the end of the scene, as the as-yet-unidentified attacker throws the Comedian through the glass window, from which he falls to his death. The shot—which is also a mimetic composition—begins in slow motion as the Comedian first makes contact with the window; as the glass shatters, the speed decreases almost to the point of stasis. The frame-per-second rate decreases—that is, the speed of the shot increases—as the Comedian begins his descent to the streets below, until the smiley face pin that he had been wearing on his bathrobe falls into the frame. When this pin, which is one of the most iconic images associated with the graphic novel, is facing the camera, the speed once again ramps up nearly to the point of stasis, giving us the second panel moment of the shot. The film again ramps down into real time mere instants before cutting away to the Comedian's dead body on the sidewalk, and then to the opening credits.

The opening credits sequence that follows is similarly worthy of extended investigation and arguably contains the film's most unique contribution to comic book film style. As David Bordwell notes, "Credit sequences are very important narrational gestures. These extrafictional passages usually present information in highly self-conscious and omniscient fashion."[62] Like *Scott Pilgrim*, wherein the opening credits served multiple purposes, the six-minute credits sequence in *Watchmen* sets the stage for the narrative, fleshing out the details of the alternate history in which the film is set—as Bob Dylan sings on the soundtrack, "the times they are a-changin'," literally—while also establishing the film's highly self-conscious style. The former point is worth elaborating on. The revisionist history of *Watchmen* inserts superheroes into key historical moments—including the assassination of JFK (the Comedian did it) and the moon landing (Dr. Manhattan was there)—while also marking the trajectory of superhero culture itself: early in the sequence, superheroes are seen fighting alongside police, and later, one is seen dead with his cape stuck in a revolving door, before yet another is shown being institutionalized against his will. Such events seemingly set history down a

FIGURES 5.25, 5.26,
AND 5.27. Stills from
Watchmen

darker path, exemplified by military police gunning down peaceful Vietnam
protesters and Nixon's reelection as president for a third term. Superheroes ultimately become just another part of this world's pop cultural landscape, depicted as the subject for an Andy Warhol screen printing and as a
guest of honor at Studio 54. Composed primarily of extreme slow-motion
shots, each of which represents an entire scene in microcosm, this sequence
takes the panel moment to the limit by excising the real-time bookends; as
a result, the sequence reads more as a slow-motion variation of panel time
as represented in *Scott Pilgrim*, since it doesn't visualize closure so much as a
series of disconnected (panel) moments.

The eagle-eyed reader may have noticed that the credits in figure 5.28
attribute authorship of the graphic novel to illustrator Dave Gibbons only;

FIGURE 5.28. Still from *Watchmen*

no mention is made of its writer, Alan Moore, who has become notorious for his confrontational, even malevolent stance with regard to cinema in general and film adaptations of his comics in particular. In an interview with *The Guardian*, he clarifies his issue with such works:

> "There is something about the quality of comics that makes things possible that you couldn't do in any other medium," he says, with just a hint of the exasperated schoolteacher. "Things that we did in Watchmen on paper could be frankly horrible or sensationalist or unpleasant if you were to interpret them literally through the medium of cinema. When it's just lines on paper, the reader is in control of the experience—it's a tableau vivant. And that gives it the necessary distance. It's not the same when you're being dragged through it at 24 frames per second."[63]

While Moore may have a great deal of expertise in the unique artistic qualities of comics, I'd argue that he doesn't fully understand the nuances or expressive potential of cinema: he seems to imply that all films are necessarily literal in meaning, incapable of providing a sense of aesthetic distance from their subject matter, and that their viewers are entirely passive receivers of audiovisual information. The first ten minutes of *Watchmen* alone are enough to prove him wrong on all fronts, given the film's liberal use of mimetic compositions (which encourage active, intertextually minded viewing) and use of film style (which remediates comics in a figural rather than literal way, resembling the very *tableau vivant* tradition that Moore evokes).

In the documentary *The Mindscape of Alan Moore* (2005), the cantankerous comics creator elaborates on the specific aspects of his work that supposedly make it "unfilmable": "The way in which a tremendous amount of information could be included visually in every panel, the juxtapositions between what a character was saying and what the image that the reader was looking at would be."[64] Again, the film frame and the comics panel are equally capable of containing information-dense images, and film's synchronous soundtrack can similarly provide an ironic aural counterpoint to the visual information on screen. What exactly about *Watchmen*, then, is so "unfilmable"? Perhaps Moore means to refer to *Watchmen*'s paratexts: a film may be able to remediate a comic book, but surely it will not also be able to incorporate autobiography, essays, journalism, interviews, psychological profiles, and police case reports, all of which can be printed as prose within the graphic novel format. It is here that we'll turn our attention away from the film itself and toward its paratexts, wherein *Watchmen*'s polymediality truly lies.

In anticipation of the film's theatrical release, stand-alone adaptations of *Watchmen*'s paratextual materials were released to DVD and Blu-ray as a separate commercial product, thereby transforming these elements of the graphic novel into a transmedia storytelling and marketing strategy. Adapting *Under the Hood* into a short faux-television documentary, featuring interviews with Hollis Mason (Nite Owl I), among other retired superheroes, was the filmmakers' original way to convey the content of the graphic novel's prose sections while radically transforming their form; *Tales of the Black Freighter*, an animated short, adapted the pirate comic-within-the-comic that runs throughout *Watchmen* and provides an allegorical commentary on the events of the main narrative provided in the film. The realization of these two peripheral elements of *Watchmen*'s storyworld simultaneously performed a variety of functions: announcing the filmmakers' dedication to the minutiae of the original text (contributing to the fidelity discourse discussed earlier); creating hype for the forthcoming theatrical release of the film; introducing and deepening fans' engagement with the diegetic world; and, most importantly for my argument here, remediating the paratextual strategy first seen in the graphic novel, wherein supplemental elements like *Under the Hood* and *Black Freighter* were textually present but nevertheless separate from the main narrative and also presented in an idiom that marked them as distinct from the main text: the comic's autobiographical prose section becomes a 1970s television newsmagazine, similar to *60 Minutes* (1968–), while the comic-within-a-comic becomes a stand-alone animated film.

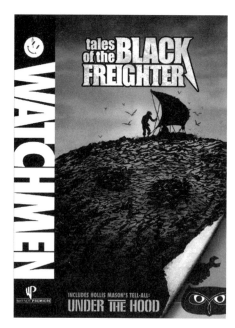

LEFT
FIGURE 5.29. Cover of *Tales of the Black Freighter/Under the Hood* DVD release

ABOVE
FIGURE 5.30. Still from *Under the Hood*

Under the Hood in particular is able to elaborate on the backstories glimpsed in the film's opening credits, rewarding viewers with extra information and thus providing a unique contribution to the transmedia narrative.

Tales of the Black Freighter has been considered a central part of Moore and Gibbons's *Watchmen* comics, arguably providing the moral center of the text via an allegorical version of the narrative. Richard Reynolds summarizes the relationship between the text and its imaginary intertext thusly:

> *Watchmen* is at bottom about the intentions and fictions employed by everybody either to achieve power and control or simply to get through their daily lives. The youth reading the *Black Freighter* comic fails to grasp the significance of the story before he is obliterated in Adrian Veidt's attack on New York—an event which, for the alert reader of *Watchmen*, is echoed by the story of the marooned mariner. There are no privileged cases: superheroes, presidents, psychiatrists, newsvendors, journalists, admen; all are presented as consumers of their own self-serving fictions.[65]

Black Freighter also presents a key part of *Watchmen*'s revisionist history that is not otherwise covered in the film: seemingly as a direct result of superheroes appearing on the streets of New York in the wake of Superman's debut in *Action Comics*, the genre fails to make a comeback in postwar comics culture. Instead, it would seem that EC Comics—best known today for their gruesome early-1950s horror stories—continued to dominate the marketplace, with pirate-themed comics in particular. But taken separately from the central narrative, *Black Freighter* is itself somewhat marooned. Much of its meaning emerges from the specific ways in which the narration of the pirate comic intersects with the main plot, at times echoing Rorschach's trajectory in the story and at others commenting on Adrian's use of mass destruction to achieve world peace. Disconnected from the film proper in a stand-alone home video release, these specific thematic parallels are barely implicit. In the *TUC* version of the film, however, *Tales of the Black Freighter* is incorporated into the feature itself, providing a running commentary on the main narrative. In this way, the evocative connections between film and paratext are made much more explicit. In an even more literal way than Gray imagines, the paratextual becomes explicitly textual here, just as it was in the comics. For instance, an animated scene detailing the mariner's isolation and his increasingly tenuous grip on sanity is inserted between Rorschach's arrest and subsequent psychological examination, suggesting that the vigilante is also becoming (or has become) mentally unmoored, even if his intentions are good. The mariner's raft, buoyed by the dead bodies of his former crew, also echoes Rorschach's placement in a prison in which he's surrounded by the very criminals that he himself brought to justice.

For the purposes of this chapter, however, the way in which these animated sequences are incorporated into the film is more relevant than their thematic bearing on the text.[66] The *Black Freighter* segments of *Watchmen* are presented as an animated representation of a comic book: we see young Bernard reading a floppy issue of *Tales of the Black Freighter* on the street; the camera cuts to an over-the-shoulder shot, showing a double-page spread before (virtually) tracking into one particular panel which, once it takes up the entire frame, comes to life in full-motion animation. Though not all of the sequences are introduced in this way—some, like the aforementioned Rorschach scene, are not diegetically introduced—enough of them are that the viewer understands this subnarrative's place in the overall story. As discussed in chapter 3, this technique is very similar to that seen in the prologue to *Superman* or in the framing devices of *Creepshow*, and indeed produces the same effect, marking the scenes thereafter as a figurative remediation of not just *a* comic, but *this* comic in particular as animated film. *Superman* places this device outside of the diegesis, thereby framing the entire film as

FIGURES 5.31 AND
5.32. Stills from
Watchmen

a live-action comic; the subtler strategies of remediation employed in *Watchmen*'s live-action scenes, however, also mark them as a cinematic version of comics, thereby remediating the "comic-within-a-comic" framework of the original graphic novel.

Black Freighter, Under the Hood, and *TUC* are all only accessible on home video, which speaks to the evolving role of theatrical release in a film's life. Richard Grusin has described DVD releases of films as a form of remediation that "marks a fundamental change in the aesthetic status of the cinematic artefact," because

> the DVD release of a feature film is no longer seen as an afterthought, a second-order distribution phenomenon aimed at circulating the original film to a wider audience. Today the production, design and distribution of DVD versions of feature films are part of the original contractual (and thus artistic) intention of these films.[67]

According to Jared Gardner, Snyder had always intended to utilize the home video market to fully realize his adaptation of *Watchmen*, paratexts and all.[68] In the new paradigm embodied by such complex long-term release strategies, we must increasingly recognize that "a film does not end after its closing credits"[69] but rather continues through "multiply networked, distributed forms of cinematic production and exhibition."[70] Grusin dubs this, retooling Tom Gunning, the digital cinema of interactions, though the concept is not dissimilar to transmedia storytelling insofar as the viewer ultimately chooses his or her own path through the narrative by selecting which parts of the metatext to consume and in what order. (Like Jenkins, Grusin invokes *The Matrix* franchise as an example.)

The kind of control that DVD gives viewers is not unlike that of the comic book reader, who at any given moment assumes a perspective that encompasses past, present, and future on a single page and in a single view. The original graphic novel allegorizes the act of comic book reading through the superpowers of Dr. Manhattan, whose perception of linear time as simultaneous mirrors the perception of the comic book reader. As Gardner interprets the character:

> Dr. Manhattan is capable of taking in past, present, and future in a glance, of moving back and forward between them effortlessly, even of making choices in the gaps between slivers of time that might impact if not the conclusion at least its ultimate meaning. Dr. Manhattan, that is, sees time like a comic reader. . . . If there was ever a comic book that could not be adapted to film, it was surely this one.[71]

Indeed, a theatrical release would have difficulty remediating this aspect of the medium (as we saw in earlier discussions of split-screen imagery), but this kind of temporal control is old hat to home video viewers, specifically in scene selection menus that simultaneously present them with an array of scenes and moments in time—each represented, as they are in comics, through a single privileged instant. Viewers are thereby "invited to excavate the layers through multiple viewings using . . . [their] new powers (like Dr. Manhattan) to stop time, to study a film frame by frame, byte by byte—powers consequent to the DVD."[72] Both as an adaptation of Moore and Gibbons's comics series and a remediation of the comics medium, *Watchmen* only becomes richer as a text in its home video afterlife. Contrary to Gardner's conclusion about the impossibility of adapting the comic to film, I arrive at a different conclusion about the potential of the graphic novel's remediation: indeed, if ever there was a comic book film that was meant for DVD, it was surely *Watchmen*.

FIGURE 5.33. Still from
Watchmen DVD menu

Thus we see how the remediation of a multilayered comic book like *Watchmen* can be detected at every stage of the film's distribution, from before its theatrical exhibition to its home video afterlife. Considering the franchise as a single polymedial object, the various texts—the film itself and its paratexts in their various configurations—each maintain their autonomy through aesthetic differentiation while also, following the logic of transmedia storytelling, combining to form a coherent whole. As Grusin suggests, it is increasingly important to pay attention to the ways in which films are remediated to home video formats, since they determine the means through which most people will see a film after its comparatively brief theatrical release window. These packages are texts in themselves that don't only remediate theatrical films but may also contribute to and extend the aesthetic choices made in the film itself. In the case of *TUC*, the package is more worthy of discussion than the theatrical film on its own, transforming the film into a much more complicated polymedial object than it was in its initial theatrical presentation.

But if we're considering *TUC* as a text in and of itself, one final element warrants some brief commentary, namely, *Watchmen: The Complete Motion Comic* (2008). Motion comics are a hybrid medium that combines formal attributes associated with comics and animation. As Morton has rightly pointed out, however, the particular attributes remediated tend to differ on a case-by-case basis, making defining the medium's essential characteristics difficult.[73] Like the live-action comic book film itself, the motion comics format can result in some confusion between the categories of adaptation and remediation, especially since the most well-known motion comics—those that are produced and distributed by large media conglomerates in order to further monetize existing intellectual properties and works—adapt specific comics while also remediating the comics medium more generally. *Watchmen: The Complete Motion Comic* (hereafter *TCMC*) certainly falls into this category. Unlike *Under the Hood* or *Black Freighter*, *TCMC* stands apart from the transmedia narrative contained in the *TUC* box set and instead represents an alternative stand-alone adaptation of the graphic novel. At five hours and twenty-five minutes in length and boasting the same twelve-episode structure as the graphic novel, *TCMC*'s titular "complete" might be interpreted in either of two ways: (1) that the disc in question contains the motion comic in its entirety, or (2) that the motion comic presents the *comic book* in its entirety, albeit with the addition of motion. Like other motion comics that adapt pre-existing works,[74] the overwhelming majority of the images in *TCMC* are digitally scanned, manipulated, and animated versions of Gibbons's original comics art, including conventional elements like caption boxes and speech balloons that are rendered superfluous by the audiobook-like voiceover narration (performed entirely by Tom Stechschulte). This begs the question: if Snyder's *Watchmen* can be considered a "hyper faithful" adaptation of the graphic novel by treating the comics images as storyboards for a comparatively small percentage of its compositions, what does that make *TCMC*?

The question, of course, is rhetorical, but it seems clear that within *TUC*, *TCMC* occupies an intermediary space between the original graphic novel and its live-action film adaptation: for those unsatisfied with the aesthetic and narrative liberties taken by Snyder et al. in "hyper faithfully" adapting *Watchmen* to live action, the motion comic exists as an even *more* hyper faithful adaptation.[75] Of course, the motion comic has received some scrutiny along these very lines: as one review cited by Craig Smith in his article describing the production of motion comics goes, "What's the point of watching a barely animated version of [the graphic novel]? . . . If you're really that interested in seeing the story come to life, just watch the movie when it hits theaters this Friday."[76] While the merits of *TCMC* as an adaptation of the graphic novel are certainly debatable—as are the merits of motion comics in general[77]—I would suggest that this is beside the point of its inclusion in the *TUC* box set. While *TCMC* was initially released episodically on iTunes and later collected as a stand-alone commodity (released just prior to the theatrical release of *Watchmen*, concurrent with but separate from the *Under the Hood/Tales of the Black Freighter* disc), its inclusion in *TUC*—where it exists alongside a hardcover printing of Moore and Gibbons's graphic novel, two cuts of Snyder's film adaptation, and a host of bonus material for both—recontextualizes it. As Sara J. Van Ness puts it in her description of the film's critical reception:

Viewing the film as an entity separate from the graphic novel was as challenging for those who admired the graphic novel as it was for those who
disliked the original text. Some had preconceived notions about the film
because of their dislike for the graphic novel; others found problems with
its applicability to a modern-day audience or how it compared to other
superhero films, and still other reviewers sided with Moore, deciding that
any film adaptation of *Watchmen* was a second-rate *Watchmen*. That is, the
film never should have been made.[78]

To an even greater extent than other comic book films, then, *Watchmen*
tended to be assessed relative to its source material, a comparison that the
film's marketing seemed to encourage both before and after its theatrical
release. Taken as a whole, *TUC* seems intended to undermine the entire
enterprise of adaptation, insofar as its usual goal is to create a new text that
can stand on its own, separate and autonomous from (if always still haunted
by) the original. Both *TCMC* and Snyder's adaptations of *Watchmen* instead
devote considerable energy to redirecting the viewer's attention back to the
graphic novel in ways that go beyond concerns regarding fidelity, and their
inclusion alongside the graphic novel in the *TUC* box set unmoors all three
versions from any sense of textual primacy. Rather than a film adaptation of
a notable work or even a transmedia narrative, what *TUC* truly packages is
a never-ending cycle of intertextual and polymedial circulation where each
element directs the reader/viewer forward and backward to other versions
of the story.

Watchmen: TUC represents a limit case for comic book film style and the
logical endpoint for the present investigation: as a multimedia object that
curates and collects multiple texts, it doesn't merely challenge the limits
of cinema and comics but truly transcends them, assembling original and
adaptations, mediation and remediations, into a single package wherein they
interact in a variety of ways. The ostensible goal of comic book film style is
to retain something of the comic book medium—be it the graphic interaction of word and image, the dynamism of the panel and the multipanel grid,
or the creative intervention of the reader—in a way that takes full advantage
of cinema's expressive potential, free from the restrictive leash of classical
continuity style. *TUC*, however, goes a step further: not only does it include a
live-action film that adapts and remediates comics, it also retains the graphic
novel in its entirety and adapts it in animated form as literally as possible.
While each of these texts might stand alone in other contexts, their inherent

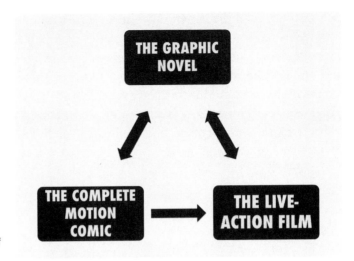

FIGURE 5.34. Graph of
Watchmen franchise

concern with remediation—and certainly each of the three distinct versions of *Watchmen* is concerned with remediation to a significant degree—enables them to speak to one another. The lenticular art that adorns the box set is thus both revealing and evocative of *TUC*'s intervention: as you tilt the box set in your hands, the character portraits change from the live-action actors of Snyder's film to Gibbons's cartooned drawings and back again. In this dynamic image, there is no originary state, and neither is given primacy over the other: the nature of the images and the relationship between them is entirely a matter of perspective, and literally rests in the hands of the viewer/reader.

The result is truly polymedial, though in a very different way from this chapter's other case study: whereas *Scott Pilgrim* incorporates a variety of media into its cinematic form, switching between them to create particular aesthetic effects, narrative meanings, and nostalgic/thematic resonances, *Watchmen*'s theatrical cut is a more traditional example of comic book film style, albeit a particularly dense one. Beyond its theatrical context, however, the paratextual materials used to market and extend Snyder's film remediate the pseudo-paratexts contained in the original graphic novel in different ways, turning *Watchmen* into a transmedial narrative. The *TUC* box set, which collects the various artifacts that inspired, extended, and marketed the film into a single commodity, allows us to consider the transmedia franchise *in toto* as one massive polymedial object, as a single text. In both cases, polymedia is employed to similar ends. To paraphrase Madianou and

Miller, the film (or the larger franchise it creates) switches between media to achieve its purposes: what cannot be achieved by film can be accomplished by animation, video games, or television. Comics are not simply comics; they are defined relationally as also not film, not animation, and not video games. With an entire media ecology available to remediate cinematically, polymedia encourages an *à la carte* approach to film style, resulting in films that are more heterogeneous and stylistically ambitious than classical film style has traditionally allowed.

CONCLUSION

While the breadth of case studies analyzed over the previous chapters indicates comic book film style's significant presence in contemporary American filmmaking, it nevertheless remains the case that not every comic book adaptation will necessarily betray an interest in remediating the formal qualities of comics. While there are numerable exceptions, from *Batman: The Movie* to *Watchmen*, contemporary superhero films have actually been surprisingly hesitant to embrace comic book film style. In the wake of Stephen Norrington's *Blade* (1998) and Bryan Singer's *X-Men* (1999)—both of which pared away the neon-bright excess associated with previous superhero films like Joel Schumacher's *Batman & Robin* (1997) in favor of a muted color palette and a more restrained approach to the genre's more fantastical elements—superhero cinema has chased a brand of realism that is most often defined by buzzwords like "dark" and "gritty." Looking back at the *American Cinematographer* profiles of the first two *X-Men* films, it's striking how forcefully the film's director of photography, Newton Thomas Sigel, denounces the aesthetics of comics and the influence they might have on his cinematographic approach. On the first *X-Men* film, for instance, he deliberately "avoided using a lot of color. . . . I instead wanted the colors to be balanced and fairly muted and subdued, to go against that primary-color, comic-book look. In fact, I pull-processed most of the film to desaturate everything."[1] For the sequel, *X2: X-Men United*, Sigel elaborated that "for Bryan, it was important for the films to have a very classical, naturalistic look, and yet have an other-worldliness and also an energy that's very modern. He did not want them to feel like comic books. In many ways, I think we're trying to make films that are closer to *Road to Perdition* than, say, *Gone in 60 Seconds*."[2] For good or ill, the effects of this paradigm shift in terms of developing a different cinematic approach to comic book material can still be felt today, both in the still-ongoing *X-Men* series and beyond.

These superhero films' comparative lack of interest in remediating comics can also be detected on the level of narrative. As Alexander Huls observes for the *A.V. Club*,

> Between Bryan Singer's first *X-Men* movie and Jon Favreau's *Iron Man*, superhero movies were wary about adopting anything that was too comic book-like—especially narrative tropes like crossovers, multiverses, events, and team-ups. It wasn't only that they were too cumbersome, even ambitious, to implement; studios also generally feared that mainstream audiences wouldn't accept them.[3]

In the summer of 2008, however, another paradigm shift occurred with the release of Marvel Studios' *Iron Man* and *The Incredible Hulk*. Together, the two films functioned as the opening salvo of the Marvel Cinematic Universe (MCU): a massive shared storyworld boasting an ever-expanding cast of comic book characters in a potentially never-ending serial narrative.[4] This synergistic approach to serialization and world-building was itself adapted from Marvel Comics, which established an interconnected storyworld to unite its various publications as early as 1961 with the publication of *Fantastic Four* #1.[5] As Bart Beaty summarizes:

> Until the 1960s, American comic book stories were largely independent of each other, so that any one Superman adventure might be read by some-one with only the scantest knowledge of other Superman adventures. The comic books produced by Marvel Comics under the editorship of Stan Lee in the 1960s transformed this model. Lee created stories with stron-ger serial components, thus heightening the stakes of the shared-universe storytelling that had been introduced by rival DC Comics two decades prior.[6]

Between Marvel and DC, the company-wide shared narrative universe quickly became a central feature and pleasure of superhero comics. And yet it wasn't until Marvel Studios' ambitious plan to combine the *Iron Man*, *Incredible Hulk*, *Thor*, and *Captain America* franchises in *The Avengers* that this narrative approach was attempted in film. While it is difficult to overstate the impact that Marvel Studios' success has had on the company, which went from filing for bankruptcy in 1996 to being purchased by Disney for $4 billion in 2009, even more significant is its impact on the American film industry more broadly. In the wake of Marvel's unprecedented success with this world-building gambit, other film studios (and the conglomerates that own them) rapidly sought to rejuvenate their own intellectual properties (IP) by placing them into similarly conceived shared universes, including what has come to be known as the "DC Extended Universe" (DCEU). Anticipating this outcome, Beaty correctly claimed that "the narrative model on which Marvel Comics built its success in the 1960s will have an important impact on the Hollywood blockbuster logic of the 2010s."[7] At the time of this prediction, *The Avengers* was still a year away from release, and a separate interconnected cinematic universe exploiting DC Comics' deep stable of characters was but a glimmer in Warner Bros.' eye. Since then, however, both companies have established and expanded these serialized cinematic storyworlds in a variety of films, publicly announced plans for future films, and laid claim to multiple release dates per year up to 2020,[8] committing to expanding their megafranchises through a savvy combination of character-centric films and larger-scale crossover events. Following suit, Universal announced plans to rejuvenate their "Universal Monster" IPs in the Marvel style,[9] while Paramount has taken early steps to exponentially expand its *Transformers* franchise *and* introduce a separate "Hasbro Cinematic Universe" combining IPs such as G.I. Joe, Micronauts, and M.A.S.K.[10]

With crossovers and shared universes becoming increasingly *de rigueur* in contemporary mainstream cinema, scholars and critics (not to mention industry insiders) have rightly begun to interrogate what's unique about Marvel Studios' operation.[11] Martin Flanagan, Mike McKenny, and Andy Livingstone, for instance, have concisely defined Marvel Studios as "a company with a strong vision in pursuit of a clear house style, dominant in its 'genre' zone, and expressing all this through a [unique selling point] (the shared universe) that has its competitors scrambling in emulation."[12] While the latter two aspects of this tripartite definition have already been discussed, the suggestion that Marvel Studios cultivates a distinctive "house style" is also crucial. The concept is closely associated with the classical Hollywood era, wherein each film studio sought to develop an identifiable visual design and consistent mode of production that would both streamline film production and contribute to a unique brand identity (often strongly associated with particular genres: e.g., Universal with expressionistic horror,[13] Warner Bros. with street-level gangster pictures[14]). In the contemporary postindustrial and poststudio era, however, production has become increasingly decentralized, and the major studios often function primarily as distributors. In this context, Marvel Studios' success as a brand and as a legitimate film studio seems to harken back to the classical era in more ways than one.[15]

It is precisely against the landscape of studio-mandated aesthetic standardization that the concept of the "auteur" initially emerged, as only truly "visionary" directors were able to transcend the strictures of a house style to put a distinctive stamp on their work. These concepts of house style (and classical studio filmmaking more generally) and auteurism have always existed in tension, such that Flanagan et al. suggest that Marvel's "insistence on house style" necessitates "the quasi-classical reining-in of authorship."[16] As the president of Marvel Studios and executive producer on all Marvel Studios films, Kevin Feige is often singled out as the "auteur" behind the MCU, with various directors realizing his vision in the same way that television directors report to an executive producer (or "showrunner"). Marvel's dismissal of directors like Patty Jenkins (from *Thor: The Dark World* [2013]) and *Scott Pilgrim*'s Edgar Wright (from *Ant-Man* [2015], a film he himself pitched, developed, and wrote before leaving the project due to creative differences[17]) suggests that the studio prefers to work with directors that are willing to color within the lines already established by previous entries in the MCU.

Given the ascendency of Marvel Studios and the adoption of its all-inclusive approach to world-building by its competitors, one might reasonably ask if narrative will displace aesthetics as comics' primary influence on contemporary filmmaking—that is, if it hasn't already. Is there room for the eccentricities of comic book film style in "quasi-classical" shared narrative universes such as the MCU? In an article for the website *Film School Rejects*, PhD candidate Landon Palmer wonders if Marvel's insistence on a house style might well preclude the possibility of innovative and stylized filmmaking:

As Marvel's calendar grows, and as it continues to form a cinematic universe that its executives feel must cohere under the umbrella of a narratively integrated house style, what room is there for distinctive filmmaking? What room is there for excess and flourish when the overt studio ideal requires not only the generic expectations of conventional heroic storytelling and the demands of summer-ready cinematic spectacle, but also that each film fulfill the requirements of an ambitious narrative network that must continually operate as a platform for new material?[18]

While Liam Burke has argued that Marvel Studios' films actually do evince some comic book influence on the level of style, most of the characteristics that he cites are among the defining attributes of David Bordwell's intensified continuity style, including "asymmetrical compositions," "exaggerated depth of field," and "a variety of angles," none of which fall under the umbrella of remediation.[19] This shouldn't be surprising: if Marvel Studios' goal is to establish a unified and coherent cinematic universe that is *separate and distinct* from that of the comics, it seems unlikely that the intermedial and nonnarrative effects of comic book film style would play any significant role. Indeed, aside from the occasional slow-motion panel moment (e.g., see figure 4.24, from *Avengers: Age of Ultron*), Marvel Studios' interest in comics has been mostly relegated to intertextual, rather than intermedial, appropriation.

So does the ascendency of Marvel Studios and its generic intensified continuity aesthetic sound the death knell of comic book film style? Can the fundamentally classical concept of house style be reconciled with the inherently nonclassical effects inherent in comic book film style? Even while the most popular and prolific purveyor of comic book superhero adaptations largely eschews the kind of stylization that would visually evoke the medium of sequential art, comic book film style can still be found in cinemas today, enriching the visual experience and intermedial complexity of superhero and nonsuperhero films alike. I would like to conclude this study with three brief case studies of films too recent to have received extended consideration elsewhere in the book. Collectively, these films illustrate the role of comic book film style at the present moment and also suggest what the future may hold for this highly influential mode of intermediality in the age of crossovers, serialization, and shared narrative universes.

Batman v Superman: Dawn of Justice

While the DCEU technically began with *Man of Steel* (2013), a film that intro-duced a new cinematic Superman more in line with the "gritty realism" of Christopher Nolan's influential Dark Knight trilogy, its storyworld expanded exponentially with its sequel, *Batman v Superman: Dawn of Justice*. Unlike the MCU's inaugural *Iron Man*, there was no hint of a "bigger universe" full of superheroes (or "metahumans") in *Man of Steel* (beyond a blink-and-you'll-miss-it Wayne Enterprises satellite and other such Easter eggs that would only be meaningful to eagle-eyed comics readers). As Mark J. P. Wolf notes, this is a fairly standard world-building strategy, whereby a world conceived for one story or character later grows to accommodate more and more nar-rative content.[20] More pressing for the purposes of this study is whether the DCEU adheres to or eschews an overarching house style, or, more point-edly: Does the DCEU have room for comic book film style? It may be too early to tell definitively, but the discourse coming from Warner Bros. and its DC Films division certainly wants to create the impression that its shared universe will be more amenable to stylistic variation and individual artistic visions than the MCU. As Sam Adams summarizes in a report from the set of *Justice League* (2017), "DC's mantra is that its movies are 'filmmaker driven,' a pointed contrast to the Marvel Cinematic Universe, where individuality takes a back seat to house style. (Just ask Edgar Wright.)"[21] The fact that DC hired Marvel Studios' cast-off Patty Jenkins to helm *Wonder Woman* (2017) strongly suggests that the former is willing to accept filmmakers' visions with fewer qualifications than the latter.[22]

If *Batman v Superman* is any indication, however, there may not be much more room for comic book film style in the DCEU than there has been in the MCU. Despite being directed by *300* and *Watchmen*'s Zack Snyder—the reigning king of comic book film style—*Batman v Superman*'s stylistic sys-tem has much more in common with Nolan's Dark Knight trilogy and Sny-der's own *Man of Steel* than the "fanboy auteur's"[23] more remediation-heavy adaptations.[24] Following the stylistic template established in *Man of Steel*, many of the action scenes in *Batman v Superman* are defined by shaky, hand-held camerawork, punctuated by quick zooms presumably meant to impart a pseudo-documentary feel; the film's re-creation of *Man of Steel*'s climax from Bruce Wayne's perspective certainly adheres to this model. Other scenes, however, are shot in a markedly different style. For instance, the "Knightmare" sequence at the center of the film can be productively com-pared to *300*'s "Crazy Horse" shot analyzed in chapter 4. Both present highly choreographed, CGI-heavy action scenes that play out within a seemingly unbroken take, feature blown-out lighting in keeping with their similar desert settings, and offer a dynamic sense of perspective on the action. This, however, is where the similarities between the two end. Whereas *300*'s sense of visual dynamism is created through speed ramping, digital zooms, and morphs between different perspectives, the "Knightmare" plays out within what appears to be a true long take captured by a smoothly moving camera. As *American Cinematographer* reveals, however, the

> elaborate camera move . . . is actually comprised of multiple moves stitched together in post. The shot is part of an apocalyptic dream sequence in which the Earth is laid to waste by alien forces. It begins with Batman fighting a squad of enemy troopers in the back of a big-rig trailer. The camera follows the skirmish out the back of the trailer, then tracks 360 degrees around Batman as he is finally overwhelmed[25]

by a horde of flying Parademons. In contrast to the handheld aesthetic favored in *Man of Steel* and elsewhere in *Batman v Superman*, the shots that compose this "shot" are steadied by forty feet of track and a Technocrane.[26] Whereas *Man of Steel* creates a realist aesthetic through handheld camera work, this shot favors a mode of realism more akin to a film like Alfonso Cuarón's *Children of Men* (2006), which Stephen Prince has compared to *300* thusly:

> Unlike the extended camera moves in *300* that present themselves as part of a visual effects sequence, the long takes in *Children of Men* unfold in a more naturalistic manner and are perceptually indistinguishable from true long takes. I make this distinction because, while Cuarón did shoot the film with extended takes, he lengthened these by digitally conjoining several takes to create scenes that unfold in a single, unbroken camera perspective. The joins between the shots cannot be seen even if the viewer knows where they are. The digital stitching is that perfect.[27]

The crucial difference that Prince alludes to but does not articulate in this passage is that *300* calls attention to the processes of (re)mediation inherent in the representation through the use of speed ramping and other techniques; in stark contrast to Snyder's liberal use of panel moments in *300* and *Watchmen*, no such temporal manipulation or self-reflexivity can be found in *Batman v Superman*'s "Knightmare" scene, which plays out entirely in real time.

In both *Man of Steel* and *Batman v Superman*, film style and digital visual effects are mostly employed synergistically to create an increased sense of verisimilitude. This is not to say that the film is devoid of anything resembling comic book film style, but rather that Snyder's typical tendencies toward this brand of stylization are considerably toned down. For instance, the film is bookended with funeral scenes—the former for Thomas and Martha Wayne, the latter for Clark Kent/Superman—both of which are replete with expressive slow-motion cinematography. The murder of the Waynes in particular strongly recalls the nearly static *tableaux* seen in the opening credits of *Watchmen*. Despite the use of slow motion in these scenes and elsewhere, however, the film only contains two true panel moments across its two-and-a-half hour running time, both of which occur in quick succession during a chase sequence involving the Batmobile. And despite the film's obvious debt to specific comic book narratives like *Batman: The Dark Knight Returns*, *The Death of Superman*, and "Must There Be a Superman?" (*Superman* #247, January 1972), the film boasts very few mimetic compositions that directly recall specific images and comic book panels; this is particularly surprising given Snyder's consistent predilection toward compositional intertextuality throughout *300* and *Watchmen*. In summation, *Batman v Superman* is only marginally more inclined toward comic book film style than *Man of Steel* and feels more like a step toward establishing what will ultimately become solidified as the "dark" and "gritty" DCEU house style.

Such an analysis is in keeping with the oft-expressed feeling that the DCEU—at least in its nascence—is not governed by a strong authorial voice or long-term plan, but is rather being made up on the fly, with each subsequent film in the storyworld designed as a direct response to and (over) correction of what audiences and critics didn't like about the previous one. As a case in point, the "dark" and "gritty" aesthetic of *Batman v Superman* is largely maintained in the third DCEU film (and the first to be directed by someone other than Snyder), David Ayer's *Suicide Squad*, but with some significant departures that were possibly added in postproduction (that is, after *Batman v Superman*'s release and critical drubbing).[28] Aside from a handful of Snyder-esque panel moments and slow-motion shots, *Suicide Squad*'s increased stylization compared to other DCEU films—its frequent use of garish neon colors, expository onscreen text, and a torrent of popular music cues, all of which are particularly concentrated in the first act—creates a somewhat bipolar aesthetic sensibility, like *Batman v Superman* by way of *Spring Breakers* (2012). Looking to the DCEU's future, the teaser trailer for

Wonder Woman features hints of an action sequence that contains at least three Snyder-esque panel moments—more than in the entirety of *Batman v Superman*—despite being directed by Jenkins rather than Snyder. (Whether these moments of temporal elasticity will be retained in the film's final cut, however, is at this point indeterminable.) In any case, further work is certainly warranted on the DCEU, its world-building approach compared to the MCU, and especially the relationship between its evolving house style and comic book film style.

The Diary of a Teenage Girl (2015)

In 2013, Abdellatif Kechiche's *Blue Is the Warmest Color*, a dramatic film adapted from a French graphic novel by Julie Maroh, won the prestigious Palme d'Or at the Cannes Film Festival. While the film's one-sheet recalls the restricted color palette of *Sin City* and appropriates the inking of its comic book source material with splashes of bright blue on an otherwise grayscale image, the movie itself is largely devoid of the self-reflexive or intermedial gestures that characterize comic book film style. Two years later, however, another female-penned graphic bildungsroman, Phoebe Gloeckner's semiautobiographical *Diary of a Teenage Girl: An Account in Words and Pictures*, was also adapted to film. Marielle Heller's adaptation would tackle subject matter somewhat comparable to Kechiche's film—both are coming-of-age narratives about teenage girls struggling with their nascent sexuality during times of social and political turbulence—but with a strong infusion of explicit intermediality in the vein of *American Splendor*. The film opens with two non-diegetic bits of hand-drawn animation, one locating the narrative in time and place ("San Francisco 1976") and the other announcing the film's title. Similar flourishes appear throughout, functioning alternately as vehicles for narrative exposition or as representations of the protagonist Minnie Goetze's artistic sensibility and inner life. Significantly, the character's journey includes her discovery of Aline Kominsky's underground "comix," and Minnie is often seen wearing a "Mickey Rat" T-shirt (including in the opening scene).[29] Both of these narrative choices signal the character's and the film's interest in the underground comix movement that flourished as part of San Francisco's counterculture at this time. The medium of comics—and specifically comix such as those produced by Kominsky, Robert Armstrong (of "Mickey Rat" fame), and their contemporaries—thus become a crucial part of the film's narrative world and its aesthetic approach, providing diegetically motivated opportunities for explicit intermediality. As the narrative progresses, the style of the animation evolves as well, beginning in stark black-and-white and becoming more sophisticated and colorful, culminating in a representation of a drug trip that recalls the dense hallucinogenic imagery of LSD-inspired comix.

While the cinematic afterlife of underground comix has largely been confined to animation so far—think *Fritz the Cat* (1972) or *Heavy Metal* (1981)—the distinct styling of underground and alternative comics also works well in a live-action context, as films like *The Diary of a Teenage Girl* and *American Splendor* demonstrate.[30] Narratively, both films center on the inner lives of characters who become directly involved in the creation of comics. To experience the world as Harvey Pekar and Minnie Goetze do is to see it as potential fodder for comics, if not as comics themselves. To convey this worldview, the filmmakers represent live-action worlds that are infiltrated and adorned by drawings that exist solely within their respective protagonist's mind. In this regard, both films owe a debt to Alain Resnais's *I Want to Go Home*, another film about an American comic strip writer/artist that positions imaginary animated avatars of comic strip characters into otherwise live-action environments. While *Diary* and *Splendor* both use this technique to align the viewer's perspective with the characters, Carolyn A. Durham argues that Resnais's explicit intermediality also serves a satirical purpose, turning "the comic strip into a particularly insightful tool of cultural analysis by establishing a double equation between American and 'low' or popular culture, on the one hand, and between French and 'high' or elite culture, on the other."[31] "Resnais uses the comic strip," she continues, "at the opposite end of the hierarchical scale of cultural art forms from Flaubert, to mediate between American culture as a whole and the Hollywood film industry, whose paradoxical ability to dominate the international market with a reportedly mediocre product makes it the ideal example of 'American cultural imperialism.'"[32] This sounds quite similar to Drew Morton's analysis of Jean-Luc Godard's deployment of comics imagery (specifically explicit intermediality) in *La Chinoise* (1967), where comic book images of Batman, Captain America, and Nick Fury are deployed as part of the film's Marxist ideological critique.[33] The comparisons to Resnais and Godard certainly suggest the potential of comic book film style in more experimental contexts than those in which it is usually deployed. While my decision to focus on American filmmaking placed these *nouvelle vague* filmmakers beyond the scope of this book, it's clear that comic books—including *bandes dessinées*, *fumetti*, and manga—have been and will continue to be remediated in other cultural and national filmmaking contexts, potentially creating alienating effects, discourses, and commentaries beyond those suggested here. With superhero films increasingly embracing interconnected storyworlds governed by restrictive house styles, the intermedial and inherently nonclassical effects of comic book film style may find their ideal home in the art house rather than the multiplex, both in adaptations of alternative comics like *The Diary of a Teenage Girl* and beyond.

Deadpool (2016)

While films like *Blue Is the Warmest Color* and *The Diary of a Teenage Girl* are welcome reminders that "comic book adaptation" need not be synonymous with Hollywood's continuing superhero obsession, the cape-and-cowl genre nevertheless remains an important potential site of remediation and stylistic innovation. Tim Miller's *Deadpool*, which was released a month prior to *Batman v Superman*, in some respects plays like a bog standard superhero outing intent on checking off a list of genre prerequisites: origin story that pins the creation of the superhero on the villain—check; montage showing the creation and evolution of the superhero costume—check; love interest that is kidnapped by the villain to lure the superhero to a climactic battle—check; sequel-teasing post-credits stinger—double check. Yet despite its conventional narrative, *Deadpool* is perhaps the most innovative and heavily stylized superhero film since *Watchmen*, owing largely to its commitment to comedic self-reflexivity. While comic book film style is inherently self-reflexive insofar as it forces viewers to be mindful of the medium-specific differences between cinema and comics, *Deadpool* goes further in this regard than any of the case studies explored over the previous chapters. In large part, this is a result of maintaining the titular character's metafictional traits from the comics. As executive producer Aditya Sood puts it in a documentary about the film's production, "One of the traditions of Deadpool from the comics is that he kind of exists in his own metanarrative where he is aware of the fact that he is in the comic, that he comments on the fact that he's in the comic."[34] In practice, this allows him to comment directly on nondiegetic attributes of the comic book medium (e.g., speech balloons, caption boxes, etc.) from within the fiction. In the film, this characteristic is adapted rather conventionally as a kind of direct address to the viewer that is by no means unique in terms of cinematic narration. (In a post-credits sequence, the film even explicitly pays homage to *Ferris Bueller's Day Off* [1986], a film with which it shares its style of fourth wall–breaking direct address.) Producer Simon Kinberg suggests that this potentially alienating approach to narration doesn't just provide humor but also effectively "[exposes] the process of making movies to the audience. It's pretty radical and something that the audience loves."[35] On the face of it, Kinberg's suggestion that the film's narration is radical may seem overblown, but *Deadpool*'s use of direct address does accomplish more than just elicit cheap laughs from its viewers. Whereas the trend in superhero cinema since 1998 has been toward fostering a kind of generic verisimilitude defined by "gritty" realism and muted colors, *Deadpool* is intent on laying bare its own artifice through comic book film style.

As in *Watchmen*, the opening credits sequence provides a rich starting point for an analysis of the film's visual design, narrative approach, and interest in self-reflexivity. The movie opens with diegetic time at a complete standstill. The (virtual) camera moves fluidly through coffee cup lids and various other obstacles that are suspended in perfect stasis, creating a statuesque three-dimensional *tableau*. The visual density of the scene is impressive: while onscreen text offers a parodic treatment of traditional cinematic opening credits (star Ryan Reynolds is credited only as "God's Perfect Idiot" while Miller's credit reads "Directed by an Overpaid Tool"), the mise-en-scène includes metatextual references to the comics (a stray Starbucks cup bearing the name "Rob L." refers to Deadpool creator Rob Liefeld) and an explicit reference to the film's star and his profilmic celebrity (in the form of a 2010 issue of *People Magazine* declaring Reynolds as the "Sexiest Man Alive"). In both cases, this will be the first of several such references: Liefeld's name is later given to a character within the fiction, and his name can be seen located elsewhere in the film's mise-en-scène; Reynolds's famously good looks and acting ability are further travestied in Deadpool's dialogue when the hideously scarred superhero (which is, of course, Reynolds himself buried under layers of makeup and latex) sarcastically quips: "Do you think Ryan Reynolds got this far on his superior acting method?" In short, this 106-second opening shot sequence primes the viewer for the kind of self-reflexive humor and approach to stylization that will set *Deadpool* apart from straight-faced superhero films.

Familiar markers of comic book film style are also scattered throughout the film, such as a caption box (reading "2 years ago . . .") and various manifestations of figural intermediality, including action sequences that are punctuated by multiple panel moments.[36] Deadpool's fourth wall–breaking narration warrants special mention here, as it—and indeed the character more generally—is essentially untethered from the diegetic world. A comparison to *Wanted* is helpful here. For instance, both films have scenes where cars flip over; both films use panel moments as a means of emphasizing the spectacular nature of this stunt; and both films even have their central characters speak from within the slow motion. But whereas *Wanted*'s Wesley yells "I'm sorry!" in a protracted manner that is synchronized with the slowed visual representation, Deadpool is able to move and speak in "real time" despite the slow motion all around him ("Oh shit—did I leave the stove on?"). Elsewhere, diegetic time halts completely—for instance, in the scene where Deadpool uses his swords to turn one goon into "a fucking kebab"— while Deadpool continues his narration in voiceover. Both strategies use cinema's potential for temporal elasticity to remediate comics' contradictory treatment of time within individual panels, which can squeeze a large amount of dialogue or narration into a panel that seems to visualize only a brief instant of diegetic time. Recall also that comic book film style is itself nondiegetic, insofar as its effects do not exist within the storyworld but only on the level of its representation. Such moments therefore incorporate the character's metafictional awareness of and mastery over the media that represent him into a standard trope of comic book film style.

Given the film's willingness to embrace such artifice and alienation effects, it may come as a surprise that *Deadpool* ostensibly occurs within the same diegetic universe as Twentieth Century Fox's *X-Men* films, including those mentioned at the outset of this conclusion. But just as Deadpool himself exists both inside and outside of the fictional world simultaneously, *Deadpool* both expands the diegesis previously established in the various *X-Men* films while also parodying the franchise's increasingly convoluted serial narrative. For instance, when metallic mutant muscleman Colossus asks Deadpool to visit the X-Men's leader, Professor Xavier, Deadpool's response betrays a metafictional awareness of the different actors that have played the character in the franchise's two competing timelines: "McAvoy or Stewart? These timelines are so confusing!" Deadpool also possesses a metatextual awareness of Reynolds's own history (and, to put it generously, mixed success) with superhero cinema, spoofing his appearances in *X-Men Origins: Wolverine* and *Green Lantern* (2011) at various points.[37] The *Green Lantern* reference—a pre-superheroic Wade Wilson/Deadpool pleads with his captors, "Please don't make the supersuit green . . . or animated!"—is an obvious gibe at the all-CG costume Reynolds sported in the aforementioned failed franchise-starter.[38] The character even mocks at multiple points the budget of the film in which he stars, which is extremely low by the standards of superhero tentpoles. While these metafictional gestures allow the film to transcend the limitations of the established *X-Men* universe in which it is

set—as suggested earlier, the style adhered to in Fox's *X-Men* films is arguably even more restrictive than the house styles of the MCU or DCEU—the
film's box office success may indicate that audiences are hungry for more
playfulness and stylization in superhero films going forward. In terms of
domestic box office, *Deadpool* actually outgrossed the hyperserious *Batman v
Superman*—despite a more restrictive R rating, less built-in character recognition, and a *much* lower budget.[39] The increased stylization and decreased
self-seriousness of DCEU films post *Batman v Superman* may reasonably be
interpreted as a response to *Deadpool* and its unique combination of self-
reflexive humor and comic book film style. For risk-averse Hollywood studios, *Deadpool* proves that departing from the quasi-classical house styles
seemingly necessitated by massive shared universes in favor of the idiosyn-
crasies and experimental attitude of comic book film style may be viable, if
not vital to the cinematic superhero genre's ongoing success.

This book has shown that live-action cinema has a tremendous capacity
to remediate a broad array of formal qualities associated with comic books
in a variety of innovative ways. From the speech balloon and the caption box
to the multipanel matrix and the privileged instant of the panel, remediating
the comic book medium using the resources of film style has undoubtedly
expanded the expressive vocabulary of cinema with a multitude of intermedial and polymedial effects. The three additional film analyses presented in
this short conclusion further suggest that comic book film style is very likely
to continue to play a significant role in the way filmmakers adapt comic book
material going forward, irrespective of genre or narrative approach. But in
transforming silence to sound, panel to frame, and stasis to movement, comic
book film style doesn't (or doesn't only) enable one medium's narrative content to adapt more smoothly to another; it totally reshapes the inherent
and conventionalized elements from comics within an ontologically alien
moving audio-image environment, challenging us to reconsider how these
aesthetic and narrative tools function, and how those functions necessarily
change depending on the context in which we encounter them. Crucially,
the results of this intermedial approach to film style are not merely flashy
or ostentatious departures from convention, nor can they be waved away as
"style for style's sake." In fact, comic book film style illuminates the nature
of cinema as a medium—ever changing, ever evolving—as much as it does
that of comics.

NOTES

INTRODUCTION

1. Tudor, "Walter Hill—Director."
2. See Brooker, *Hunting the Dark Knight*, 29–34, for a summary of critical and audience reactions to the film.
3. Ebert, "*Superman III*," n.p.
4. Faraci, "Joss Whedon on How to Make a Good Comic Book Movie," n.p.
5. Bolter and Grusin, *Remediation*, 45.
6. Ibid., 19.
7. Gardner, *Projections*, Kindle loc. 563.
8. Thompson, "Concept of Cinematic Excess," 523.
9. Bordwell, *On the History of Film Style*, 4.
10. Burke, *Comic Book Film Adaptation*, 267.
11. Bordwell, *The Way Hollywood Tells It*, 54.
12. King, *New Hollywood Cinema*, 74–75.
13. Ibid., 113.
14. Ibid., 1.
15. The Fader, "New York Mythology," n.p.
16. Horsley, *The Blood Poets*, 36.
17. Ibid., 37.
18. Johnson, *The Action Cinema Handbook*, 42.
19. Tudor, "Walter Hill—Director," n.p.

20. Chaplin, "Walter Hill," 241.

21. Gardner, *Projections*, Kindle loc. 1732.

22. McCloud, *Understanding Comics*, 9.

23. Wolk, *Reading Comics*, Kindle loc. 223.

24. The inverse mistake is also possible: for instance, a chapter devoted to super-hero films in Eric Lichtenfeld's *Action Speaks Louder* includes a discussion of *Sin City*, presumably because it's a comic book adaptation. Since the film is a neo-noir with no real ties to the superhero genre, it seems likely that the author is conflating the two categories. See Lichtenfeld, *Action Speaks Louder*, 309–312.

25. Burke, *Comic Book Film Adaptation*, 8.

26. King, *New Hollywood Cinema*, 80.

27. Hughes, *Comic Book Movies*, 1.

28. See chapter 8 of Leitch, *Film Adaptation and Its Discontents*.

29. Bordwell, *The Way Hollywood Tells It*, 54.

30. Leitch, "Adaptation Studies at a Crossroads," 63.

31. Ibid., 64; italics added.

32. Stam, "Beyond Fidelity," 54.

33. Smith, "Shaping *The Maxx*," 33.

34. Rehak, "*Watchmen*: Stuck in the Uncanny Valley."

35. Stam, "Beyond Fidelity," 54.

36. Hassler-Forest, "The *300* Controversy," n.p.

37. See Lefèvre, "Incompatible Visual Ontologies?"

38. Burke, *Comic Book Film Adaptation*, 18.

39. Ibid.

40. Ibid., 106.

41. Ibid., 99.

42. Ibid., 117.

43. Tudor, quoted in Neale, *Genre and Hollywood*, 17–18; emphasis in original.

44. See Bakhtin's discussion of heteroglossia, a concept that would later become the basis for literary intertextuality, in "Discourse in the Novel." See Bakhtin, *The Dialogic Imagination*, 259–422.

45. Bolter and Grusin, *Remediation*, 65.

46. Ibid., 26.

47. Ibid., 65.

48. Ibid., 19.

49. Shklovsky, *Theory of Prose*, 6; emphasis in original.

50. Bolter and Grusin, *Remediation*, 44.

51. Bolter, "Transference and Transparency," 24; italics added.

52. Lefèvre, "Incompatible Visual Ontologies?," 12.

53. Bolter and Grusin, *Remediation*, 15; italics added.

CHAPTER 1. THE SIX MODES OF INTERACTION BETWEEN COMICS AND FILM

1. Burke, *Comic Book Film Adaptation*, 23.
2. The British film *Tamara Drewe*, adapted from Posy Simmonds's graphic novel, was also released in 2010. It is excluded from this list based only on the fact that it was produced outside of the Hollywood system.
3. Bordwell, *The Way Hollywood Tells It*; Shaviro, *Post-Cinematic Affect*.
4. Bordwell, *The Way Hollywood Tells It*, 137.
5. Shaviro, *Post-Cinematic Affect*, 123.
6. Ibid., 67.
7. Beaty, *History of Violence*, 27.
8. Bluestone, *Novels into Film*, ix.
9. Burke, *Comic Book Film Adaptation*, 140–141.
10. Julia Round has argued that even while the filmmakers adapting comics often claim to use panels as storyboards, the images that result are never perfectly equivalent to the original panel. This is due to the various medium-specific differences that necessarily shape the ways in which images are presented and experienced for film (or television) and comics, respectively. See Round, "Revenant Landscapes in *The Walking Dead*," 3.
11. Tweedie, "Moving Pictures, Still Lives," 256.
12. Burke, *Comic Book Film Adaptation*, 18.
13. Of course, one needs to be fairly familiar with the comics intertexts being evoked to even recognize that remediation is taking place in these instances. As Neil Rae and Jonathan Gray put it, comic book film viewers who aren't also comic book readers are "intertextually 'poor'" compared to the "intertextually 'rich'" readers. The latter category would be more likely to have the kind of specialized knowledge required to recognize compositional mimesis at work. See Rae and Gray, "When Gen-X Met the X-Men," 89.
14. See, for example, Perry, "From Comics to Movies: Visual References in The Dark Knight Trilogy" and Perry, "From Comics to Movies: Visual References in The X-Men Franchise."
15. In the comic, this occurs in *The Losers* #4 (November 2003); it takes place around 1:15:30 in the Blu-ray edition of the film.
16. This scene takes place in *The Losers* #3 (October 2003) and at 54:33 in the Blu-ray edition of the film.
17. Groensteen, *Comics and Narration*, 146.
18. Some comic book films that employ a montage of comic book art during their opening credits include *Superman*, *Flash Gordon* (1980), *Brenda Starr* (1989), *The Return of Swamp Thing* (1989), *Tank Girl* (1995), *Judge Dredd* (1995), *G-Men from Hell* (2000), *American Splendor*, *Spider-Man 2*, *Sin City*, *Ultraviolet*, and *Super*.

Spider-Man 2, for example, features a montage of art by comics painter Alex Ross that summarizes the plot of the previous film in the franchise. It should also be noted that both Marvel Studios and DC Films have short animations that precede the opening credits in many film versions of their properties. These are modified for each film to include comics art featuring the characters being adapted onscreen.

19. Burke, *Comic Book Film Adaptation*, 151.
20. Ibid., 149.
21. Rae and Gray, "When Gen-X Met the X-Men," 98.
22. Lefèvre, "Incompatible Visual Ontologies?," 4.
23. Ibid., 9.
24. Bazin, *What Is Cinema?*, 7.
25. Cohen, "Dick Tracy," 16.
26. Bazin, *What Is Cinema?*, 8.
27. Prince, *Digital Visual Effects in Cinema*, Kindle loc. 46.
28. Groensteen, *System of Comics*, 19.
29. Manovich, *Language of New Media*, 322.
30. Lefèvre, "Incompatible Visual Ontologies?," 6.
31. See Ecke, "Spatializing the Movie Screen."
32. Gardner, *Projections*, Kindle loc. 91.
33. McCloud, *Understanding Comics*, 92.
34. Pedler, "The Fastest Man Alive," 253.
35. McCloud, *Understanding Comics*, 63.
36. Carrier, *Aesthetics of Comics*, 51.
37. Groensteen, *System of Comics*, 10.
38. Ibid., 11.
39. Scott, "Dawn of the Undead Author," 450.
40. Indeed, Costas Constandinides, Drew Morton, and Liam Burke have all erroneously conflated the staccato rhythm of panel moments with bullet time. See Constandinides, *From Film Adaptation to Post-Celluloid Adaptation*, 87; Burke, *Comic Book Film Adaptation*, 196–197; and Morton, "Comics to Film," 47. (Morton has since revised his dissertation as the book *Panel to the Screen*, which was published as this book was going to press.)
41. Rehak, "Migration of Forms," 34.
42. These occur between 5:07 and 5:37 on the Blu-ray version.
43. This scene takes place between 49:10 and 49:22 on the Blu-ray version.
44. McCloud, *Understanding Comics*, 67.
45. Lefèvre, "Incompatible Visual Ontologies?," 6.

CHAPTER 2. VANDALIZING THE FOURTH WALL

1. Carrier, *Aesthetics of Comics*, 4.
2. Ibid., 38.
3. Gravett, *Comics Art*, 22. Until that point, Richard Outcault had written the Yellow Kid's "dialogue" on his oversized shirt or elsewhere in the mise-en-scène. Perhaps not recognizing his own innovation, he would largely abandon the speech balloon and return to his earlier convention with subsequent strips (24).
4. McCloud, *Understanding Comics*, 12.
5. Groensteen, *System of Comics*, 12.
6. Lefèvre, "Incompatible Visual Ontologies?," 11.
7. Ibid. Lefèvre doesn't interrogate the issue further, concluding that silence and sound are fundamentally different means of communication and that "the change from a 'silent medium' to a 'sound medium' poses also a lot of problems for the adaptation" (12).
8. Khordoc, "Comic Book's Soundtrack," 159.
9. Carrier, *Aesthetics of Comics*, 45.
10. Ibid., 44.
11. Shklovsky, *Theory of Prose*, 6.
12. Bordwell, Staiger, and Thompson, *Classical Hollywood Cinema*, 3.
13. Gardner, *Projections*, Kindle loc. 560.
14. Ibid., Kindle loc. 664.
15. Chion, *Audio-Vision*, 170.
16. Eisner, *Comics and Sequential Art*, 24.
17. Bordwell, Staiger, and Thompson, *Classical Hollywood Cinema*, 187.
18. Ibid., 186.
19. Altman, *Silent Film Sound*, 372.
20. Bordwell, Staiger, and Thompson, *Classical Hollywood Cinema*, 301.
21. Kirchoff, "Beyond Remediation," 27.
22. Kirchoff recognizes this, justifying his position by examining only comic *books* rather than *strips* (ibid., 42). However, since comic books began in the late nineteenth century as collected reprints of daily strips, the distinction between strips and books doesn't hold. Moreover, the differences between strips and books is not formal but rather narrative in nature (e.g., length of individual episodes, reliance on seriality). Whether a newspaper or a standalone magazine/pamphlet/book, the venue or form of publication doesn't affect how comics captions function.
23. Carrier, *Aesthetics of Comics*, 29.
24. McCloud, *Making Comics*, 142.
25. Altman, *Silent Film Sound*, 168.
26. Ibid.

27. See Røssaak, "Figures of Sensation."

28. Tomasovic, "The Hollywood Cobweb," 315.

29. This shot warrants a bit of clarification. While *The Great Train Robbery* is largely narrative in its orientation, this final shot is not easily reconciled with what has come before, since the gun-toting cowboy in question is no longer alive at the end of the film. Coupled with the direct address to the viewer, the shot is most persuasively identified as an attraction that lies beyond the scope of the narrative.

30. Gunning, "Cinema of Attraction[s]," 382.

31. Ibid., 383.

32. Ibid., 384.

33. *Scott Pilgrim vs. the World*, which uses text to an even greater extent than any of these four films, is discussed in detail in chapter 5 and is therefore excluded from consideration in this chapter.

34. Gardner, *Projections*, Kindle loc. 108.

35. Warner, "*Phew! Whaam! Aaargh! Boo!*," 120–121.

36. Rowsell, Pedersen, and Trueman, "Playing as a Mutant," 51.

37. See Baudrillard, *Simulacra and Simulation*.

38. Chion, *Audio-Vision*, 9.

39. Warner, "*Phew! Whaam! Aaargh! Boo!*," 108.

40. For the sake of comprehensiveness (and no other reason), I present a complete list of the onomatopoeias included in this sequence: BIFF, BAP!, ZWAPP!, SPLOOSH, KLONK, URKK, SWOOSH, SWA-A-P, EEE-YOW, OUCH!, KAPOW!, KER-SPLOOSH, SPLA-A-T, PLOP, URKKK!!, BLURP!, and finally, KER-PLOP!

41. Wartenberg, "Wordy Pictures," 100.

42. Chion, *Audio-Vision*, 60.

43. Warner, "*Phew! Whaam! Aaargh! Boo!*," 121.

44. Young, *Colonial Desire*, 21.

45. For camp readings of *Batman*, see Medhurst, "Batman, Deviance and Camp"; Torres, "The Caped Crusader of Camp"; Brooker, *Batman Unmasked*; and Yockey, *Batman*.

46. Gardner, *Projections*, Kindle loc. 46.

47. Ibid., Kindle loc. 55.

48. Genette, *Palimpsests*, 20.

49. Gunning, "Cinema of Attraction[s]," 382.

50. While *Super* arguably represents the zenith of this subgenre, other films have tackled similar subject matter, including *Mystery Men* (1999), *Unbreakable* (2001), *Special* (2006), *Defendor* (2009), the HBO documentary *Superheroes* (2011), and most notably *Kick-Ass* and *Kick-Ass 2*.

51. See Cohn, *Visual Language of Comics*, 41.

52. Carrier, *Aesthetics of Comics*, 4.

53. Kinder, "Playing with Power," 261.

54. The film's use of the comics panel, specifically in its innovative opening credits sequence, is discussed in the following chapter.

55. See, for instance, Hight, "*American Splendor*"; Bolton, "Narrativity, Purpose, and Visible Adaptation"; and Sperb, "Removing the Experience."

56. Bolton, "Narrativity, Purpose, and Visible Adaptation."

57. Ibid.

58. Morton, "Comics to Film (and Back Again)," 159.

59. Otto Pächt, quoted in Carrier, *Aesthetics of Comics*, 29.

60. Gunning, "Cinema of Attraction[s]," 382.

61. Jim Carrey, who appears in *Kick-Ass 2* as Colonel Stars and Stripes, notoriously boycotted the film for its high level of gun violence. The 2012 shooting at Sandy Hook Elementary School, which occurred between production and the film's release, was the catalyst for his change of heart. See Petri, "Jim Carrey Refuses to Promote Kick-Ass 2."

62. See Khordoc, "Comic Book's Soundtrack," 156–173.

63. Curti, "Beating Words to Life," 201–202.

64. McClarty, "In Support of Creative Subtitling," 597–598.

65. Khordoc, "Comic Book's Soundtrack," 157.

66. McClarty, "In Support of Creative Subtitling," 593.

67. While this scene is present in Mark Millar and John Romita Jr.'s *Kick-Ass 2* comics, the gangsters therein speak English. The Chinese dialogue is specific to the film, opening up the possibility for creative subtitling. In the commentary track on the Blu-ray release of the film, director Jeff Wadlow takes credit for the idea of presenting the subtitles as speech balloons.

68. For instance, Anna Foerster suggests that *Night Watch*'s dynamic subtitles seem to have been produced by "someone inexperienced, who might not understand the underlying reasons for the conventions applied in standard subtitling practice." See Foerster, "Towards a Creative Approach in Subtitling," 88.

69. McClarty, "In Support of Creative Subtitling," 593.

70. Ibid., 598.

71. Rodowick, *Reading the Figural*, 3.

72. Gardner, *Projections*, Kindle loc. 3584.

73. See McCloud, *Understanding Comics*, 9; and Groensteen, *System of Comics*, 19.

CHAPTER 3. THESE PANELS HAVE BEEN FORMATTED TO FIT YOUR SCREEN

1. See the episode of *Siskel & Ebert* streaming online at http://siskelandebert.org/video/9WMU5YX115WB/What8217s-Wrong-With-Home-Video.

2. Aumont, *The Image*, 106.

3. Mitry, *Aesthetics and Psychology of the Cinema*, 75.

4. Groensteen, *System of Comics*, 30–31.

5. Cook, "Why Comics Are Not Films," 173.

6. Bolter and Grusin, *Remediation*, 45.

7. Mitry, *Aesthetics and Psychology of the Cinema*, 80.

8. Friedberg, *The Virtual Window*, 4–5.

9. Mitry, *Aesthetics and Psychology of the Cinema*, 80.

10. Stork, "Chaos Cinema."

11. Pratt, "Making Comics into Film," 153.

12. Groensteen, *System of Comics*, 25–26.

13. The storyboard, a pretext to many films, is also often equated with comics, specifically in films that prominently feature mimetic compositions. Insofar as the storyboard represents a drawn template for a particular film composition, comics panels may be *treated* as storyboards, but they are not themselves storyboards per se. A comics panel is not an intermediary step between conception and representation, but is itself the final representation in its own medium: it is text, not pretext. Nevertheless, the fact that many shots require more than one storyboard to previsualize provides further evidence that sequential static images, like those of comics, are not necessarily equivalent to an equal number of cinematic shots.

14. McCloud, *Understanding Comics*, 66–72.

15. Smith, "Shaping *The Maxx*," 34.

16. Groensteen, *Comics and Narration*, Kindle loc. 2595.

17. Ecke, "Spatializing the Movie Screen," 15.

18. Ibid.

19. Ibid., 7.

20. Deleuze, *Cinema 1*, 13–14.

21. Ecke, "Spatializing the Movie Screen," 15.

22. I can only speculate that the lack of symmetry here is a deliberate attempt to suggest that the character of Superman has fully transcended the medium of his origin to become a figure of the cinema.

23. Perhaps the best-known instance of this effect in American comics is Spider-Man's "spider-sense," a superpower that serves to warn the character of urgent dangers. In the 2002 film featuring the character, this power was conveyed using a variation on "bullet time." See chapter 4 for an analysis of this effect in the context of comic book film style.

24. The placement of photographic images within the architecture of comics also calls to mind the related medium of the photonovel, which combined the narrative and visual conventions of comics (panels, word balloons, expository captions, etc.) with photographic stills from live-action films or television programs. This hybrid medium was most popular as an inexpensive alternative to

dubbing or subtitling films, or as a means of distributing filmic and televisual texts prior to the advent of home video technologies.

25. Bolter and Grusin, *Remediation*, 45.

26. Bordwell and Thompson, *Film Art*, 187.

27. Friedberg, *The Virtual Window*, 191.

28. Bordwell and Thompson, *Film Art*, 187.

29. Manovich, *Language of New Media*, 323.

30. Friedberg, *The Virtual Window*, 198.

31. Ibid., 3.

32. For scholarship concerning the use of split screen in Lee's film, see Booker, *May Contain Graphic Material*, xxxi; Ecke, "Spatializing the Movie Screen," 17–19; Morton, "Comics to Film (and Back Again)," 120–132; and Rauscher, "Workshop IV," 265–273.

33. Such disruptions in traditional continuity can be read for their symbolic meaning—the characters literally do not see "eye to eye"—or as symptomatic of the comparative lack of continuity from panel to panel in a comic book. Groensteen writes that "in a comic, narrative *continuity* is assured by the *contiguity* of images" (*System of Comics*, 117) rather than by cinematic devices like eyeline matches, match cuts, sound bridges, etc.

34. Manovich, *Language of New Media*, 322.

35. Groensteen, *System of Comics*, 31.

36. Lefèvre, "Incompatible Visual Ontologies?," 6.

37. Gardner, *Projections*, Kindle loc. 91.

38. Morton, "Comics to Film (and Back Again)," 126.

39. Michael Cohen, quoted in Bizzocchi, "The Fragmented Frame."

40. Burke, *Comic Book Film Adaptation*, 184–185.

41. Morton, "Comics to Film (and Back Again)," 127.

42. Ibid., 127–129.

43. Rauscher, "Workshop IV," 269.

44. Morton, "Comics to Film (and Back Again)," 127.

45. There are also consequences in terms of how point of view is constructed. As Aumont writes, "The notion of framing, by way of the fantasy of the visual pyramid, invites us to establish an equivalence between the eye of the image-maker and that of the spectator. It is this assimilation of one to the other that also informs the many forms of the concept of point of view" (*The Image*, 115). Moments such as the one seen in figure 3.17 make this equivalence more complex, given the plurality of perspectives offered by the film. Friedberg's invocation of cubism and its multiple simultaneous perspectives is also apt here (*The Virtual Window*, 191).

46. Hagener, "Aesthetics of Displays."

47. Bizzocchi, "The Fragmented Frame."

48. Paul Feig's *Ghostbusters* (2016) creates a similar effect by having digital arti-facts (ghosts, proton streams, and even something as banal as a necklace in one scene) extend beyond the 2.35:1 photographic space and into the letterboxed negative space at the top and bottom of the screen. This accentuates the effect of the 3-D presentation, and gives the impression that these effects transcend the reality of the diegetic world.

49. The next chapter is concerned with temporal effects, such as slow motion, as a means of remediating comics.

50. This incredibly novel sequence is impossible to adequately describe in prose. On the Blu-ray release of the film, the sequence begins at 1:12:06 and ends at 1:13:47. In its theatrical 3-D presentation, the subshots were further distin-guished from one another by their varying depths, an effect that is lost in its 2-D version.

51. Groensteen, *Comics and Narration*, Kindle loc. 1437.

52. Ibid., Kindle loc. 616.

CHAPTER 4. THE PRIVILEGED INSTANT

1. The Flash had previously been introduced in the "Golden Age" with the alter ego Jay Garrick in *Flash Comics* #1 (January 1940). The "Silver Age" saw the reintroduction and refinement of the superhero genre about ten years after its popularity fell sharply with the end of World War II.

2. Wolk, *Reading Comics*, Kindle loc. 96.

3. Ibid., Kindle loc. 104.

4. Bukatman, "Comics and the Critique of Chronophotography," 86.

5. Ibid., 88.

6. Scott McCloud would classify such Muybridge-esque panel transitions as "moment-to-moment," which his research reveals to be among the least used transition types in all of comics; their scarcity is rivaled only by "non-sequitur" transitions (*Understanding Comics*, 74–75).

7. Bukatman, "Comics and the Critique of Chronophotography," 89.

8. In moving-image representations of the character, such as *The Flash* television series (2014–) and the teaser trailer for *Justice League* (2017), superspeed is often represented using extreme slow motion through which the character moves at a regular or heightened speed. While 24 frames per second may be insuffi-cient to represent the Flash, significantly increased shooting speeds may prove adequate.

9. For an analysis of character and franchise reboots in comics and cinema, including a discussion of the Flash, see Proctor, "Beginning Again."

10. Burke, *Comic Book Film Adaptation*, 194.

11. Arnheim, *Art and Visual Perception*, 384; italics added.

12. Ndalianis, "Frenzy of the Visible," 238.

13. Ibid.

14. Pedler, "The Fastest Man Alive," 253. Comic book artists need to be especially careful to differentiate between movement and stasis, since both states are represented via static images. Pedler notes that this is the reason why Captain Cold or Mr. Freeze's victims must be visibly covered in icicles; without such explicit signifiers, readers wouldn't be able to tell who's frozen in place, since from the reader's perspective everybody's motion in the comic book is "frozen" already.

15. Ibid., 250.

16. Doane, *Emergence of Cinematic Time*, 60.

17. Bukatman, "Comics and the Critique of Chronophotography," 90.

18. Doane, *Emergence of Cinematic Time*, 33.

19. Ibid., 4.

20. Pedler, "The Fastest Man Alive," 253.

21. Gardner, *Projections*, Kindle loc. 274.

22. Doane, *Emergence of Cinematic Time*, 189.

23. Deleuze, *Cinema 1*, 4.

24. Ibid., 5.

25. See https://twitter.com/DavidAyerMovies/status/586347483955142656 and https://twitter.com/DavidAyerMovies/status/591761248859123713.

26. Carroll, "The Future of Allusion," 53.

27. Ibid., 56.

28. Ibid., 57.

29. Lefebvre, "The Art of Pointing," 221.

30. Prince, "True Lies," 273.

31. Manovich, *Language of New Media*, 295.

32. Lefebvre, "The Art of Pointing," 231–232.

33. Ibid., 389n34.

34. Bergson, quoted in Doane, *Emergence of Cinematic Time*, 77.

35. All of these events have been narrativized numerous times in the comics, but perhaps most notably in *Daredevil* #1 (April 1964), *Daredevil: The Man Without Fear* #1 (October 1993), and *Daredevil: Yellow* #1–6 (August 2001–January 2002).

36. From *Daredevil* #168 (January 1981).

37. From *Daredevil* #181 (April 1982).

38. Kirby is played by Kevin Smith, who wrote the "Guardian Devil" arc for which Quesada provided the pencils. See *Daredevil* Vol. 2, #1–8 (November 1998–June 1999).

39. See Jeffries, "Spotting Stan."

40. To call this image the "opening shot" of the film is somewhat misleading, since it is a digitally assisted tracking shot that begins at ground level, then scales up

the side of a church, and finally settles on Daredevil clutching the crucifix at its spire. In the midst of the upward camera movement, five brief flash-forwards to various of the film's fight scenes occur. Though the trajectory of the camera is consistent, sometimes we are closer to the church upon returning from these cutaways (notably in the seventh shot, which is a close-up on a stained glass portrait). A strict shot-by-shot analysis would technically identify this as the eleventh shot of the film (beginning after the digitally animated opening credits sequence).

41. If not from "the text" more generally, which would encompass the film itself as well as an assemblage of paratexts that influence the film's reception. As Jonathan Gray argues in *Show Sold Separately*, "A film or [television] program is but one part of the text, the text always being a contingent entity, either in the process of forming and transforming or vulnerable to further formation or transformation" (Kindle loc. 197).

42. See *Daredevil* #227–233 (February–August 1986) and *Daredevil: The Man Without Fear* #1–5 (October 1993–February 1994), respectively.

43. A film like *Tank Girl* takes this practice to another level, using actual comic book art to transition between scenes.

44. Doane, *Emergence of Cinematic Time*, 94.

45. McCloud, *Understanding Comics*, 113.

46. Owano, "High Frame Rate Cinema Booed."

47. Cohn, *Visual Language of Comics*, 10.

48. Ibid., 134.

49. Constandinides, *From Film Adaptation to Post-Celluloid Adaptation*, 84.

50. See McCloud, *Understanding Comics*, 111, and Ndalianis, "Frenzy of the Visible," 245.

51. Gardner, *Projections*, Kindle loc. 91.

52. Pratt, "Narrative in Comics," 111.

53. McCloud, *Understanding Comics*, 67.

54. Ibid., 68.

55. Groensteen, *System of Comics*, 11; italics added.

56. Ibid., 66.

57. Ironically, it is precisely this aspect of comics that the psychologist Fredric Wertham singled out as damaging to young minds in his infamous anti-comics crusade of the 1950s. Predictably, Wertham was far less generous than McCloud in ascribing a creative or even active role to readers. As Gardner puts it, "Where Wertham gets it wrong is in his embrace of a comic book version of the 'intentional fallacy,' imagining that [the] process [of closure] is controlled by producers determined to dictate specific pathological responses," rather than by the readers themselves in active negotiation with the text (*Projections*, Kindle loc. 1929). For more on Wertham, see Nyberg, *Seal of Approval*, and Beaty, *Fredric Wertham and the Critique of Mass Culture*.

58. Gardner associates the gutter between panels with the cultural "gutter" in which comics has existed for most of its history. In filling the gutters between panels, it seems that McCloud's theory of closure hopes to pull comics out of the cultural gutter as well. See Gardner, *Projections*, Kindle loc. 91.

59. Obviously, this doesn't include "motion comics," which ought to be considered separately as "an emerging form of digital animation that typically appropriates and remediates an existing comic book narrative and artwork into a screen-based animated narrative" (Smith, "Motion Comics," 357). Motion comics will be considered in the next chapter with regard to *Watchmen*'s motion comic adaptation.

60. Somigli, "Superhero with a Thousand Faces," 280–281.

61. See Powell, *Stop the Clocks!*, 11–31, for a discussion of "real time" films from Alfred Hitchcock's *Rope* (1948) to Joel Schumacher's *Phone Booth* (2002).

62. Doane, *Emergence of Cinematic Time*, 172.

63. Powell, *Stop the Clocks!*, 18.

64. Rehak, "The Migration of Forms," 26.

65. The lenses were 85mm, 35mm, and 18mm, giving radically different depths of field and perspectives on the action despite a consistent shooting position.

66. If projected at the normal playback rate of 24 frames per second, each second of profilmic reality shot at this rate would take over six seconds to view.

67. Fordham, "A Beautiful Death," 78.

68. Prince, *Digital Visual Effects in Cinema*, Kindle loc. 1279.

69. Ibid., Kindle loc. 1265.

70. Burke, *Comic Book Film Adaptation*, 196.

71. Constandinides, *From Film Adaptation to Post-Celluloid Adaptation*, 87; italics in original.

72. McCloud, *Understanding Comics*, 67.

73. The aforementioned slow-motion sequences in *X-Men: Days of Future Past* and *X-Men: Apocalypse* operate similarly, speeding up and slowing down in a visually dynamic way that is not strictly tied to Quicksilver's subjectivity.

74. Stork, "Chaos Cinema."

75. There's also something to be said for comics' natural ability to render actions in their most hyperbolic and impressive state, distilling lengthy sequences down to their most aesthetically striking moments. Spider-Man comics, for instance, are practically catalogues of the character's most intricate, acrobatic poses, which don't maintain their sense of grandiosity when presented as fleeting instants within larger movements. The number of panel moments in *The Amazing Spider-Man 2*, which isolate and emphasize precisely these kinds of poses, seems to be a direct response to this problem.

76. Watercutter, "Video."

77. Doane, *Emergence of Cinematic Time*, 27.

CHAPTER 5. THE POLYMEDIAL COMIC BOOK FILM

1. This is distinct from what Drew Morton has dubbed "re-remediation," which refers specifically to film remediations of comic books that have themselves remediated cinema. As a representative example, Morton claims that Frank Miller, *Sin City*'s comic book writer/artist and codirector of its film adaptation, uses "film to re-remediate his initial comic book remediation of noir visual style." This is more a case akin to a snake eating its own tail, and doesn't represent a more complex phenomenon than standard remediation, in my view, since film and comics remain the only media involved in the intermedial exchange. See Morton, "Comics to Film (and Back Again)," 30.

2. Madianou and Miller, "Polymedia," 170.

3. Ibid., 175.

4. Shaviro, *Post-Cinematic Affect*, Kindle loc. 1495.

5. Madianou and Miller, "Polymedia," 171.

6. Ibid., 172.

7. Gaudreault and Marion, *The End of Cinema?*, Kindle loc. 688.

8. Bolter and Grusin, *Remediation*, 6.

9. Rodowick, *Reading the Figural*, 3.

10. Gardner, *Projections*, Kindle loc. 3029.

11. Ibid., Kindle loc. 3644.

12. Shaviro, *Post-Cinematic Affect*, Kindle loc. 28.

13. Ibid., Kindle loc. 103.

14. Kadner, "Girl Trouble," 46.

15. See Murphy, "Virtual Canadian Realities," 502; Murray, "Scott Pilgrim vs the Future of Comics Publishing," 130; and Pino, "Sound Affects," 89.

16. Shaviro, *Post-Cinematic Affect*, Kindle loc. 103.

17. See Pino, "Sound Affects."

18. At a glance, the *Scott Pilgrim* series might be mistaken for manga, given the dimensions of each book, the graphic style (including large *kawaii* [cute] eyes), and the black-and-white printing. Nevertheless, the relationship between the *Scott Pilgrim* graphic novels and manga is a contentious one. While some categorize them as Original English Language manga, O'Malley himself rejects this and prefers the designation "manga-influenced comic." I prefer the latter categorization as well, since it recognizes the hybridity and transnationality of the series' style. See Berninger, "'Scott Pilgrim Gets It Together,'" 247.

19. Wolf, *Building Imaginary Worlds*, 247.

20. Murray, "Scott Pilgrim vs. the Future of Comics Publishing," 130.

21. Shaviro, *Post-Cinematic Affect*, Kindle loc. 974.

22. Ibid., Kindle loc. 980.

23. For instance, see Lascelles, "'Scott Pilgrim vs. the World'"; Semansky, "*Scott Pilgrim vs. the World* Is Almost Sensory Overload . . . "; Waterhouse, "'Scott Pilgrim vs. the World' Succeeds in Sensory Overload."

24. Juul, *Half-Real*, 35.

25. Ibid., 1.

26. Jeff Thoss, quoted in Murray, "Scott Pilgrim vs. the Future of Comics Publishing," 136.

27. "Chiptune" refers to the style of synthesized electronic music found in older (1990s and before) video games, arcade machines, and computers. "Eight-bit" refers to the computing power of the microprocessor found in systems such as the Nintendo Entertainment System (NES).

28. In an interview, Wright noted that Quentin Tarantino had suggested to him that viewers needed "a title sequence at the start to let people settle in and hint more about what we were about to see" after screening an early cut of the film with a different opening credits sequence. See Ulloa, "*Scott Pilgrim vs the World* (2010)."

29. The sequence is bookended by shots of Knives looking on in amazement. Wright has suggested that "the animation is a manifestation of how cool the music is in Knives' head." See ibid.

30. The sequence was actually produced by scratching on sheets of acetate, which were kicked around the floor to add scratches, dirt, and hairs before being scanned into a computer and divided into frames. See ibid.

31. Manovich, *Language of New Media*, 306.

32. Ibid., 307.

33. Pino, "Sound Affects," 100.

34. The title of the comic book is itself a reference to the Smashing Pumpkins' 1995 double-album *Mellon Collie and the Infinite Sadness*. Throughout the comic and the film, Scott wears different Smashing Pumpkins T-shirts, including one with their shared initials "SP" inside a crudely drawn heart.

35. McCloud, *Understanding Comics*, 67.

36. Each of the shots in this sequence also represents a mimetic composition. See chapter 3 of *Scott Pilgrim's Precious Little Life*, "This One Girl . . ."

37. This aesthetic strategy has also been appropriated by Japanese anime, through which it has been taken up and remediated in films (e.g., *Kill Bill Vol. 1* [2003]).

38. Cossar, "Shape of New Media," 6.

39. Murray argues that "the comic's nostalgic preoccupation with old technologies such as eight-bit gaming and arcade games betrays an anxiety regarding format irrelevance and obsolescence, as well as about big business and media conglomeration." The film maintains this ambivalence toward contemporary technologies, particularly through Scott's sense of obliviousness to contemporary

technology and media. For instance, Scott needs to ask his roommate the web address for "Amazon.ca." The preference for "old" media (e.g., Young Neil plays an original Nintendo GameBoy rather than its current-generation equivalent, the Nintendo 3DS) is also a key component of the film's address to "geek" culture. See Murray, "Scott Pilgrim vs. the Future of Comics Publishing," 139.

40. Ahn, "Animated Subjects," 30.

41. Lamarre, *The Anime Machine*, 19.

42. These sequences—flashbacks to Ramona's previous relationships with Evil Exes numbers one and three—feature character designs directly ported over from the comics. This does constitute explicit intermediality, insofar as these scenes feature literal comic book art, including panels that are read sequentially. However, these sequences are also *animated*, which makes them more similar to another noncinematic remediation of comics known as the motion comic. The inclusion of these hand-drawn animated segments certainly contributes to the film's dense polymediality; indeed, because these scenes are framed within the story as subjective, narrated flashbacks, their nonphotographic status further confirms my thesis that the wide array of media incorporated into *Scott Pilgrim*'s textuality mirrors the hypermediated subjectivities of its characters and their experiences of the world.

43. See http://www.scottpilgrimtheapp.com.

44. See Murphy, "Virtual Canadian Realities"; Eveleth, "Crucial Convergence."

45. Jenkins, *Convergence Culture*, 95–96.

46. Significantly, the film was written before the graphic novel series was complete. As a result, the conclusions of the two versions are markedly different.

47. Previously released cuts of *Watchmen* clock in at 162 minutes for the theatrical cut and 186 minutes for the director's cut.

48. Berger, *Tensions in the Struggle*, 70.

49. No issue was released in June 1987.

50. Genette, *Paratexts*, xviii.

51. The French title of Genette's book is *Seuils*, which simply means "thresholds."

52. Genette, *Paratexts*, 2.

53. Gray, *Show Sold Separately*, Kindle loc. 192.

54. This status is conferred by a combination of factors: the fact that these sections are not presented as comics but as prose, as well as their placement at the end of each issue (or, in the collected version, between chapters), gives them a sense of otherness and distance from the main narrative. They also represent a diegetic pause in which the investigation of the story's central mystery comes to a halt.

55. Their closest equivalent in *TUC* would be the audio commentaries and "video journals" that describe the making of the film, which describe the process of the film's production in a way analogous to the inclusion of Gibbons's preliminary sketches.

56. Bluestone, *Novels into Film*, ix.

57. Rehak, "Adapting *Watchmen* after 9/11," 154.

58. Morton, "Comics to Film (and Back Again)," 99.

59. Overall, *Watchmen*'s critical reception was characterized by the claim that it was "too faithful" to its source material, illustrating the damned-if-you-do, damned-if-you-don't logic of fidelity discourse. See Owen, "*Watchmen* Is Too Faithful to Alan Moore's Book"; Lemire, "Review: 'Watchmen' Almost Too Faithful to Book"; Sancton, "Did Zack Snyder Love *Watchmen* Too Much?"; and Roeper, "*Watchmen*," for representative examples. Arguably, the film's self-effacing stance is best revealed by the titles of the different released cuts, with the Director's Cut's definitive status—typically such versions are considered as the "real work of art" and the "true version of the film"—having been thoroughly supplanted by the Ultimate Cut. The Director's Cut is thereby implicitly reduced to *penultimate* status, indicating the franchise's overall preference for the original vision of the graphic novel over the cinematic intervention made by Snyder. See Gray, *Show Sold Separately*, Kindle loc. 1687.

60. Rehak, "Adapting *Watchmen* after 9/11," 154.

61. It's worth reiterating here that while fidelity may be the goal, implicit or not, of adaptations, the same cannot—or at least should not—be said of remediation, which recognizes and embraces the differences between media. Panel moments and mimetic compositions don't attempt to reproduce the comic book medium but to hybridize it with the cinema.

62. Bordwell, *Narration in the Fiction Film*, 66.

63. Rose, "Alan Moore: An Extraordinary Gentleman."

64. Moore, quoted in Van Ness, *Watchmen as Literature*, 172.

65. Reynolds, *Super Heroes*, 114.

66. With regard to the narrative meaning of *Black Freighter*, Reynolds's reading is, in my view, absolutely adequate: see ibid., 110–114, in particular.

67. Grusin, "DVDs, Video Games and the Cinema of Interactions," 214.

68. Gardner, *Projections*, Kindle loc. 3818.

69. Grusin, "DVDs, Video Games and the Cinema of Interactions," 214.

70. Ibid., 210.

71. Gardner, *Projections*, Kindle loc. 3792.

72. Ibid., Kindle loc. 3818.

73. Morton, "The Unfortunates," 357.

74. In the first piece of published scholarship on motion comics, Craig Smith too narrowly defines them as adaptations. As Morton notes, however, there have been a wide variety of original works that have no basis in a preexisting comics text. See Smith, "Motion Comics," 358, and Morton, "The Unfortunates," 349.

75. Significantly, among the motion comic's aesthetic interventions are the addition of "lens" effects (flares, selective focus) and the removal of the paneled

grid in favor of a unified frame. These choices more closely align the motion comic's style with cinema or animation than with comics, reinforcing its intermediary status between the graphic novel and Snyder's film.

76. Smith, "Motion Comics," 358–359.

77. See Morton, "The Unfortunates," 348 and 364, for some particularly biting comments on the format from Mark Waid and Scott McCloud.

78. Van Ness, *Watchmen as Literature*, 186–187.

CONCLUSION

1. Williams, "Unusual Suspects," 38.

2. Silberg, "A Universe X-pands," 37. The titles cited by Sigel here are particularly ironic, given that *Road to Perdition* (2002) is itself adapted from a graphic novel whereas *Gone in 60 Seconds* (2000) is not. The visual style of the comic—defined by chiaroscuro crosshatching and near-photographic levels of detail—would certainly challenge Sigel's reductive conception of how comics look.

3. Huls, "Golden Age of Superhero Movies."

4. For an in-depth analysis of the narrative logic underlying Marvel Studios' approach, see Jeffries, "The Worlds Align."

5. Flanagan, McKenny, and Livingstone, *Marvel Studios Phenomenon*, 6.

6. Beaty, "Introduction," 109.

7. Ibid.

8. In 2014, Marvel Studios' president Kevin Feige claimed to have a rough sketch of their film slate that stretched to 2028. See McMillan, "Kevin Feige."

9. Fleming, "Universal Taps Alex Kurtzman."

10. Gonzales, "Paramount's 'Transformers' Story Room."

11. See, for instance, Flanagan, McKenny, and Livingstone, *Marvel Studios Phenomenon*, and Yockey, *Make Ours Marvel*.

12. Flanagan, McKenny, and Livingstone, *Marvel Studios Phenomenon*, 197.

13. Schatz, *Genius of the System*, 354.

14. Ibid., 136.

15. It's worth noting that the shared comics universe first established in *Fantastic Four* #1 was also in part facilitated by a house style that had Marvel's stable of artists emulating Jack Kirby's distinctive art, while consistency of tone across titles was easily maintained under Stan Lee's editorship. See Hatfield, *Hand of Fire*, Kindle loc. 222, and Howe, *Marvel Comics*, Kindle loc. 898.

16. Flanagan, McKenny, and Livingstone, *Marvel Studios Phenomenon*, 125.

17. Masters and Kit, "Why 'Ant-Man' Director Edgar Wright Exited Marvel's Superhero Movie."

18. Palmer, "Is There Room for Auteurs in the Marvel Cinematic Universe?"

19. Burke, *Comic Book Film Adaptation*, 262.

20. Wolf, *Building Imaginary Worlds*, 198.

21. Adams, "'Justice League' Set Report."

22. As was the case with Wright, the reason cited for Jenkins's departure from the project was "creative differences." See Kit, "'Thor 2' Director Patty Jenkins Exits."

23. Scott, "Dawn of the Undead Author."

24. See Marcks, "A Clash of Titans."

25. Ibid.

26. Ibid.

27. Prince, *Digital Visual Effects in Cinema*, Kindle loc. 1289.

28. On the difficulties surrounding *Suicide Squad*'s production, see Masters, "'Suicide Squad's' Secret Drama."

29. Mickey Rat is a grotesque parody of Mickey Mouse created by Robert Armstrong.

30. Terry Zwigoff's adaptations of Daniel Clowes's work, namely, *Ghost World* (2001) and *Art School Confidential* (2006), are also noteworthy in this regard, as is *Crumb* (1994), his documentary about the underground comix artist Robert Crumb, who features as a character in *American Splendor* and, coincidentally, is married to Aline Kominsky.

31. Durham, *Double Takes*, 27.

32. Ibid., 33.

33. Morton, "Godard's Comic Strip Mise-en-Scène."

34. See the documentary "From Comics to Screen . . . to Screen" on the *Deadpool* Blu-ray release.

35. Ibid.

36. The film was shot on 4K digital cameras capable of shooting at up to 1,800 frames per second. See ibid.

37. Regrettably, the film doesn't find room to parody Reynolds's appearances in comic book adaptations like *Blade: Trinity* (2004) or *R.I.P.D.* (2013).

38. The insult is also ironic insofar as the most distinctive and visually interesting aspect of the superhero costume in *Deadpool* is its digitally animated eyes. Impossibly expressive superhero masks—which allow characters to visibly emote despite having their faces completely obscured—have been an accepted convention of superhero comics for decades but had not been attempted in a live-action film prior to *Deadpool*, presumably out of an interest in maintaining verisimilitude wherever possible. For more on the strange compromises made between comic book accuracy and verisimilitude in superhero costume design, see Jeffries, "From the Top of the Cowl to the Tip of the Cape."

39. *Deadpool* grossed $363 million on a $58 million production budget, compared to *Batman v Superman*'s $330 million on a $250 million production budget. When worldwide box office is taken into account, however, *Batman v Superman* did outgross *Deadpool*, but only marginally: $872 million compared to $782 million. Box office and budgetary figures are taken from www.boxofficemojo.com.

BIBLIOGRAPHY

Adams, Sam. "'Justice League' Set Report: How Zack Snyder Is Attempting to Rescue a Franchise." *IndieWire*, June 21, 2016. http://www.indiewire.com/2016/06/justice-league-ben-affleck-zack-snyder-batman-v-superman-1201691050/.

Ahn, Jiwon. "Animated Subjects: Globalization, Media, and East Asian Cultural Imaginaries." PhD diss., University of Southern California, 2008. ProQuest (304809649).

Altman, Rick. *Silent Film Sound*. New York: Columbia University Press, 2004.

Arnheim, Rudolf. *Art and Visual Perception: A Psychology of the Creative Eye*. Expanded and revised ed. Berkeley: University of California Press, 1974.

Aumont, Jacques. *The Image*. Translated by Claire Pajackowska. London: British Film Institute, 1997.

Bakhtin, Mikhail M. *The Dialogic Imagination: Four Essays*. Edited by Michael Holquist. Translated by Caryl Emerson and Michael Holquist. Austin: University of Texas Press, 1981.

Baudrillard, Jean. *Simulacra and Simulation*. Translated by Sheila Faria Glaser. Ann Arbor: University of Michigan Press: 1994.

Bazin, André. *What Is Cinema?* Translated by Timothy Barnard. Montreal: Caboose, 2009.

Beaty, Bart. *Fredric Wertham and the Critique of Mass Culture*. Jackson: University Press of Mississippi, 2005.

———. *A History of Violence*. Toronto: University of Toronto Press, 2008.

————. "Introduction." *Cinema Journal* 50, no. 3 (Spring 2011): 106–110.

Berger, Nico J. *Tensions in the Struggle for Sexual Minority Rights in Europe: Que(e)rying Political Practices.* Manchester: Manchester University Press, 2004.

Berninger, Mark. "'Scott Pilgrim Gets It Together': The Cultural Crossovers of Bryan Lee O'Malley." In *Transnational Perspectives on Graphic Narratives: Comics at the Crossroads,* edited by Shane Denson, Christina Meyer, and Daniel Stein, 243–255. London: Bloomsbury, 2013.

Bizzocchi, Jim. "The Fragmented Frame: The Poetics of the Split-Screen." Burnaby, BC: School of Interactive Arts and Technology, Simon Fraser University, 2009. http://web.mit.edu/comm-forum/mit6/papers/Bizzocchi.pdf.

Bluestone, George. *Novels into Film.* Baltimore: Johns Hopkins University Press, 1957.

Bolter, Jay David. "Transference and Transparency: Digital Technology and the Remediation of Cinema." *Intermediality: History and Theory of the Arts, Literature and Technologies* 6 (2005): 13–26.

Bolter, Jay David, and Richard Grusin. *Remediation: Understanding New Media.* Cambridge, MA: MIT Press, 2000.

Bolton, Matthew. "Narrativity, Purpose, and Visible Adaptation in Shari Springer Berman and Robert Pulcini's *American Splendor* (2003)." *Miranda* 8 (2013). http://miranda.revues.org/3537.

Booker, M. Keith. *May Contain Graphic Material: Comic Books, Graphic Novels, and Film.* Westport, CT: Praeger, 2007.

Bordwell, David. *Narration in the Fiction Film.* Madison: University of Wisconsin Press, 1985.

————. *On the History of Film Style.* Cambridge, MA: Harvard University Press, 1997.

————. *The Way Hollywood Tells It: Story and Style in Modern Movies.* Berkeley: University of California Press, 2006.

Bordwell, David, Janet Staiger, and Kristin Thompson. *The Classical Hollywood Cinema: Film Style and Mode of Production to 1960.* London: Rutledge and Kegan Paul, 1985.

Bordwell, David, and Kristin Thompson. *Film Art: An Introduction.* 8th ed. New York: McGraw-Hill Higher Education, 2007.

Brooker, Will. *Batman Unmasked: Analyzing a Cultural Icon.* New York: Continuum, 2000.

————. *Hunting the Dark Knight: Twenty-First Century Batman.* London: I. B. Tauris, 2012.

Brubaker, Ed, Matt Fraction, et al. *The Immortal Iron Fist.* New York: Marvel Comics, 2007.

Bukatman, Scott. "Comics and the Critique of Chronophotography, or 'He Never Knew When It Was Coming!'" *Animation: An Interdisciplinary Journal* 1, no. 1 (2006): 83–103.

Burke, Liam. *The Comic Book Film Adaptation: Exploring Hollywood's Leading Genre.* Jackson: University Press of Mississippi, 2015.

Carrier, David. *The Aesthetics of Comics.* University Park: Pennsylvania State University Press, 2000.

Carroll, Noël. "The Future of Allusion: Hollywood in the Seventies (and Beyond)." *October* 20 (Spring 1982): 51–81.

Cavell, Stanley. *The World Viewed: Reflections on the Ontology of Film.* Cambridge, MA: Harvard University Press, 1979.

Chaplin, Elayne. "Walter Hill." In *Contemporary North American Film Directors: A Wallflower Critical Guide,* edited by Yoram Allon, Del Cullen, and Hannah Patterson, 241–243. London: Wallflower, 2002.

Chion, Michel. *Audio-Vision: Sound on Screen.* Translated by Claudia Gorbman. New York: Columbia University Press, 1994.

Cohen, Michael. "Dick Tracy: In Pursuit of a Comic Book Film Aesthetic." In *Film and Comic Books,* edited by Ian Gordon, Mark Jancovich, and Matthew P. McAllister, 13–36. Jackson: University Press of Mississippi, 2007.

Cohn, Neil. *The Visual Language of Comics: Introduction to the Structure and Cognition of Sequential Images.* London: Bloomsbury, 2013.

Constandinides, Costas. *From Film Adaptation to Post-Celluloid Adaptation: Rethinking the Transition of Popular Narratives Across Old and New Media.* New York: Continuum, 2010.

Conway, Gerry, Ross Andru, et al. *The Amazing Spider-Man.* New York: Marvel Comics, 1973.

Cook, Roy T. "Why Comics Are Not Films: Metacomics and Medium-Specific Conventions." In *The Art of Comics: A Philosophical Approach,* edited by Aaron Meskin and Roy T. Cook, 165–187. Chichester: Wiley-Blackwell, 2012.

Cossar, Harper. "The Shape of New Media: Screen Space, Aspect Ratios, and Digitextuality." *Journal of Film and Video* 61, no. 4 (2009): 3–16.

Curti, Giorgio Hadi. "Beating Words to Life: Subtitles, Assemblage(s)capes, Expression." *GeoJournal* 74, no. 3 (June 2009): 201–208.

Deleuze, Gilles. *Cinema 1: The Movement-Image.* Translated by Hugh Tomlinson and Barbara Habberjam. Minneapolis: University of Minnesota Press, 1986.

Diggle, Andy, Jock, et al. *The Losers.* New York: Vertigo, 2003.

Doane, Mary Ann. *The Emergence of Cinematic Time: Modernity, Contingency, The Archive.* Cambridge, MA: Harvard University Press, 2002.

Durham, Carolyn A. *Double Takes: Culture and Gender in French Films and Their American Remakes.* Hanover, NH: University Press of New England, 1998.

Ebert, Roger. "*Superman III.*" *RogerEbert.com,* June 17, 1983. http://www.rogerebert.com/reviews/superman-iii-1983.

Ecke, Jochen. "Spatializing the Movie Screen: How Mainstream Cinema Is Catching Up on the Formal Potentialities of the Comic Book Page." In *Comics as a Nexus of Cultures: Essays on the Interplay of Media, Disciplines and International Perspectives,* edited by Mark Berninger, Jochen Ecke, and Gideon Haberkorn, 7–20. Jefferson, NC: McFarland, 2010.

Eisner, Will. *Comics and Sequential Art: Principles and Practices from the Legendary Cartoonist.* New York: W. W. Norton, 2008.

Eveleth, Kyle. "Crucial Convergence: *Scott Pilgrim* as Transmedial Test Case." *Textual Overtures* 1, no. 1 (2013): 1–14.

Fader, The. "New York Mythology." *The Fader*, October 3, 2005. http://www.thefader .com/2005/10/03/new-york-mythology.

Faraci, Devin. "Joss Whedon on How to Make a Good Comic Book Movie." *Birth. Movies. Death*, April 20, 2012. http://birthmoviesdeath.com/2012/04/20 /joss-whedon-on-how-to-make-a-good-comic-book-movie.

Flanagan, Martin, Mike McKenny, and Andy Livingstone. *The Marvel Studios Phenomenon: Inside a Transmedia Universe.* London: Bloomsbury, 2016.

Fleming, Mike Jr. "Universal Taps Alex Kurtzman, Chris Morgan to Relaunch Classic Movie Monster Franchises." *Deadline Hollywood*, July 16, 2014. http://deadline .com/2014/07/universal-classic-movie-monsters-805169/.

Foerster, Anna. "Towards a Creative Approach in Subtitling: A Case Study." In *New Insights into Audiovisual Translation and Media Accessibility: Media for All 2*, edited by Jorge Díaz Cintas, Anna Matamala, and Josélia Neves, 81–98. Amsterdam: Rodopi, 2010.

Fordham, Joe. "A Beautiful Death." *Cinefex* 109 (April 2007): 61–108.

Fox, Gardner, Harry Lampert, et al. *Flash Comics.* New York: DC Comics, 1940.

Friedberg, Anne. *The Virtual Window: From Alberti to Microsoft.* Cambridge, MA: MIT Press, 2001.

Gardner, Jared. *Projections: Comics and the History of Twenty-First-Century Storytelling.* Stanford: Stanford University Press, 2012.

Gaudreault, André, and Philippe Marion. *The End of Cinema? A Medium in Crisis in the Digital Age.* Translated by Timothy Barnard. New York: Columbia University Press, 2015.

Genette, Gérard. *Palimpsests: Literature in the Second Degree.* Translated by Channa Newman and Claude Doubinsky. Lincoln: University of Nebraska Press, 1997.

———. *Paratexts: Thresholds of Interpretation.* Translated by Jane E. Lewin. Cambridge: Cambridge University Press, 1997.

Gonzales, David. "Paramount's 'Transformers' Story Room Will Pitch at Least a Dozen New Movies." *Forbes*, June 8, 2015. http://www.forbes.com/sites/davegon zales/2015/06/08/paramounts-transformers-story-room-will-pitch-at-least-a -dozen-new-movies/#5e838aea59b6.

Gravett, Paul. *Comics Art.* London: Tate Publishing, 2013.

Gray, Jonathan. *Show Sold Separately: Promos, Spoilers, and Other Media Paratexts.* New York: New York University Press, 2010.

Groensteen, Thierry. *Comics and Narration.* Translated by Ann Miller. Jackson: University Press of Mississippi, 2013.

———. *The System of Comics.* Translated by Bart Beaty and Nick Nguyen. Jackson: University Press of Mississippi, 2007.

Grusin, Richard. "DVDs, Video Games and the Cinema of Interactions." In *Multimedia Histories: From the Magic Lantern to the Internet*, edited by James Lyons and John Plunkett, 209–221. Exeter, UK: University of Exeter Press, 2007.

Gunning, Tom. "The Cinema of Attraction[s]: Early Film, Its Spectator and the Avant-Garde." In *The Cinema of Attractions Reloaded*, edited by Wanda Strauven, 381–388. Amsterdam: Amsterdam University Press, 2006.

Hagener, Malte. "The Aesthetics of Displays: How the Split Screen Remediates Other Media." *Refractory: A Journal of Entertainment Media* 14 (2008). http://refractory.unimelb.edu.au/2008/12/24/the-aesthetics-of-displays-how-the-split-screen-remediates-other-media-%E2%80%93-malte-hagener/.

Hassler-Forest, Dan. "The 300 Controversy: A Case Study in the Politics of Adaptation." *Film & History* (2012). http://www.uwosh.edu/filmandhistory/controversial_films/films/300.php.

Hatfield, Charles. *Hand of Fire: The Comics Art of Jack Kirby.* Jackson: University Press of Mississippi, 2012.

Hight, Craig. "*American Splendor*: Translating Comic Autobiography into Drama-Documentary." In *Film and Comic Books*, edited by Ian Gordon, Mark Jancovich, and Matthew P. McAllister, 180–198. Jackson: University Press of Mississippi, 2007.

Horsley, Jake. *The Blood Poets: A Cinema of Savagery 1958–1999.* Vol. 2, *Millennial Blues from "Apocalypse Now" to "The Matrix."* Lanham, MD: Scarecrow Press, 1999.

Howe, Sean. *Marvel Comics: The Untold Story.* New York: Harper, 2012.

Hughes, David. *Comic Book Movies.* London: Virgin Books, 2003.

Huls, Alexander. "The Golden Age of Superhero Movies Has Yet to Face Its Greatest Threats." *A.V. Club*, August 5, 2016. http://www.avclub.com/article/golden-age-superhero-movies-has-yet-face-its-great-239826.

Jeffries, Dru. "From the Top of the Cowl to the Tip of the Cape: The Cinematic Superhero Costume as Impossible Garment." *Cinephile* 9, no. 2 (Fall 2013). http://cinephile.ca/wp-content/uploads/9.2-WEB-VERSION.pdf.

———. "Spotting Stan: The Fun and Function of Stan Lee's Cameos in the Marvel Universe(s)." In *Make Ours Marvel: Media Convergence and a Comics Universe*, edited by Matt Yockey, 297–318. Austin: University of Texas Press, 2017.

———. "The Worlds Align: Media Convergence and Complementary Storyworlds in Marvel's *Thor: The Dark World.*" In *World Building: Transmedia, Fans, Industries*, edited by Marta Boni, Martin Lefebvre, and Marc Steinberg. Amsterdam: University of Amsterdam Press, forthcoming.

Jenkins, Henry. *Convergence Culture: Where Old and New Media Collide.* New York: New York University Press, 2006.

Johnson, Andy. *The Action Cinema Handbook.* Raleigh, NC: Lulu Press, 2015.

Jurgens, Dan, Jerry Ordway, et al. *The Death of Superman.* New York: DC Comics, 1993.

Juul, Jesper. *Half-Real: Video Games between Real Rules and Fictional Worlds.* Cambridge, MA: MIT Press, 2005.

Kadner, Noah. "Girl Trouble." *American Cinematographer* (August 2010): 42–55.

Kanigher, Robert, Carmine Infantino, et al. *Showcase.* New York: DC Comics, 1956.

Khordoc, Catherine. "The Comic Book's Soundtrack: Visual Sound Effects in *Asterix.*" In *The Language of Comics: Word and Image,* edited by Robin Barnum and Christina T. Gibbons, 156–173. Jackson: University Press of Mississippi, 2001.

Kinder, Marsha. "Playing with Power on Saturday Morning Television and on Home Video Games." In *American Television: New Directions in History and Theory,* edited by Nick Browne, 255–286. Langhorne, PA: Harwood Academic Publishing, 1994.

King, Geoff. *New Hollywood Cinema: An Introduction.* New York: Columbia University Press, 2002.

Kirchoff, Jeffrey S. J. "Beyond Remediation: Comic Book Captions and Silent Film Intertitles as the Same Genre." *Studies in Comics* 3, no. 1 (2012): 25–45.

Kit, Borys. "'Thor 2' Director Patty Jenkins Exits." *The Hollywood Reporter,* December 6, 2011. http://www.hollywoodreporter.com/heat-vision/thor-2-patty-jenkins-270210.

Lamarre, Thomas. *The Anime Machine: A Media Theory of Animation.* Minneapolis: University of Minnesota Press, 2009.

Lascelles, Robert. "'Scott Pilgrim vs. the World': Highly Stylized Comedy." *The Orange County Register,* August 19, 2010. http://www.ocregister.com/articles/scott-262718-moment-movie.html.

Lee, Stan, Jack Kirby, et al. *The Fantastic Four.* New York: Marvel Comics, 1961.

Lee, Stan, John Romita, et al. *The Amazing Spider-Man.* New York: Marvel Comics, 1967.

Lefebvre, Martin. "The Art of Pointing: On Peirce, Indexicality, and Photographic Images." In *Photography Theory,* edited by James Elkins, 220–244. New York: Routledge, 2007.

Lefèvre, Pascal. "Incompatible Visual Ontologies? The Problematic Adaptation of Drawn Images." In *Film and Comic Books,* edited by Ian Gordon, Mark Jancovich, and Matthew P. McAllister, 1–12. Jackson: University Press of Mississippi, 2007.

Leitch, Thomas. "Adaptation Studies at a Crossroads." *Adaptation* 1, no. 1 (2008): 63–77.

———. *Film Adaptation and Its Discontents: From "Gone with the Wind" to "The Passion of the Christ."* Baltimore: Johns Hopkins University Press, 2007.

Lemire, Christy. "Review: 'Watchmen' Almost Too Faithful to Book." *Fox News,* March 2, 2009. http://www.foxnews.com/printer_friendly_wires/2009Mar02/0,4675,FilmReviewWatchmen,00.html.

Lichtenfeld, Eric. *Action Speaks Louder: Violence, Spectacle, and the American Action Movie.* Middletown, CT: Wesleyan University Press, 2007.

Loeb, Jeph, Jim Lee, et al. *Batman.* New York: DC Comics, 2002.

Loeb, Jeph, Tim Sale, et al. *Daredevil: Yellow.* New York: Marvel Comics, 2001.

Madianou, Mirca, and Daniel Miller. "Polymedia: Towards a New Theory of Digital Media in Interpersonal Communication." *International Journal of Cultural Studies* 16, no. 2 (2012): 169–187.

Maggin, Elliot S., Curt Swan, et al. *Superman*. New York: DC Comics, 1972.

Manovich, Lev. *The Language of New Media*. Cambridge, MA: MIT Press, 2001.

Marcks, Iain. "A Clash of Titans." *American Cinematographer*, April 2016. http://www
.theasc.com/ac_magazine/April2016/ClashTitans/page1.php.

Masters, Kim. "'Suicide Squad's' Secret Drama: Rushed Production, Competing
Cuts, High Anxiety." *The Hollywood Reporter*, August 3, 2016. http://www.holly
woodreporter.com/heat-vision/suicide-squads-secret-drama-rushed-916693.

Masters, Kim, and Borys Kit. "Why 'Ant-Man' Director Edgar Wright Exited Marvel's Superhero Movie." *The Hollywood Reporter*, May 28, 2014. http://www.holly
woodreporter.com/news/why-ant-man-director-edgar-707374.

McClarty, Rebecca. "In Support of Creative Subtitling: Contemporary Context
and Theoretical Framework." *Perspectives: Studies in Translatology* 22, no. 4 (2014):
592–606.

McCloud, Scott. *Making Comics: Storytelling Secrets of Comics, Manga and Graphic Novels*.
New York: Harper, 2006.

——. *Understanding Comics: The Invisible Art*. New York: HarperPerennial, 1993.

McMillan, Graeme. "Kevin Feige: Marvel Has Plotted Films through 2028." *The
Hollywood Reporter*, April 3, 2014. http://www.hollywoodreporter.com/heat-vision
/kevin-feige-marvel-has-plotted-693317.

Medhurst, Andy. "Batman, Deviance and Camp." In *The Many Lives of the Batman*,
edited by Roberta E. Pearson and William Uricchio, 149–163. New York: Routledge, 1991.

Micheline, David, Todd McFarlane, et al. *The Amazing Spider-Man*. New York: Marvel Comics, 1988.

Millar, Mark, J. G. Jones, et al. *Wanted*. Los Angeles: Top Cow Productions, 2003.

Miller, Frank, Klaus Janson, et al. *Batman: The Dark Knight Returns*. New York: DC
Comics, 1986.

Miller, Frank, David Mazzucchelli, et al. *Daredevil*. New York: Marvel Comics, 1986.

Miller, Frank, John Romita Jr., et al. *Daredevil: The Man Without Fear*. New York: Marvel Comics, 1993.

Mitry, Jean. *The Aesthetics and Psychology of the Cinema*. Translated by Christopher
King. Bloomington: Indiana University Press, 1997.

Morton, Drew. "Comics to Film (and Back Again): A Study in Stylistic Remediation
from 1978–2009." PhD diss., University of California Los Angeles, 2012. ProQuest
(1013442267).

——. "Godard's Comic Strip Mise-en-Scène." *Senses of Cinema* 53 (December
2009). http://sensesofcinema.com/2009/feature-articles/godards-comic-strip
-mise-en-scene/.

——. *Panel to the Screen: Style, American Film, and Comic Books during the Blockbuster
Era*. Jackson: University Press of Mississippi, 2016.

——. "The Unfortunates: Towards a History and Definition of the Motion
Comic." *Journal of Graphic Novels and Comics* 6, no. 4 (2015): 347–366.

Moore, Alan, Brian Bolland, et al. *Batman: The Killing Joke.* New York: DC Comics, 1988.

Moore, Alan, Dave Gibbons, et al. *Watchmen.* New York: DC Comics, 1986.

Murphy, David. "Virtual Canadian Realities: Charting the Scott Pilgrim Universe." *International Journal of Canadian Studies* 45–46 (2012): 495–507.

Murray, Padmini Ray. "Scott Pilgrim vs the Future of Comics Publishing." *Studies in Comics* 3, no. 1 (2012): 129–142.

Ndalianis, Angela. "The Frenzy of the Visible in Comic Book Worlds." *Animation: An Interdisciplinary Journal* 4, no. 3 (2009): 237–248.

Neale, Steve. *Genre and Hollywood.* London: Routledge, 2000.

Nyberg, Amy Kiste. *Seal of Approval: The History of the Comics Code.* Jackson: University Press of Mississippi, 1998.

O'Malley, Bryan Lee. *Scott Pilgrim's Precious Little Life.* Portland, OR: Oni Press, 2004.

Owano, Nancy. "High Frame Rate Cinema Booed but Shows Will Go On." *Phys,* May 4, 2012. http://phys.org/news/2012-05-high-cinema-booed.html.

Owen, Paul. "*Watchmen* Is Too Faithful to Alan Moore's Book." *The Guardian,* July 22, 2009. http://www.theguardian.com/film/filmblog/2009/jul/22/watchmen-book-film-alan-moore.

Palmer, Landon. "Is There Room for Auteurs in the Marvel Cinematic Universe?" *Film School Rejects,* July 28, 2015. https://filmschoolrejects.com/is-there-room-for-auteurs-in-the-marvel-cinematic-universe-4d1bd4fccbec#.9wi90v74m.

Pedler, Martyn. "The Fastest Man Alive: Stasis and Speed in Contemporary Superhero Comics." *Animation: An Interdisciplinary Journal* 4, no. 3 (2009): 249–263.

Pekar, Harvey, Robert Crumb, et al. *American Splendor.* Cleveland, OH: Harvey Pekar, 1978.

Perry, Spencer. "From Comics to Movies: Visual References in The Dark Knight Trilogy." *SuperHeroHype,* March 26, 2015. http://www.superherohype.com/features/334663-from-comics-to-movies-visual-references-in-the-dark-knight-trilogy#/slide/1.

———. "From Comics to Movies: Visual References in The X-Men Franchise." *SuperHeroHype,* May 25, 2015. http://www.superherohype.com/features/341787-from-comics-to-movies-visual-references-in-the-x-men-franchise#/slide/1.

Petri, Alexandra. "Jim Carrey Refuses to Promote Kick-Ass 2, on the Grounds of Violence. Can You Do This?" *The Washington Post,* June 25, 2013. https://www.washingtonpost.com/blogs/compost/wp/2013/06/25/jim-carrey-refuses-to-promote-kick-ass-2-on-the-grounds-of-violence-can-you-do-this/.

Pino, Camilo Diaz. "Sound Affects: Visualizing Music, Musicians and (Sub)cultural Identity in *BECK* and *Scott Pilgrim.*" *Studies in Comics* 6, no. 1 (July 2015): 85–106.

Powell, Helen. *Stop the Clocks! Time and Narrative in Cinema.* London: I. B. Tauris, 2012.

Pratt, Henry John. "Making Comics into Film." In *The Art of Comics: A Philosophical*

Approach, edited by Aaron Meskin and Roy T. Cook, 147–164. Chichester, UK: Wiley-Blackwell, 2012.

———. "Narrative in Comics." *Journal of Aesthetics and Art Criticism* 67 (2009): 107–117.

Prince, Stephen. *Digital Visual Effects in Cinema: The Seduction of Reality*. New Brunswick: Rutgers University Press, 2012.

———. "True Lies: Perceptual Realism, Digital Images and Film Theory." In *Film Theory and Criticism*, edited by Leo Braudy and Marshall Cohen, 6th ed., 270–282. New York: Oxford University Press, 2004.

Proctor, William. "Beginning Again: The Reboot Phenomenon in Comics and Film." *Scan: Journal of Media Arts Culture* 9, no. 1 (2012). http://scan.net.au/scan/journal/display.php?journal_id=163.

Rae, Neil, and Jonathan Gray. "When Gen-X Met the X-Men: Retextualizing Comic Book Film Reception." In *Film and Comic Books*, edited by Ian Gordon, Mark Jancovich, and Matthew P. McAllister, 86–100. Jackson: University Press of Mississippi, 2007.

Rauscher, Andreas. "Workshop IV: Teaching Comics and Film Studies—Ang Lee's *The Hulk* (USA 2003)." In *Comics as a Nexus of Cultures: Essays on the Interplay of Media, Disciplines and International Perspectives*, edited by Mark Berninger, Jochen Ecke, and Gideon Haberkorn, 265–273. Jefferson, NC: McFarland, 2010.

Rehak, Bob. "Adapting *Watchmen* after 9/11." *Cinema Journal* 51, no. 1 (2011): 154–159.

———. "The Migration of Forms: Bullet Time as Microgenre." *Film Criticism* 32, no. 1 (2007): 26–48.

———. "*Watchmen*: Stuck in the Uncanny Valley." *Graphic Engine*, March 9, 2009. https://graphic-engine.swarthmore.edu/watchmen-stuck-in-the-uncanny-valley/.

Reynolds, Richard. *Super Heroes: A Modern Mythology*. Jackson: University Press of Mississippi, 1994.

Rodowick, D. N. *Reading the Figural, or Philosophy after the New Media*. Durham, NC: Duke University Press, 2001.

Roeper, Richard. "*Watchmen*." *Richard Roeper and the Movies*. http://www.richardroeper.com/reviews/watchmen.aspx.

Rose, Steve. "Alan Moore: An Extraordinary Gentleman." *The Guardian*, March 16, 2009. http://www.theguardian.com/books/2009/mar/16/alan-moore-watchmen-lost-girls.

Røssaak, Eivind. "Figures of Sensation: Between Still and Moving Images." In *The Cinema of Attractions Reloaded*, edited by Wanda Strauven, 321–336. Amsterdam: Amsterdam University Press, 2006.

Round, Julia. "Revenant Landscapes in *The Walking Dead*." Bournemouth, UK: Faculty of Media and Communication, Bournemouth University, 2015. http://eprints.bournemouth.ac.uk/22873/1/Round%20-%20PCA%20paper%20for%20IJOCA%20-%20Revenant%20Landscapes%20in%20TWD.pdf.

Rowsell, Jennifer, Isabel Pedersen, and Douglas Trueman. "Playing as a Mutant in a Virtual World: Understanding Overlapping Story Worlds in Popular Culture Video Games." *Literacy* 48, no. 1 (April 2014): 47–53.

Sancton, Julian. "Did Zack Snyder Love *Watchmen* Too Much?" *Vanity Fair*, March 4, 2009. http://www.vanityfair.com/online/daily/2009/03/did-zach-snyder-love-watchmen-too-much.

Schatz, Thomas. *The Genius of the System: Hollywood Filmmaking in the Studio Era.* New York: Pantheon, 1988.

Scott, Suzanne. "Dawn of the Undead Author: Fanboy Auteurism and Zack Snyder's 'Vision.'" In *A Companion to Media Authorship*, edited by Jonathan Gray and Derek Johnson, 440–462. Malden, MA: Wiley-Blackwell, 2013.

Semansky, Matt. "*Scott Pilgrim vs. the World* Is Almost Sensory Overload . . ." *The Coast*, August 12, 2012. http://www.thecoast.ca/halifax/scott-pilgrim-vs-the-world-is-almost-sensory-overload/Content?oid=1772714.

Shaviro, Steven. *Post-Cinematic Affect.* Winchester, UK: Zero Books, 2010.

Shklovsky, Viktor. *Theory of Prose.* Translated by Benjamin Sher. Champaign: Dalkey Archive Press, 1990.

Silberg, Jon. "A Universe X-pands." *American Cinematographer* (April 2003): 36–47.

Smith, Craig. "Motion Comics: Modes of Adaptation and the Issue of Authenticity." *Animation Practice, Process & Production* 1, no. 2 (2011): 357–378.

Smith, Greg M. "Shaping *The Maxx*: Adapting the Comic Book Frame to Television." *Animation Journal* 8, no. 1 (Fall 1999): 32–53.

Smith, Kevin, Joe Quesada, et al. *Daredevil.* New York: Marvel Comics, 1998.

Somigli, Luca. "The Superhero with a Thousand Faces: Visual Narratives on Film and Paper." In *Play It Again, Sam: Retakes on Remakes*, edited by Andrew Horton and Stuart Y. McDougal, 279–294. Berkeley: University of California Press, 1998.

Sperb, Jason. "Removing the Experience: Simulacrum as an Autobiographical Act in *American Splendor*." *Biography* 29, no. 1 (Winter 2006): 123–139.

Stam, Robert. "Beyond Fidelity: The Dialogics of Adaptation." In *Film Adaptation*, edited by James Naremore, 54–76. New Brunswick, NJ: Rutgers University Press, 2000.

Stork, Matthias. "Chaos Cinema: The Decline and Fall of Action Filmmaking." *IndieWire*, August 22, 2011. http://blogs.indiewire.com/pressplay/video_essay_matthias_stork_calls_out_the_chaos_cinema.

Thompson, Kristin. "The Concept of Cinematic Excess." In *Film Theory and Criticism*, edited by Leo Braudy and Marshall Cohen, 6th ed., 513–524. New York: Oxford University Press, 2004.

Tomasovic, Dick. "The Hollywood Cobweb: New Laws of Attraction (The Spectacular Mechanics of Blockbusters)." In *The Cinema of Attractions Reloaded*, edited by Wanda Strauven, 309–320. Amsterdam: Amsterdam University Press, 2006.

Torres, Sasha. "The Caped Crusader of Camp: Pop, Camp, and the *Batman* Television Series." In *Camp: Queer Aesthetics and the Performing Subject: A Reader*, edited by Fabio Cleto, 330–343. Ann Arbor: University of Michigan Press, 1999.

Tudor, Andrew. "Walter Hill—Director." *Film Reference*. http://www.filmreference.com/Directors-Ha-Ji/Hill-Walter.html.

Tweedie, James Andrew. "Moving Pictures, Still Lives: Neobaroque Cinema, Visual Culture, Theory." PhD diss., University of Iowa, 2002. ProQuest (305515295).

Ulloa, Alexander. "*Scott Pilgrim vs the World* (2010)." *Art of the Title*, January 3, 2011. http://www.artofthetitle.com/title/scott-pilgrim-vs-the-world/.

Van Ness, Sara J. *Watchmen as Literature: A Critical Study of the Graphic Novel.* Jefferson, NC: McFarland, 2010.

Warner, Marina. "*Phew! Whaam! Aaargh! Boo!*: Sense, Sensation, and Picturing Sound." *The Soundtrack* 1, no. 2 (2008): 107–125.

Wartenberg, Thomas E. "Wordy Pictures: Theorizing the Relationship between Image and Text in Comics." In *The Art of Comics: A Philosophical Approach*, edited by Aaron Meskin and Roy T. Cook, 85–104. Malden, MA: Blackwell Publishing, 2012.

Watercutter, Angela. "Video: How *Dredd 3D* Shot Its Brain-Melting Slow-Mo." *Wired*, January 4, 2013. http://www.wired.com/2013/01/dredd-3d-slow-mo/.

Waterhouse, Jon. "'Scott Pilgrim vs the World' Succeeds in Sensory Overload." *AJC.com*, August 10, 2010. http://www.accessatlanta.com/news/entertainment/movies/scott-pilgrim-vs-the-world-succeeds-in-sensory-ove/nQ4TY/.

Williams, David E. "Unusual Suspects." *American Cinematographer* (July 2000): 36–47.

Wolf, Mark J. P. *Building Imaginary Worlds: The Theory and History of Subcreation*. New York: Routledge, 2012.

Wolk, Douglas. *Reading Comics: How Graphic Novels Work and What They Mean*. Philadelphia: Da Capo Press, 2007.

Yockey, Matt. *Batman*. Detroit: Wayne State University Press, 2014.

———, ed. *Make Ours Marvel: Media Convergence and a Comics Universe*. Austin: University of Texas Press, 2017.

Young, Robert J. C. *Colonial Desire: Hybridity in Theory, Culture, and Race*. London: Routledge, 1995.

INDEX